Robert Louis Stevenson and the Art of Collaboration

Robert Louis Stevenson and the Art of Collaboration

Audrey Murfin

EDINBURGH
University Press

Edinburgh University Press is one of the leading university presses in the UK. We publish academic books and journals in our selected subject areas across the humanities and social sciences, combining cutting-edge scholarship with high editorial and production values to produce academic works of lasting importance. For more information visit our website: edinburghuniversitypress.com

© Audrey Murfin, 2019, 2021

Edinburgh University Press Ltd
The Tun – Holyrood Road,
12(2f) Jackson's Entry,
Edinburgh EH8 8PJ

First published in hardback by Edinburgh University Press 2019

Typeset in 11/13 Adobe Sabon by
IDSUK (DataConnection) Ltd

A CIP record for this book is available from the British Library

ISBN 978 1 4744 5198 7 (hardback)
ISBN 978 1 4744 5199 4 (paperback)
ISBN 978 1 4744 5200 7 (webready PDF)
ISBN 978 1 4744 5201 4 (epub)

The right of Audrey Murfin to be identified as the author of this work has been asserted in accordance with the Copyright, Designs and Patents Act 1988, and the Copyright and Related Rights Regulations 2003 (SI No. 2498).

Contents

List of Illustrations	vi
Acknowledgements	vii
Introduction: Collaboration in Theory and Practice	1
1. Criminal Collaborators: *Deacon Brodie* and *Strange Case of Dr Jekyll and Mr Hyde*	29
2. Collaboration and Marriage: *The Dynamiter*	53
3. Counterpoint: Fanny's and Louis's Pacific Diaries	81
4. *Disjecta Membra*: Collaboration and the Body of the Text in *The Wrong Box* and *The Master of Ballantrae*	119
5. 'A kind of partnership business': *The Wrecker* and *The Ebb-Tide*	150
Bibliography	181
Index	193

List of Illustrations

Figure 1.1 William Henley. Photograph by Frederick Hollyer. © Victoria and Albert Museum, London.   30

Figure 1.2 Actor Richard Mansfield as Jekyll and Hyde (*c.* 1895). Photograph by Henry Van der Weyde (1838–1924; London, England). Pach Brothers. *Richard Mansfield as Dr. Jekyll and Mr. Hyde*. https://www.loc.gov/item/96511898/   39

Figure 2.1 Fanny Stevenson at Bournemouth, 1885. Beinecke Rare Book and Manuscript Library.   55

Figure 3.1 Butaritari native dance. This image is from the photograph album entitled 'The Cruise of the Equator' of Robert Louis Stevenson's travels around the Gilbert Islands and Samoa in 1889. The City of Edinburgh Museums and Galleries; Writers' Museum.   89

Figure 3.2 'Samoan Girl: Sosophina'. Photograph by Lloyd Osbourne, 1889. This image is from the photograph album entitled 'The Cruise of the Equator' of Robert Louis Stevenson's travels around the Gilbert Islands and Samoa in 1889. The City of Edinburgh Museums and Galleries; Writers' Museum.   110

Figure 4.1 Robert Louis Stevenson (right), Lloyd Osbourne (centre) and Joe Strong (right). Untitled, from the photograph album entitled 'The Cruise of the Casco' of Robert Louis Stevenson's travels around Hawaii and French Polynesia in 1888. The City of Edinburgh Museums and Galleries; Writers' Museum.   121

Figure 5.1 Self-portrait of artist Will H. Low, Stevenson's friend and the original for Loudon Dodd in *The Wrecker*. William H. Low, *Self-Portrait at Montigny*, 1876, oil on canvas, Smithsonian American Art Museum, Bequest of Henry Ward Ranger through the National Academy of Design.   165

Acknowledgements

I am grateful to have received funding to work on this project from Sam Houston State University's Enhancement Research Grant, which allowed me to travel to the Robert Louis Stevenson Museum to look at Fanny Stevenson's diary and other material. I am also grateful to the Huntington Library for granting me the John Brockway Huntington Foundation Fellowship, allowing me to view Stevenson's diaries from the Pacific Islands as well as other items from their vast Stevenson collection.

This book would not be possible without support and feedback from other scholars, especially Stephen Arata, Erik Hage and Caroline McCracken-Flesher. I am grateful to the English Department at Sam Houston State University and especially to my colleagues who have assisted me with responses to drafts, writing advice and institutional support, including Tracy Bilsing, Jake Blevins, Bill Bridges, Julie Hall, Helena Halmari, Paul Child and April Shemak, and to my students at Sam Houston, especially Jenny Seay, who assisted me with research on this project. My interest in Stevenson began during the writing of my dissertation at Binghamton University, which included some of the ideas contained in Chapter 2, and I and I wish to thank Nancy Henry for her encouragement and mentorship. I am very grateful for Ersev Ersoy and Michelle Houston at Edinburgh University Press, and for the thoughtful feedback from anonymous reviewers.

I appreciate the invaluable assistance of the many librarians who have helped me to access all the materials that have gone into the writing of this book: at the Robert Louis Stevenson Museum in St. Helena, California; at the Stevenson House in Monterey, California; at the Huntington Library in San Marino, California; and at the Beinecke Rare Book and Manuscript Library at Yale University. I am particularly grateful to Marissa Schleicher at the Robert Louis Stevenson Museum who generously allowed me to share her office; Kris Quist and Corrine Mendoza at the Stevenson House for granting me access to their collection; and Mary Ellen Budney at the Beinecke for sending material I had missed. I also wish to thank Michelle Hoogterp, English subject librarian at the Newton Gresham Library at Sam Houston State University for her dedication in finding difficult sources.

I wish to thank my family, especially Justin, Melissa and Reid Murfin, who graciously opened their New Haven home to me, allowing me to spend long days reading at the Beinecke Library. I could not have written this book without Michael Demson, who has been an active participant in this project from its earliest stages, and to whom I dedicate this book.

Introduction

Collaboration in Theory and Practice

In 1893 Henry James dispatched two volumes of new stories to Samoa, to his friend Robert Louis Stevenson. Stevenson had already (too late) written James a letter, advising him 'I have written and ordered your last book, *The Real Thing*, so be sure and don't send it',[1] demonstrating both how eager Stevenson was to read James, and how eager James was to be read by him. The volumes, *The Real Thing and Other Tales* and *The Private Life*, contain some of James's most cynical reflections on the profession of the writer. Thematically, most of the stories focus on the contrast between the idealised writer as inspired artist and the more humdrum reality of writing as a profession. (This topic would recur through much of Stevenson's work, too.) One story from *The Real Thing*, 'Greville Fane', describes a prolific and popular, but insufficiently literary, female novelist. The narrator, a journalist tasked with writing her obituary, is simultaneously embarrassed by her career and respectful, admitting in the first paragraph 'I didn't admire her, but I liked her',[2] exemplifying the reaction of the average reader to her many novels. While 'Greville Fane' (the novelist Mrs Stormer's pen name) toils at producing three novels a year while living the restricted life of a middle-class widow, her children harbour more upper-class aesthetics and tastes. Although she works hard to apprentice her son, Leolin, to her craft, he proves to be an unproductive writer, all the while disparaging his mother's lack of sophistication in both art and society. In the end, the narrator alleges, Leolin only ever uses his mother's work, while simultaneously appropriating her increasingly diminishing earnings. She does not see it this way. Instead, she distinguishes between the 'form' and the 'substance' of art, fondly crediting her profligate son with providing the latter by means of his extravagant living:

> Leolin had been obliged to recognise insuperable difficulties in the question of *form*, he was so fastidious; so that she had now arrived at a definite understanding with him (it was such a comfort) that *she* would do the form if he would bring home the substance. That was now his position – he foraged for her in the great world at a salary.[3]

There is much to say here about James's ironic treatment of the work of art being split into 'substance' and 'form'. I will limit myself to pointing out the obvious: that within mimetic practice (and Greville Fane is a Trollopian realist) only form can be art, since 'substance' would merely be life.

Robert Louis Stevenson and the fictional Greville Fane were both popular, but in most other ways they were opposite: she is 'matronly, mild, inanimate' while he was a lean, charismatic bohemian; she had 'not contributed a sentence to the language'[4] while he was considered a preeminent stylist. But in 1893 when he received *The Real Thing*, Stevenson was actively bemoaning the lack of success of his latest and longest novel, *The Wrecker* (1892), co-written with his stepson, Lloyd Osbourne. Many of his acquaintances, including his publishers at Scribner's, blamed the disappointment on the upstart young man. According to Barry Menikoff, Scribner's believed that

> Stevenson's collaboration with Lloyd Osbourne on *The Wrong Box* and *The Wrecker* was having a deleterious effect on sales: readers assumed that Stevenson was allowing his name to be used to help sell his stepson's work, or else that Osbourne's work was corrupting Stevenson's. In either case, Stevenson was the loser – both in prestige and in his pocketbook.[5]

James's story prompts us to ask many questions about the situation of the author in the late nineteenth century. There is first the question, as I have mentioned, of the discrepancy between the writer as an artist and the writer as a professional catering to a specific market. Greville Fane is adept at only the latter, and sometimes Stevenson worried that he was the same way. It also shows us the discrepancy between the illusion of the author-celebrity writing above the fray, and the reality of that person embedded in a web of relationships and beset by domestic squabbles and difficulties. Finally, most literally, is Robert Louis Stevenson as fond and naive as Greville Fane? Is Lloyd Osbourne Leolin Stormer? Is, in short, collaboration a con?

On the contrary, by looking at a selection of texts both collaborative and not, I will argue that understanding literary collaboration is essential to understanding Stevenson's writings. Stevenson often collaborated with family and friends. Early collaborations include three plays with his friend W. E. Henley. Later, he and his wife Fanny co-authored a volume of linked stories, *More New Arabian Nights*, also titled *The Dynamiter* (1885). He collaborated most extensively with his stepson, Lloyd Osbourne, with whom he wrote three novels: *The Wrong Box* (1889), *The Wrecker* and *The Ebb-Tide* (1894). Stevenson's collaborations with Osbourne typify the critical problem my project addresses. Like Fanny Stevenson's, Osbourne's literary reputation has not been notable. Furthermore, there is evidence that Stevenson's collaborations with Osbourne became frustrating. Why would this famous and successful author practise a writing process that burdened him with inexpert collaborators? The answer to this question can be found in Stevenson's novels, essays and plays, which dramatise the process of collaboration. Stevenson creates an alternate narrative of what it means to write – one that challenges commonly held assumptions about the celebrity cult of the author in Victorian Britain, and notions of authorship more generally.

This book is structured around critical readings of major Stevenson texts, supported and contextualised by archival research into unpublished manuscripts and letters by both Stevenson and his associates. I argue that it is not merely that Stevenson collaborated, but that his work is *about* collaboration – its benefits, but also its pitfalls. Stevenson's self-reflective body of work reimagines authorship by examining the ways that authors choose material, negotiate the marketplace and, ultimately, maintain power over their own words, or let that power go. Characteristically, Stevenson's exploration will not come to firm conclusions; for every moment in which he cedes authority, there is another in which he wants it back. Writing to his cousin Robert Alan Mowbray Stevenson about his co-written novel *The Wrecker*, he allows that collaborative writing leads to 'greater richness of purview, consideration, and invention', but claims the final ownership of the project, calling himself the 'one person being responsible and giving the *coup de pouce* to every part of the work' (*Letters* 8: 364–5). Stevenson's work explores the tensions of the author, the space between the concept of the author as infallible producer of clear and unitary meaning, and the author as a medium through which the ideas of others are made to speak. What does it mean to be an author at the end of the nineteenth century? Stevenson's fictions dramatise the process of collaboration and create an alternate narrative of what it means to write – one that challenges commonly held assumptions about the celebrity cult of the author in Victorian Britain, replacing the subjectivity of the author with an ever shifting, multifaceted perspective.

Collaborative Criticism

Contemporary thought on collaboration and authorship begins with two foundational articles: Roland Barthes's 1967 essay 'The Death of the Author' challenges the idea that the background or intention of the author has any special authority over the interpretation of a literary text,[6] and Michel Foucault's response, 'What is an Author?' (1969), endorses the creation of what Foucault calls the 'author-function' – an idea of the author separate from the historical personage.[7] Less acknowledged in criticism on collaboration, but equally important, is M. M. Bakhtin, whose notion of heteroglossia, or a multiplicity of voices or discourses, within the novel frees readers from having to think of novelistic style as emerging from a single and entirely unified consciousness.[8] Bakhtin's playful notions of discourse came close to the aesthetic values Stevenson expressed through his literary career, from his multi-plotted experimental works like *New Arabian Nights* and *The Dynamiter* to, near the end of his life, his fascination with the linguistic diversity he found in the Pacific islands.

The most notable subsequent development in criticism on collaboration is Wayne Koestenbaum's 1989 discussion of the erotic nature of male/male literary collaboration. Koestenbaum finds that collaborative writing attained its zenith during the sexually contentious years of the *fin de siècle* as authors enact on the page desires they are forbidden in life. There is something to this – my reading of *The Wrecker* specifically will examine the romance of the male partnership. However, Koestenbaum's discussion of the Stevenson–Osbourne partnership specifically is quite literal, and his claim that '[Stevenson] understood the sexual implications of his relationship with Lloyd' (146) is not borne out in the biographical studies.[9] Not surprisingly, Koestenbaum is also dismissive of Stevenson's collaborations with Fanny.

Related to Koestenbaum's book in approach is a great deal of work that takes on collaboration as a specifically feminist problem, from Bette London's *Writing Double*, which looks at collaborations between women, to Holly Laird's *Women Coauthors*, which looks at female co-authors, regardless of the gender of their writing partner.[10] These feminist approaches elucidate Stevenson's professional relationship with his wife, and in particular the prickly ways in which the pair negotiated, and not always successfully, the discrepancy between his fame and her literary ambitions. But because Stevenson did not collaborate with one person, or in one type of relationship, but in three, a more multivalent approach is required.

Other works that deal with literary production and the networks and negotiations involved in publication are relevant to my thinking about collaboration, though they may not specifically address the kind of partnered collaboration I look at in this study. Jack Stillinger's challenge to the romantic conception of the 'solitary genius' and Jerome McGann's observations that texts reflect a series of negotiations rather than the intent of a single author both argue that literary production involves a vast network of players, including editors and publishers, a network obscured by any focus on authorial intent (McGann) or on genius (Stillinger).[11]

Adding to this discussion, I posit that in order to define collaboration, we must consider four essential questions: is it acknowledged? is it mutual? is it equal? and is it separable? All authors receive advice from others, making all texts in a sense collaborative, but I propose that texts in which the collaboration is mutually undertaken and overtly acknowledged differ fundamentally from traditionally authored texts. On the other hand, I argue that criticism of collaboration has been hampered by the assumption that true collaboration must be evenly divided (all of Stevenson's collaborations were, in one way or another, unequal ones), and that the business of the critic is to solve the 'problem' of who has written what, a project which I argue shows an a priori scepticism about the possibility of collaboration at all. Like Stevenson and his associates, I believe that collaborative writing encompasses more than the sum of its parts.

Is it acknowledged?

Literary labour, by its nature, is almost always collaborative in some sense or other. Every author responds to the influence of literary history, speaks back to his or her contemporaries, and gets feedback from family, friends, editors and publishers. Authors are social beings after all. Jerome McGann argues that texts come not from a single author but from a series of discussions and compromises between authors, editors, publishers and others tasked with turning an author's earliest ideas into a book.[12] This shows how central collaboration is to authorship, but it also threatens our ability to look at collaboration as a focused and specific endeavour. In seeing the collaborative nature of all writing (or at least all published writing), we must also take care to distinguish this ordinary, unavoidable kind of collaboration from that work that is undertaken from the beginning in a collaborative process, which therefore remains differently thought of from its very conception. Koestenbaum finds the dual author title page to be a significant boundary of collaboration:

> A text is most precisely and satisfyingly collaborative if it is composed by two writers who admit the act by placing both of their names on the title page. A double signature confers enormous interpretive freedom: it permits the reader to see the act of collaboration shadowing every word in the text. Collaborative works are intrinsically *different* than books written by one author alone: even if both names do not appear, or one writer eventually produces more material, the decision to collaborate determines the work's contours, and the way in which it can be read. Books with two authors are specimens of a relation and show writing to be a quality of motion and exchange, not a fixed thing.[13]

Focusing on the decision to collaborate within a specific relationship means that the kinds of collaborations that I am most interested in are primary collaborations between author and author, and not the ways in which the literary marketplace is collaborative, although this is of course true, and important for Stevenson as well. Critics have long noted the interventions of various of his friends, family and associates in the final form his texts took, and with varying levels of consent from Stevenson himself.

The most important figure in this context is Stevenson's friend Sidney Colvin, who has often been credited with, or accused of, editing or censoring Stevenson's work. In Barry Menikoff's re-edited version of Stevenson's late Pacific novella, *The Beach of Falesá* (1892), for instance, Menikoff writes:

> But in truth he had become the source of production with little control over the final product. Stevenson was a machine whose creative workings were alien to all those around him. He supplied the art: a variety of producers were integral in its finishing, marketing, and distribution.[14]

Menikoff critiques Colvin's decision to edit *The Beach of Falesá* in such a way as to bring it more in line with a late-Victorian sense of propriety by revising the fake marriage certificate with which the young Pacific Islander Uma is married to the ugly white colonial trader

Wiltshire. In the earlier version the certificate had Uma married to Wiltshire for one night, but periodical publications either left this out or changed the duration to one week, which seems hardly better.[15] Menikoff's own work was to reissue the novel in order to restore Stevenson's original intentions more fully. However, as McGann points out, intentions need not be everything, because editors routinely surpass or undermine authorial intentions by, for example, publishing work that was never intended for publication, even as they gesture to authorial intention as a final goal.[16] If we follow McGann instead of Menikoff, perhaps Colvin should truly be seen as a collaborator, and *The Beach of Falesá*, as originally published, a co-authored text. There is much to say about the Stevenson/Colvin relationship, but I have not, in my analysis, chosen to view Sidney Colvin as one of Stevenson's collaborators, for the simple reason that Stevenson appears not to have viewed him that way, and thus the writing is not relational in the same way as his explicit, acknowledged collaborations.

Arguments such as McGann's or Stillinger's are necessary and important because they highlight that the ways we have conventionally thought of authorship, one person as the single originator of meaning and text, is wrong. Writing has always been social, and so the collaborative mode of writing is not as revolutionary as some might have it. And yet, this is not to say that there should be no distinction between writing intended as collaborative and that which merely, as all writing must, shows the influence of other people. Not every text I will consider in this book bears the name of two authors. And yet, many of Stevenson's books *do* bear the names of two authors, and this merits consideration, because it represents a deeper commitment to collaboration throughout the writing process.

This question of acknowledged or unacknowledged collaborators has been an especially fraught one within feminist criticism, where it has long been recognised that women's labour is not acknowledged at the same rate as men's, and that the work of many men of genius has been aided by wives or other female family members who have received little credit for their talents. The evidence for this is in the renewed interest in thinkers such as Dorothy Wordsworth, whose journals formed a significant portion of the writings of her better-known brother.[17] Stevenson was unusual in crediting his wife Fanny for her co-authorship of *The Dynamiter*. He certainly didn't have to, as far the world was concerned, and it might have been better received if he had not. It is in a way ironic that Stevenson is an unacknowledged collaborator on his wife's own publication, *The Cruise of the*

Janet Nichol *among the South Sea Islands*, published years after his death, her purportedly private diary which describes one of the family's cruises in the Pacific.

Is it mutual?

Another reason that I have decided to exclude Sidney Colvin's influence on Stevenson's work from this work on collaboration is that collaboration minimally requires a mutual conversation between collaborators. Where I have found it in some cases relevant to consider contributors who were unacknowledged, in all cases they were working with Stevenson's consent and feedback. In her discussion of Colvin's work on Stevenson's Complete Works, for instance, biographer Jenni Calder notes that while Stevenson was in Samoa and far away from the publishing world, 'it was virtually impossible for him to be more involved than he was, but he was also willing to leave editorial problems to Colvin – in spite of the fact that he did not trust Colvin on some issues.'[18] This editing after the fact, with or without Stevenson's approval, does not rise to the level of working together because there is little give and take. Still less do I consider posthumous revisions such as Sir Arthur Quiller-Couch's completion of Stevenson's unfinished novel *St. Ives*. Stevenson had no thought, when he died, that this was a collaborative novel, nor did Quiller-Couch have the benefit of feedback and conversation with Stevenson about it. One cannot, as a rule, collaborate with the dead, and collaboration is not the same thing as influence (Bette London's choice to include mediums in her study of collaborations notwithstanding). When, in his essay 'My First Book' (often used as the Preface to *Treasure Island*), Stevenson credits Washington Irving with originating many of the ideas in that novel,[19] it does not make *Treasure Island* a collaboration between Irving and Stevenson.

Nor is plagiarism collaboration, which seems like it should be an obvious point, and yet is a problem that caused the Stevensons some trouble. In my third chapter, on Fanny Stevenson's collaborations, I present evidence that Fanny may have believed that she was collaborating with Louis's cousin Katharine de Mattos when she published her short story 'The Nixie' in *Scribner's* in 1888. De Mattos, who claimed that the original idea for the story had been her own, was furious at the theft, and the resulting accusation of plagiarism was one of the motivating causes for the final rift between Louis and his own collaborator, W. E. Henley. This is collaborative failure.

Is it equal?

One particular problem that has dogged consideration of Stevenson's collaborations is the question of the relative talent, and contribution, of the partners. Of Stevenson's three principal collaborators, W. E. Henley, Fanny Stevenson and Lloyd Osbourne, only Henley would likely have had a respectable career in letters independent of his relationship with Stevenson. His series of poems, *In Hospital*, describing the operations on his legs at the Edinburgh hospital are still anthologised in Victorian poetry collections, and his poem 'Invictus' remains popular among readers who admire its stoic self-determinism. Its final lines, 'I am the master of my fate, / I am the captain of my soul', have made it something of a conservative rallying cry in Britain, and kept it frequently in the news.[20] As quotable as Henley's famous poem remains, his reputation has been greatly overshadowed by the more famous Stevenson. Furthermore, with the possible exception of *The Wrong Box*, which Osbourne conceived of and carried out a significant portion of before Stevenson's involvement, Stevenson saw himself as the chief author on each work on which he collaborated. Not only did he take responsibility for the final decisions on each one, but in most cases he dictated the terms of the collaboration, giving his partners assignments to fulfil and then checking them over.

This acknowledged inequality of partners has led critics to dismiss the collaborations. Edwin Eigner, for example, says that *The Wrecker* and *The Ebb-Tide* 'can be regarded as almost entirely Stevenson's own' and that he will therefore treat those texts 'without reference to the influence of his collaborator, which is anyway . . . almost impossible to perceive'.[21] After all, if Stevenson admits to having the larger part in the project, why consider the lesser partner at all? And particularly since Fanny Stevenson and Osbourne have, traditionally, found little respect among critics for their other literary productions, readers have felt that their contributions could only harm and not help any project to which they contributed. For instance, biographer Ian Bell writes of *The Wrecker*: 'Had [Stevenson] put aside his desire to help Lloyd – or quelled his own laziness – it would have been a better novel than it is.'[22] Furthermore, my reading of the criticism shows that critical evaluations of the works themselves affect the determination of whose contribution is greater, and vice versa. Critics who wish to dismiss a work from the canon inevitably claim that it is mostly the work of Stevenson's collaborator. Critics who argue for its greater significance tend to minimise this contribution. This pattern maintains across readings of all of Stevenson's works, but is particularly strong in relation to the novels *The Dynamiter* (with Fanny) and *The Wrong Box* (with Osbourne). However, it is not self-evident why readers should feel this way.

In the case of Stevenson's collaborations, all of which he undertook with authors of lesser reputations, one suspects a defensiveness at play, against readers wary of being tricked into a too positive appraisal of a hack writer. If (as in my earlier question of whether the collaboration is equal) we are able to parse out the authorship of different sections of a text, we may not have to deal with the tricky elements of collaboration at all. Any textual study I do that would identify anything as written by one author as opposed to another is from interest in the process only. I do not intend to excise the perennially unpopular Lloyd Osbourne, or any other collaborator, from Stevenson's writings. Nor do I intend to recover Fanny, Lloyd, Henley or anyone else as the true author of any of the works I discuss. Nor is it fair, in this context, to draw conclusions about the relative talents and contributions of Stevenson's collaborators, partly because it was Stevenson himself who set the terms of the partnerships and divided the labour. Ironically, for an author who is experimenting in this way with collaborative writing, Stevenson remains as authoritarian in regard to his work as he could possibly be. It is certainly worthwhile work to look at independent publications of his partners, as, for instance, Gordon Hirsch has done with regard to Osbourne and Hilary Beattie with regard to Fanny Stevenson.[23] As a poet, Henley requires no defence. But to critique their contributions to the texts on which they each collaborated is to miss the point that their roles were circumscribed by Stevenson's overarching vision. Rather, I want to discover how the work of authorship may inhere in the relationships and the space between the collaborators.

The literature on collaboration is full of other similarly unequal partners. Renaissance dramatists Beaumont and Fletcher, for instance, were famously unequal partners,[24] and Stevenson jokingly refers to their lopsided partnership in a letter to Henley (*Letters* 2: 277). This idea that collaborative labour is not relevant unless it is equal is an easy way to dismiss the collaborative because it is much easier to prove an unequal contribution than a truly equal one, which is unlikely mathematically, at least. If one person may be proved to have contributed more, he (in this case) becomes the author and authority. This tendency is more legal than descriptive, as one author simply seems easier if one person might be said to have contributed more.

A number of critical assessments of collaboration and ideas of authorship have indeed found that the idea of the author originates in the material and legal status of copyright. For instance, Peter Jaszi and Martha Woodmansee describe the ways that our idea of the author at once creates and is constrained by the law. At first the 'ideology of "authorship" informed English – and ultimately American – copyright doctrine', but this very ideology obscures the collaborative and corporate way that writing actually progresses.[25] Thus, the law becomes 'one of the most powerful vehicles of the modern authorship construct'.[26] The specifics of copyright law can have a chilling effect on experimentation with authorship. Clare Pettitt has argued that early Victorian debates about intellectual property law affected, and were affected by, nineteenth-century ideas of authorship, and that the idea of the solitary writer was

> underwritten and perpetuated by the changes in intellectual property law in the nineteenth century. The debate around the reform of intellectual property law at this time is an important one as it shows the tenacity of literary writers such as Dickens in protecting such an obsolescent idea against the arguments of the free-trade anti-monopolists who wanted to abolish both copyright and patent protections.[27]

However, this construction was at odds with the changing nature of early and mid-Victorian authorship, which was influenced by the rapidly changing technology and dispersal of novels. Pettitt argues of Dickens, for example, that

> The double-text of *Bleak House*, therefore, raises questions about the origin of art, and the ownership of the art object. Many mid-Victorian novels reflect both explicitly and silently upon such questions at a time when the Romantic notion of the single author was coming under unprecedented pressure.[28]

Meanwhile, in America during the same period, critic David Dowling argues that authorship is 'socially driven, diverse, and dependent on the economies of circulation in the literary market, a perspective that dismantles the myth of the autonomous romantic artist'.[29] The legal and financial pressures of authorship limits the creative possibilities for thinking about collaboration, and encourages both authors and critics to find, and credit, the single voice, a necessity that goes strongly against Stevenson's own broad experimentations with different modes of authorship.

The material basis for the construction of authorship could go the other way too, though, as Ernest Mehew has found in discussion of

Stevenson's collaborations with Osbourne. As an American, Osbourne was able to secure the American copyright, a treasured possession when Stevenson, like so many authors, was beset by plagiarisms from across the pond.[30] While I acknowledge the importance of economic pressures on the idea of authorship, a survey of British and American copyright effects is beyond the scope of this book, and besides, I find that Stevenson's creative practice exceeds these considerations even as it is affected by them, or as Pettitt allows, 'The aesthetic is necessarily more than an ideological category.'[31]

Is it separable?

Of all of the questions that arise when we examine collaborative writing, however, the most persistent is whether it is possible, or advisable, to separate out the true authors of different sections of a collaborative text. When faced with a collaborative text, most critics and readers will ask: who wrote what? A recent intervention into collaborative Stevenson is the work of digital scholars Anouk Lang and Robyn Pritzker, who have been using stylometric tools to analyse *The Dynamiter* (as well as other collaborative Stevenson works) to see 'where Fanny's authorial signal comes through the text most strongly'.[32] This quantitative, digital approach follows a long tradition of critics who have argued strongly for their own abilities as merely experienced readers to easily detect Fanny's 'authorial signal', as I will discuss in my own treatment of *The Dynamiter*. Where reliable manuscript evidence tells us that certain sections of text have been written by one or another author, I share it, because one of the main investigations of this book is to discover the process used by Stevenson and his collaborators. However, there are several problems with this 'separation style' of criticism as a main approach to collaborative texts.

The principal problem with separating out the authors of a collaborative work is that this kind of focus directly undermines the aim of collaboration. Consider the case of the late-Victorian poet (or poets) Michael Field – Katherine Bradley and Edith Cooper, aunt/niece and lovers who wrote under the masculine pseudonym. The pair were troubled by frequent attempts to parse their writing – to figure out who wrote what, reportedly responding to Havelock Ellis, 'As to our work, let no man think he can put asunder what god has joined.'[33] Critic Lorraine York continues, 'Authorship itself is not significantly re-theorized or rethought in this view of collaboration.

Once again the shared collaborative space must be territorialized so that the single, individuated authors can remain intact.'[34] If the usefulness of collaboration inheres in the relationship, and not in just the single work of two authors linked together, then in untying these collaborative threads, the critic will necessarily lose an important part of the picture. Maryanne Dever, in her study of the twentieth-century collaboration between Australians Marjorie Barnard and Flora Eldershaw who wrote under the pseudonym 'M. Barnard Eldershaw' likewise criticises what she terms the 'detective' model of collaborative criticism:

> This reduction of the critical exercise to one of literary detection implies a particular set of assumptions about the way literary collaboration or joint authorship functions . . . This central preoccupation with the authorial signature assumes that the collaborative enterprise will invariably leave some textual trace or clue, while denying the wider collaborative context produced through conversation, correspondence, the sympathetic hearing or reading of a manuscript, the vigorously sought opinion.[35]

Because the process of collaboration is not, in fact, two authors writing singly but takes place in a multitude of conversations, something will always be lost when collaboration is seen as two people's single compositions, combined arithmetically. In his discussion of network theory's application to the early period of literary modernism (a period that Stevenson only barely predates), Milton A. Cohen cites Ezra Pound from 1912: 'You must not only subsidize the man with work still in him, but you must gather such dynamic particles together, you must set them where they will interact, and stimulate each other.'[36] Network theory provides support for this way of viewing the greater possibilities of collaboration over and above a yoking together of individual forms because it inheres in the relationship, and not in the individual nodes.

Thinking outside of the novelistic generic box, as Stevenson always did, can also get us outside of the trap of seeing collaborative writing as comprised of two separate strands that might be untwisted. Much collaborative theory concerns drama, and for good reason.[37] Where poets and novelists working collaboratively may be rare enough to be of note, in music, drama and, more recently, film-making, collaboration is the norm, and thus the instinct to separate out the authors is virtually non-existent. It is no accident that Stevenson's first collaborative attempts, with W. E. Henley, were dramatic works, as

I discuss in my chapter on *Deacon Brodie* and *Strange Case of Dr Jekyll and Mr Hyde* (1886). Though Stevenson was ultimately never successful as a dramatist, the various roles of the theatre – on and off the stage – never ceased to fascinate him, as he discusses in, for instance, his critical essay 'Child's Play' (1878).[38] Music, too, was a lifelong interest (he played the flageolet), not only for its own sake for also for the way it functioned as a metaphor for thinking about art. Music's harmonies and discordances not only reflect collaborative work but, in fact, cannot exist without it. Stevenson's fiction, especially his later Pacific fiction written with Osbourne, is littered with scraps of popular music reflecting this fascination, but it is in his engagement with opera that he explores the way musical roles may create productive, conflictual collaborations. In my chapter on Stevenson's Pacific writings, I explore the way that he used opera to think about collaborative art and dissonance, exploring the ways that discord and argumentative voices could bring depth and complexity to narrative.

Why is there, even now that the author is dead in both the Barthesian and literal sense, still so much anxiety over the fact of collaboration? In her compelling argument about the threatening politics of Samuel Taylor Coleridge's collaborations with Robert Southey, Alison Hickey suggests that collaboration threatens our sense of the relationship between author and text in revolutionary ways, that it

> casts doubt on the authority of each [author] in relation to their jointly produced texts. Even as, in the political realm, the revolutionary refiguring of the patriarchal familial paradigm as a fraternity threatens the singular nature of political authority, so refiguring authorial paternity as fraternity jeopardizes the singular nature of writerly authority.[39]

The dangers of collaboration exceed the bounds of the collaborative moment or text itself, calling into question larger unities, between meaning and language itself: 'The anxiety about authority is associated with written language in general, whose fabrications always bear an illegitimate relation to intention.'[40] What comes out of his essays and literary criticism is that Stevenson never accepted this view of authorship in the first place in so far as he is always aware of his work being shaped by multiple forces, as he discusses most explicitly in his essay 'A Chapter on Dreams' (1888): forces including but not limited to his (pre-Freudian) unconscious dreaming self, his sense of the literary marketplace and its demands, and his acute awareness as a craftsperson, with long practice and experience, of the alarming gap between meaning and language. This gap is the most explicitly investigated in his essay 'Truth of Intercourse' (1879), which is the final essay in the series entitled *Virginibus Puerisque* (1876–81), which 'presents Stevenson's most sustained treatment of the difficulty of communication . . . The focus here is not on verbal truthfulness but on truth to one's feelings, of sincerity in one's relations to others.'[41] Stevenson explains, 'The difficulty of literature is not to write, but to write what you mean', and that, even in spoken language, 'the speech of the ideal talker shall correspond and fit upon the truth of fact – not clumsily, obscuring lineaments, like a mantle, but cleanly adhering, like an athlete's skin.'[42] The 'skin' here described is not the epidermis of the athlete, but rather the closely fitting clothes that approximate the body without being the body. It is, in other words, because Stevenson never accepts language and meaning as united, never accepts the idea of the originating genius as anything more than one of an array of sources for the creative work, that he is prepared to readily admit this radical experimentation with collaboration.

In 'My First Book' Stevenson confesses to plagiarising Washington Irving in the creation of *Treasure Island*.[43] Although the confession of plagiarism is facetious, his admission is a more enduring reflection on his artistic process. In his work on nineteenth-century plagiarism, Robert Macfarlane opposes two views of writing: *creatio* and *inventio*. *Creatio* is the notion of writing as original and divinely inspired, associated (falsely) with the Romantics. *Inventio* is the notion of 'creation as rearrangement' which is associated with the Augustans and more easily reconciled with post-structuralist views of language. Macfarlane's study is interested in 'the reappraisal of originality which occurred in Britain between 1859 and 1900'.[44] As Stevenson shows when he falsely apologises for stealing from Irving, he is engaged in experimentation with art as *inventio*, pushing boundaries in his search for more and more original raw materials. Thus, we see in 'My First Book' Stevenson seeing *Treasure Island* as a revisitation of Washington Irving, and also Ballantyne's *The Coral Island*, but in other places it is the work of his friends and family that he takes as his raw material to convert into art – whether that be W. E. Henley's fast drafts of plays early on, Fanny's tall tales in Hyères incorporated into *The Dynamiter*, or Osbourne's complete draft of *A Game of Bluff* which became the co-authored *The Wrong Box*. Furthermore, even when not working collaboratively, this *modus operandi* structures

Stevenson's thinking about his artistic process, such that he perceives even a schism in himself between the creator of raw material and the artistic interpreter, most famously in *A Chapter on Dreams*, his description of the creation of *Strange Case of Dr Jekyll and Mr Hyde* where he distinguished between the 'brownies' and 'the man with the conscience and the variable bank–account'.[45] Both, Stevenson argues, are required in the artistic process. Who has written what in Stevenson's collaboratively written texts is not always relevant. Instead, it is in the dialogic space between Stevenson and collaborators that he finds his artistic process.

Literary History, Politics and Biography

Two final issues that must be addressed in any study of late nineteenth-century collaborations are the historical and the biographical. Why the nineteenth century? There has been much work done on collaboration in Renaissance scholarship because it is the period of the drama, an inherently collaborative genre: see, for instance, Heather Hirschfeld's survey of scholarship on the topic and Jeffrey Masten's work on collaborative drama and sexualities where he asserts that collaborative writing was 'the Renaissance English theatre's dominant mode of textual production'.[46] The old idea, exploded by Jack Stillinger's work on the Romantic 'myth of the solitary genius', was that this collaborative Renaissance gave way to an author-centred Romantic period, but this model has been so far rejected that scholarly work on collaboration has come to be dominated by Romanticists, with a significant amount of work being done on William Godwin and Mary Wollstonecraft, Dorothy and William Wordsworth, Samuel Taylor Coleridge with Wordsworth and with Robert Southey, and, in America, Sophia and Nathaniel Hawthorne.[47] This now-rejected historical narrative continues by claiming that the Romantic 'age of the author' was undone by the busy marketplace of Victorian letters, and then dealt a further blow by the experiments that characterise early modernism. But collaboration has been practised in many times and cultures. Stone and Thompson note that 'collaboration was long a feature of the texts produced by African American or indigenous cultures'.[48] Stevenson himself used the model of Butaritarian opera to explore his own thinking about how art can incorporate a multiplicity of voices, as I discuss in my chapter on the Pacific diaries and *In the South Seas* (1896).

Nevertheless, in the case of Stevenson specifically, I do find that there is something 'avant-garde' and experimental in his use of collaborative composition, and thus I find it time bound and linked to literary experimentation. The dominant conception of the Victorian author is that he or she was driven by the literary marketplace. Richard Salmon describes a conception of authorship that attempts to bridge two depictions of the author, as both hero and as a labourer subject to the market, which is perhaps best embodied in the figure of David Copperfield, who is subject to the vicissitudes of the market and yet remains unshakably the hero and centre of his eponymous novel.[49] Yet at the turn of the century the identity of the author as hero was in decline. Malcolm Bradbury, who likewise notes the commercial pressures on the Victorian writer, describes the 'marked gap [by the 1890s] between serious and popular imaginative writing and a declining commercial basis for the former, with *avant-gardism* emerging in reaction at the beginning of the twentieth century in a parallel, but non-commercial, literary market'.[50] Network connections take on special and particular importance during the early years of the twentieth century. Fabio A. Durão and Dominic Williams, among others, cite the ascendency of the 'salon culture' as modernist practice[51] (though this had certainly been true in the eighteenth century and the Romantic period as well), and Cohen discusses the astonishing proliferation of groups such as the Imagists or the Futurists in the decade immediately preceding World War I, arguing that these groups served to bolster the safety and credibility of artists who might otherwise have been afraid to go it alone in opposition to their culture. He argues that in many cases belonging to these groups, led by powerful and famous authors such as Ezra Pound, might have been a requirement for young authors hoping to break into the profession.[52] We find no group around Stevenson in the sense of those mentioned above, but we do see Stevenson supported by less successful writers who support and contribute to his work and who model themselves after his style and vision. Thus, the collaborative practice that Stevenson is engaged in during the 1880s and 1890s looks forward to the experiments with authorship that would emerge in the coming decades.

Alan Sandison has argued for Stevenson as a proto-modernist, pointing out that many of his works look forward to twentieth-century modernism, as a corrective to the long-standing critical assumption that Stevenson is a romancer in the tradition of Sir Walter Scott.[53] Stevenson does both, but his most collaborative works are also the most experimental and most modern. For instance, *The Dynamiter: More New Arabian Nights*, which experiments with shifting frames and unreliable narrators and which is titled as a sequel to his *New Arabian Nights*, is one of his most experimental texts.[54] Often experimental collaborations meant sacrificing the commercial viability of the work, just as Bradbury has found in reference to similar literary experiments at the beginning of the twentieth century. In breaking away from the image of the single author as sole creator of literary authority, Stevenson proved bold in his willingness to do away with the very celebrity that contributed to some of his greatest commercial success.[55] Certainly, his name brand as the author of *Treasure Island* meant that anything he put his name to was marketable. And yet, in his choice of collaborators he eschews any who might have increased the marketability of his work, but works exclusively with people who could not have conceivably contributed to his success – who, in fact, as letters from his acquaintances and publishers attest, materially hurt it. There was, in short, no economic advantage whatsoever to listing Fanny Stevenson as a co-author on *The Dynamiter*, and whereas some have argued that Lloyd Osbourne's American citizenship would help him to hold on to American copyright, in fact Stevenson's involvement with *The Wrong Box* only hurt, and never helped, his career. Subsequent novels *The Wrecker* and *The Ebb-Tide* would have been much better received if they had been put out as single-author texts, which *The Ebb-Tide* for the most part was. In forgoing these benefits of economics and reputation, Stevenson demonstrated his commitment to pursuing a more experimental path – one that would challenge the nineteenth-century view of the author with an alternate, dialogic and relationship-based vision.

Furthermore, we can see a strong association between Stevenson's most collaborative and his contemporaneous texts. In his collaborative works with Osbourne, Stevenson leaves behind Scotland's Jacobite past and instead explores the modern world, describing *The Wrecker* as 'a tale of a caste so modern; – full of details of our barbaric manners and unstable morals; ... full of the unrest and movement of our century'.[56] Collaborative composition is vastly less pronounced in his Scottish novels such as *Kidnapped* (1886), *Catriona* (1893) or *Weir of Hermiston* (1896), though I do argue for collaborative inspiration in the narrative experiments of *The Master of Ballantrae* (1889).

A subsidiary thread I will pursue is to track Stevenson's politics as they grow in both insistence and sophistication over the course of his career. *Jekyll and Hyde* is, in my reading of it at least, only minimally concerned with the politics of the day. As Stevenson leaves behind his first partnership with Henley to work instead with his wife Fanny, his work becomes more political. In my chapter on *The Dynamiter* I assess the Stevensons' ultimately unsuccessful attempts to make sense of the Fenian dynamite campaign. More politically nuanced and interesting, however, is the pair's reflections on the sexual politics they found in the Pacific Islands, where both became interested in the intersection of sexual and colonial relations, particularly as they impacted underage girls. Both Stevensons were also doggedly concerned with the abuse of blackbirding, or the enslaving of Pacific Islanders, a topic that this book does not treat extensively but which has been treated by Roslyn Jolly among others. Archival manuscripts in Stevenson's hand held in the Huntington library (which are nearly impossible to read) dealing with slavers such as Bully Hayes provide evidence that Stevenson planned much more work on the topic, which is a central if not the central theme of Fanny's diary *The Cruise of the* Janet Nichol. In contrast to Louis's usually more thoughtful and nuanced ideas, Fanny's politics could be crude and under-thought, but the fact remains that she was his most politically interested co-author. Stevenson's growing political interests and sensibilities unfortunately coincided with his shift to working with Lloyd Osbourne as his final and exclusive collaborator. Osbourne had little interest in this mode of thought, and it contributed to a schism between the partners. Stevenson and Osbourne's *The Wrong Box*, which was originally Osbourne's conception, has an arch and impudent tone, a throwback to the dandyism of Stevenson's earlier *Jekyll and Hyde*, but without that text's moral heft. This lightness of sensibility is part of its overall failure, but has also kept it a cult classic among those who admire such things. To compare it, however, to Stevenson's simultaneous *The Master of Ballantrae* is to see how Stevenson would rather have treated the same topic: what is in *The Wrong Box* a cynical rejection and disinterest in ideas of right and wrong becomes in *The Master of Ballantrae* more of a focused challenge to conventional rules of law and morality.

Finally, Stevenson and Osbourne worked together on *The Wrecker* and *The Ebb-Tide*. These two texts are Stevenson's most political fictions, the first critiquing global capitalism especially in its impacts on the Pacific and the second critiquing imperialism and missionary zeal. The violence of the latter work greatly offended Sidney Colvin, who initially blamed what he perceived as the book's failures on Osbourne. However, as Colvin himself eventually learned, this was not true: the dark vision of *The Ebb-Tide* was Stevenson's own, and Osbourne had little to do with it.

A vexing problem in collaboration criticism is that of biography, which presents a paradoxical challenge. Critics invested in the collaborative are often seeking to demystify the cult of authorship that surrounds a particular author by demonstrating that he is not the divinely inspired *auteur* responsible for all of his work that readers have thought, but rather has been supported by a network. On the other hand, the work of analysing collaborations has sometimes pulled me deeper into the biographical by highlighting the varied relationships and personalities that make up the author's life, ironically reinforcing the kind of literary star-gazing that collaboration scholarship is meant to undermine. This problem is particularly thorny in the case of Robert Louis Stevenson because of his adventurous life, his own magnetic personality, still exerting its influence over a century later, and the strong personalities with whom he surrounded himself, all of which offers abundant material for discussion. If I have fallen into a biographical trap, at least I can say I am not alone – for all of these reasons, among Stevenson criticism it is rare to find scholarship that eschews the biographical. The difficulties of dealing with the biographical are also inextricably tied up with the question of the author as celebrity – something Stevenson certainly was in the second half of his career. And yet, in some cases I have found Stevenson himself to be acutely aware of these problems, and even turning to the work of collaboration to try to free himself from the very restrictions that fame and celebrity placed upon him, often without success.

Foucault's 'author-function' has been helpful in this regard because it reminds us that, while Stevenson the man and Stevenson the author both existed, they are not co-identical with one another. Foucault has written that 'The name of an author poses all the problems related to the category of a proper name', but it poses more problems too: 'the link between a proper name and the individual being named and the link between an author's name and that which it names are not isomorphous and do not function in the same way.'[57] Foucault's concern is that the over-identification of the biographical personage with the authorial ego may unduly influence the reception of texts. But it is worth noting that it works the other way, too – the author's name with all it brings to bear serves to obliterate the historical specificity of the life, its compromises and its connections. The politics and trends of an author's work may paint with too broad a brush our assessment of his or her messy and contradictory life. Similarly, Marjorie Stone and Judith Thompson propose that the author him- or herself be seen as a 'heterotext', in that authors are 'woven of different strands of influence and agency, absorbing or incorporating differing subjectivities, and speaking in multiple voices'.[58] We can speak of Stevenson as an author without in doing so denying the contributions of friends, families, editors, typesetters, precursors and influences.

Finally, yet another school of collaborative criticism, largely found both within feminist theory and within composition studies, suggests that the process of collaboration is a superior method of composition for scholarly and creative work alike, and 'see[s] the promotion of collaboration in many forms as a primary means to democratise institutional and social structures, including structures of writing'.[59] Composition and rhetoric scholars Lisa Ede and Andrea A. Lunsford have

> been calling on scholars in rhetoric and composition, and in the humanities more generally, to enact contemporary critiques of the author and of the autonomous individual through a greater interest in and adoption of collaborative writing practices and to do so not only in classrooms but in scholarly and professional work as well.[60]

What I have found in Stevenson's work that this reading of collaboration fails to address, however, is the cost of collaborative experimentation – the conflict, the frustration, lost sales, and some would even say the cost to his literary legacy – costs that caused him to turn away from his experiments in the end.

Chapter Overview

My analysis of Stevenson's collaborations begins with a discussion of the plays that he wrote during the 1880s with his then best friend, W. E. Henley. These plays were the foundation of Stevenson's collaborative work, even though the partnership did not last beyond them. Stevenson and Henley wrote three plays together, *Deacon Brodie* (first printed 1880 and first performed in 1882), *Beau Austin* (first printed 1884, first performed 1890) and *Admiral Guinea* (first printed 1884, and first performed in 1897), which were later collected together under the title *Three Plays* in 1892. A fourth, *Macaire*, written during the same period, was published only in 1895, after Stevenson's death. Countless others were planned. Work on *Beau Austin* and *Admiral Guinea* was sometimes conducted by notebook, giving us a fascinating glimpse into the collaborative process that Stevenson used. Although the pair were hopeful about the success of their writings on the stage, they were inevitably disappointed, and all the plays that they wrote together were failures in their own time and even less considered now.

Despite the failures of these plays, one at least, *Deacon Brodie*, has found immortality as an early source for what is perhaps Stevenson's most famous work, *Strange Case of Dr Jekyll and Mr Hyde*. Beginning with a reading of *Deacon Brodie*, I suggest that that play biographically reflects the conflicts that Stevenson and Henley were facing in their friendship and literary partnership. In shifting focus, then, to *Jekyll and Hyde* we can see that the novella bears the traces not only of the early friendship but also of its own beginnings on the stage. The dramatic origins of the *Jekyll and Hyde* story extend to its afterlife. The many successful stage and film adaptations of this famous work attest to its theatricality, and the idea of the man who shows two faces to the world is an apt description of the actor.

Jekyll and Hyde, which owes its origins to literal dual authorship, is a reflection on the collaborative space of the theatre, but also a reflection on the fragmentation of the single author. Stevenson uses the metaphor of the stage to describe his own dreaming mind in his essay 'A Chapter on Dreams', in which he describes, years later, how he came to compose *Jekyll and Hyde*. Never mentioning his earlier work and conflicts with Henley, he instead develops a theory of the author himself as split into two personalities, and then more. The dizzying and disorienting fragmentations of Stevenson's own persona in this fascinating essay provide important clues to explain why he persists in working collaboratively throughout his career. So far from himself subscribing to the idea that art is the product of a solitary mind, he already sees the mind of the artist as fractured into a multiplicity of voices. These voices contend for control just as stubbornly as a real collaborator such as Henley.

My next chapter moves to consideration of Stevenson's acknowledged collaborations with his wife Fanny, most substantially, their co-written work, *The Dynamiter*, also titled *More New Arabian Nights*, an experimental farce about the Fenian dynamite campaign that was currently in the news. Husband and wife collaborations, I argue, create subtle problems, largely because we expect a wife to assist her husband without credit. (Where a husband assists his wife, on the other hand, critics may assume the work is rightly his.) This novel, one of Stevenson's most formally experimental, draws upon the structures of the *Arabian Nights*, with their ever-receding frames and also their overt metafictionality. Just as Shahrazad makes up the stories to tell her brutal husband, Clara Luxmore, the principal narrator in *The Dynamiter*, tells inset stories that are lies. Also like *The Dynamiter*, the *Arabian Nights* is also concerned with issues of narrative and marriage. *The Dynamiter* was well regarded in the nineteenth century, but not so in the twentieth or twenty-first, precisely because recent critics have resented Fanny's involvement. However, the Stevensons may be playing a trick on us after all, because suspect, disguised and unreliable female author/narrators are pre-emptively treated within the text itself, making the structure of the tales a metafictional reflection on the circumstances of its creation.

I also consider Fanny's and Louis's co-written play, *The Hanging Judge* (1887), a thinly disguised biographical play probably meant for home production, as well as Fanny's controversial story 'The Nixie', which has been blamed for the breakup of Stevenson's friendship with Henley after Stevenson's cousin Katharine de Mattos claimed it as her own. Fanny, I hypothesise, had in fact intended to collaborate with de Mattos on the project, probably inspired by her husband's own collaborations with Henley. When Henley took the aggrieved Katharine's part, it had less to do with his loyalty to Katharine or the rightness of her own claims, and more to do with his continued resentment of the failures of the plays that he himself had written with Stevenson.

I continue to focus on the Stevenson marriage in my chapter on the couple's Pacific writings, prominently Fanny Stevenson's diary *The Cruise of the* Janet Nichol *among the South Sea Islands*, published in 1914, years after Stevenson's death, as well as Robert Louis Stevenson's travel writing from the Pacific, posthumously compiled in *In the South Seas* and his novella *The Beach of Falesá*, both of which were heavily influenced by observations from Fanny's diary. In his description of the opera on Butaritari, Stevenson lays out his theory of conflictual collaboration, prompting us to read the stress from conflicts with his sometimes-contentious wife as artistically stimulating rather than repressive. Looking at Fanny's diary reveals the extent to which much of the Stevensons' writing was a family venture. I examine the progression of several textual fragments describing Pacific Islands the Stevensons visited on the ship the *Janet Nicoll*, from their first draft as holograph manuscript fragments, to their inclusion in *The Cruise of the* Janet Nichol, and sometimes their inclusion in Louis's published non-fiction and then fiction. Remarkably, I have found that much of this material, which was originally written by Louis but later claimed by Fanny, concerns the same topic – that of the sexual exploitation of young Pacific Island girls by white traders. The shared nature of the family's diaries allowed Louis to hide in his wife's diary material on a topic that was evidently of great interest to him, but that would have negatively affected this famous author's reputation as a family-friendly author. I see Stevenson's concern with this dark side of Pacific colonisation in *The Beach of Falesá*, in which work I show that the character of Uma is quite a bit younger than more recent readers have realised. That this material proved not suitable for the Stevenson brand is supported by Sidney Colvin's zealous expurgation of *The Beach of Falesá*.

Though Stevenson did write a great deal of material with both Henley and with Fanny Stevenson, his most enduring partnership was with his stepson, Lloyd Osbourne. In addition to the three novels mentioned above, the pair planned many unfinished works, just as Stevenson had done years earlier with Henley. The work for which we have the most extensive manuscript material is *The Wrong Box*, which was revised from nineteen-year-old Osbourne's comic novel *A Game of Bluff*. For this novel we have access to a manuscript that shows Osbourne's typed pages overwritten with Stevenson's emendations and interspersed with Stevenson's handwritten pages. Even so, *The Wrong Box* presents two significant problems. First, *The Wrong Box* is atypical of Stevenson's collaborations because of just how extensive Osbourne's contributions were; Osbourne had a complete draft before Stevenson joined the project. In no other case did Stevenson give any collaborator as much leeway on a project as Osbourne had on *The Wrong Box*, nor would he ever give Osbourne such leeway again. Despite the existence of a complete manuscript that was worked on by both authors, an almost ideal situation for such archival detective work, many questions must remain for the scholar who wishes to parcel out each writer's contributions. Because Stevenson rewrote many of Osbourne's typewritten pages in his own hand, there are very few moments at which we can assign credit to Stevenson (although there are more where we can confidently assign it to Osbourne). So although *The Wrong Box* tells us the most about the process of collaboration, it also serves as an example of the impossibility and inadvisability of unbraiding the collaborative process completely.

Although *The Wrong Box* does not stand among Stevenson's most enduring works, the process that Stevenson and Osbourne used to write this novel influenced Stevenson's views about collaboration, leading him to embrace a more experimental style generally. At the end of this chapter I argue that Stevenson's concurrently written novel, *The Master of Ballantrae*, which has achieved much greater fame and respect in his canon, is a revisitation of the themes he explored with Osbourne in *The Wrong Box*, in a tragic rather than a comic mode. Even more than this, I find that the actual process of working with Osbourne became incorporated into that novel, which dramatises the collaborative experimentations and revisions that Stevenson and Osbourne were exploring.

My final chapter considers the end of Stevenson's collaborative project: his final two novels with Osbourne: *The Wrecker* and *The Ebb-Tide*. In a letter to his cousin Stevenson emphasises Osbourne's subordinate role and expresses his growing frustration: 'The great difficulty of collaboration is that you can't explain what you mean' (*Letters* 8: 364–5). Of all of Stevenson's projects, it is his wide-ranging adventure *The Wrecker* that is most in need of critical reassessment. Although inconsistent, especially because of its huge and sprawling structure, *The Wrecker* best combines the high adventure on which Stevenson had made his earlier career with the new style and concerns that he was developing late in his life: a biting critique of late-Victorian capitalism and the imperial project. I find *The Wrecker* to be the apotheosis of Stevenson's collaborative strivings throughout his career.

The Wrecker is a novel about partnerships and the compromises they require – of ethics, art and self-interest, written at a moment when Stevenson himself was the most challenged by his own difficult partnership with Osbourne. In its plot it revises themes that Stevenson had first explored with W. E. Henley in *Deacon Brodie*, when he first undertook collaborative writing: the challenges and frustrations of partnerships between men, although these topics are treated more hopefully in *The Wrecker* than they had been in *Deacon Brodie*. *The Wrecker*'s two protagonists, the American investor Loudon Dodd and English aristocratic scion Norris Carthew, are inspired but also tested by their best friends and business partners. Outside of the text, Stevenson himself was finding his own partnership with Osbourne challenging; the unequal terms of the arrangement were more difficult than he had imagined. He was also learning that the collaborative process, which had promised to be liberating, was constraining in other ways, dictating a more realistic method and forcing him to create characters based on the family's acquaintances, a thing he had often done before but only selectively.

Finally, the pair undertook *The Ebb-Tide*, but by then the process had failed. Although Stevenson began that novel with Osbourne, and Osbourne's name remains on it, Stevenson confessed that the younger man contributed little, and then only on the earlier parts. This dark novel – Stevenson's last completed one – indicates Stevenson's emerging style, a style of which we would almost certainly have had more of if not for his untimely death. As Stevenson's vision became more cynical and more political, he found himself more isolated artistically from his close associates. It seems unlikely that, in the emerging aesthetic of his late life, he would have found it possible to work with collaborators in the ways he had before. *The Ebb-Tide* is the end of his collaborative experimentations.

Notes

1. *Letters of Robert Louis Stevenson*, vol. 8, p. 159. Subsequent references to this edition will be cited parenthetically as *Letters*. Text references are to volume and page of this edition.
2. James, 'Greville Fane', p. 433.
3. Ibid. p. 451.
4. Ibid. p. 436.
5. Menikoff, *Robert Louis Stevenson and 'The Beach of Falesá'*, p. 15.
6. Barthes, 'The Death of the Author', pp. 49–55.
7. Foucault, 'What is an Author?', pp. 113–38.
8. Bakhtin, 'Discourse in the Novel', pp. 259–422.
9. Koestenbaum, *Double Talk*, p. 146.
10. London, *Writing Double*; Laird, *Women Coauthors*.
11. Stillinger, *Multiple Authorship and the Myth of the Solitary Genius*; McGann, *The Textual Condition*.
12. McGann, *The Textual Condition*.
13. Koestenbaum, *Double Talk*, p. 2.
14. Menikoff, *Robert Louis Stevenson and 'The Beach of Falesá'*, p. 8.
15. Ibid. pp. 84–9.
16. McGann, *The Textual Condition*, p. 60.
17. See, for instance, Anne Wallace, 'Home at Grasmere Again'.
18. Calder, *Robert Louis Stevenson*, p. 328.
19. Robert Louis Stevenson, 'My First Book', pp. 191–200.
20. Henley, 'In Hospital', pp. 571–86; 'Invictus', *Poetry Foundation*, https://www.poetryfoundation.org/poems/51642/invictus
21. Eigner, *Robert Louis Stevenson and the Romantic Tradition*, pp. 98n and 99n.
22. Bell, *Dreams of Exile*, p. 230.
23. Hirsch, 'The Fiction of Lloyd Osbourne'; Beattie, 'Fanny Osbourne Stevenson's Fiction'.
24. Stillinger, *Multiple Authorship*, p. 168.
25. Jaszi, 'On the Author Effect', p. 32.
26. Woodmansee, 'On the Author Effect', p. 27.
27. Pettitt, 'The Law and Victorian Fiction', p. 77.
28. Pettitt, *Patent Inventions*, p. 24.
29. Dowling, *Literary Partnerships and the Marketplace*, p. 5.

30. Mehew, Introduction to *The Wrong Box*.
31. Pettitt, *Patent Inventions*, p. 23.
32. Lang, 'Style and the Stevensons'. See also Chen et al., *Deciphering* The Dynamiter.
33. Sturgeon, *Michael Field*, p. 47, quoted in Faderman, *Surpassing the Love of Men*, p. 210 and York, 'Crowding the Garret', p. 293.
34. York, 'Crowding the Garret', p. 293.
35. Dever, '"No Mine and Thine but Ours"', pp. 66–7.
36. Pound, 'Patria Mia', p. 588, cited in Cohen, '"To Stand on the Rock of the Word 'We'"', pp. 2–3.
37. See Stone and Thompson, 'Contexts and Heterotexts', p. 17.
38. Robert Louis Stevenson, 'Child's Play'.
39. Hickey, 'Coleridge, Southey, "and Co."', p. 306.
40. Ibid. p. 306.
41. Abrahamson, ed., *Essays I*, p. 141.
42. Robert Louis Stevenson, 'Virginibus Puerisque', pp. 41 and 42.
43. Robert Louis Stevenson, 'My First Book', p. 194.
44. Macfarlane, *Original Copy*, p. 6.
45. Stevenson, 'A Chapter on Dreams', p. 248.
46. Masten, *Textual Intercourse*, p. 14.
47. For work on the Godwin–Wollstonecraft relationship, see, for instance, Rajan, 'Framing the Corpus', and Goggin, 'Editing Minervas'. For work on the Wordsworths, see Anne Wallace, 'Home at Grasmere Again' and Bellanca, 'After-Life-Writing'. For Coleridge and Wordsworth, see Jamison, 'Copyright and Collaboration'. For Coleridge and Southey, see Hickey, 'Coleridge, Southey, "and Co."'. For criticism on the Hawthornes, see Elbert, Hall and Rodier, eds, *Reinventing the Peabody Sisters*.
48. Stone and Thompson, 'Contexts and Heterotexts', p. 15.
49. Salmon, '"Farewell Poetry and Aerial Flights"'.
50. Bradbury, *The Social Context of Modern English Literature*, pp. 206, 208. More recently, critics have disputed Bradbury's sense of a disconnect between popular and elite conceptions of the author during this period; see, for instance, the discussion of the impacts of consumerism and commodity fetishism on the marketing of the work of art during modernism in Rainey, *Institutions of Modernism*, p. 4.
51. Durão and Williams, *Modernist Group Dynamics*, p. vii, and see also Hannah, 'Networks of Modernism'.
52. Cohen, '"To Stand on the Rock of the Word 'We'"', p. 5.
53. Sandison, *Robert Louis Stevenson and the Appearance of Modernism*. For a discussion of Stevenson as modernist, see also Watson, 'Modernism'. Roslyn Jolly traces the history and source of this reputation as a writer of historical romance, which is neither natural nor inevitable considering the diversity of work that Stevenson produced in his career, in *Robert Louis Stevenson in the Pacific*, p. 175.

54. Sandison, *Robert Louis Stevenson and the Appearance of Modernism*, pp. 82–121.
55. For discussion of the tensions between his artistic aspirations and the need to write for the popular market, see Ambrosini, 'R. L. Stevenson and the Ethical Value of Writing for the Market', and Norquay, *Robert Louis Stevenson and Theories of Reading*.
56. Stevenson and Osbourne, Epilogue to *The Wrecker*, p. 550. Subsequent references to this edition will be cited parenthetically as *Wrecker*.
57. Foucault, 'What is an Author?', pp. 121, 122.
58. Stone and Thompson, 'Contexts and Heterotexts', p. 19.
59. Laird, '"A Hand Spills from the Book's Threshold"', p. 346.
60. Ede and Lunsford, 'Collaboration and Concepts of Authorship', pp. 355–6.

Chapter 1

Criminal Collaborators: *Deacon Brodie* and *Strange Case of Dr Jekyll and Mr Hyde*

'When you play a good man, try to find out where he is bad, and when you play a villain, try to find where he is good.'
Constantin Stanislavski[1]

This study of Robert Louis Stevenson's collaboration begins with a work not previously understood as being collaborative. *Strange Case of Dr Jekyll and Mr Hyde* (1886) dramatises the acute struggles of the collaborative author. Stevenson may have written the actual novella single-handedly, but the life of the text tells a different story. The genesis of *Jekyll and Hyde* is collaborative, in Stevenson's persistent but ill-fated attempts to become a playwright with his friend William E. Henley. This dramatic origin retains its influence throughout the story's history: *Jekyll and Hyde* has much to say about the theatre, as this chapter will show. The afterlife of the piece is also collaborative, as Stevenson's dramatic success would be realised in the longevity *Jekyll and Hyde* has had on stage and screen. At the same time, no other piece in Stevenson's oeuvre so chillingly dramatises the dark side of collaboration. For, besides owing its origin to the stage, *Jekyll and Hyde* also emerges out of the world of nightmare, quite literally. Hyde is the enemy who seems to be our friend, the partner who shares a goal and yet appears to be working at cross-purposes. While in the light of day this might seem to be the troublesome writing partner – William Henley, say, or later Lloyd Osbourne – the dream origins of Stevenson's novella suggest that the author is himself split – that the dark collaborator may, in fact, be ourselves.

Deacon Brodie: A Theatrical Failure

William E. Henley (1849–1903) was a critic and poet. He is now best known for his poem 'Invictus' and his series of poems *In Hospital*, which describe his experience with the surgery on his foot as part of his life-long struggle with a form of tuberculosis (the other foot had been amputated years before). In some ways the opposite of Stevenson, Henley was, and is still, associated with heroic imperialism and the idealisation of the 'man of action'.[2] Though he was influential as a critic and an editor, as an imaginative writer he never reached the levels of reputation that his friend Louis did. Stevenson would use him as the original for one of his most famous characters, *Treasure Island*'s (1883) Long John Silver, with his booming voice, larger-than-life personality, and wooden leg necessitating the use of crutches. The two men met at the Edinburgh infirmary in 1875[3] and were close friends until they quarrelled in 1888. Henley was passionately devoted to Stevenson, even to the extent that he perceived a rival in Stevenson's wife Fanny, and as a result he turned just as passionately against him when the two friends had a falling out. (I describe this disagreement and its results in my next chapter.)

Figure 1.1 William Henley. Photograph by Frederick Hollyer. © Victoria and Albert Museum, London.

Stevenson published three plays with Henley, and planned many more. Three – *Deacon Brodie* (first printed 1880 and first performed in 1882), *Beau Austin* (first printed 1884, first performed 1890) and *Admiral Guinea* (first printed 1884, and first performed in 1897, after Stevenson's death) – were published together in 1892 together in the volume *Three Plays*. *Deacon Brodie* and *Admiral Guinea* are set in the eighteenth century, and *Beau Austin* in 1820, and Hultgren notes that all share 'nostalgic efforts to capture the aesthetic of an earlier time'.[4] This distinguishes them from Stevenson's later collaborations, all of which are pointedly modern in their focus. A fourth play, *Macaire*, was privately printed in 1885 and was released a year after Stevenson's death in 1895. This was an adaptation of an earlier French play, which shared *Deacon Brodie*'s interest in criminal psychology. Of all of these plays it was the first, *Deacon Brodie*, that had the most staying power. Though neglected during its run and afterwards, the themes of this play are rewritten into Stevenson's most famous work. *Deacon Brodie* tells the story of the historical William Brodie (1741–88), a cabinetmaker who moonlighted as a notorious criminal. Stevenson may have been partly inspired by the fact that his father had furniture Brodie had made[5] – a cabinet now viewable in the Writers' Museum in Edinburgh. *Deacon Brodie*'s discussion of duality is an extended meditation of the plight and difficulty of the double author. This difficulty could not be overcome, and the play's failure to achieve popular or critical success can in part be attributed to the collaborative circumstances of its creation. Nevertheless, it is from this important origin that Stevenson's solo writings go on to explore the decentring of authorship in the better-known 'The Body-Snatcher' (1884) up through his most famous work, *Strange Case of Dr Jekyll and Mr Hyde*. *Deacon Brodie* dramatises the dual nature of the titular character, but also his failure to form profitable partnerships with those around him. The contentious partnerships in the play prefigure the breakdown of Stevenson's own partnership with Henley, and the struggle between collaboration and control that would become the subject of Stevenson's later work. The theatrical origins of the story fundamentally shape its themes and its later incarnation as *Jekyll and Hyde*.

Stevenson was the master of many forms and genres. Besides his well-known novels and novellas, he changed the direction of the early British short story, his poems are still part of the established canon of the nursery, and his essays are, deservedly, undergoing a renaissance in critical attention. However, there was one genre that he never mastered, though not for lack of trying: the drama. Stevenson worked on all of his plays collaboratively, and mostly with Henley. Despite many attempts, they never had success. *Deacon Brodie*, as close as they came to a hit, was still largely considered a flop, and it contributed to the dissolution of their friendship.[6]

As the pair were working at a distance, with Henley in London and Stevenson preparing for and then returning from his French trip described in *Travels with a Donkey*, we see in Stevenson's letters his growing frustration with the process, as well as the difficulties that long-distance collaboration create. On 21 September 1878, he writes, optimistically, 'William Ernest Henley, what crowds of real, good dramatic stuff this piece contains' (*Letters* 2: 277). On his return from his travels, he responds half-teasingly to Henley's complaints that he has not done enough on the play; clearly, *Travels with a Donkey* as well as the recently completed first volume of *New Arabian Nights* (1882) were his priority. As for *Deacon Brodie*, Stevenson says it is 'not up to so much as I had hoped' (*Letters* 2: 279). In an undated letter following he says that he is working in a rush, signs his letter to Henley 'Adieu Beaumont or Fletcher / Yours Fletcher or Beaumont / Look up and see which is which – after we're played and not damned: not before' (*Letters* 2: 283), an allusion to the collaborative seventeenth-century dramatists. Fletcher is said to have written a good deal more,[7] a sly suggestion that neither collaborator may want to hog the credit until critical approval was assured. In fact, Henley explains that Stevenson's name came first on *Deacon Brodie* to 'help the play' and that Henley's would be listed first on the other plays, all of this on Stevenson's suggestion.[8] Stevenson returned to England and Scotland, working constantly at the play with Henley, but then fell sick, complaining to Charles Baxter 'The *Deacon* is quietly killing off both Henley and myself . . . but we'll push through first, and then die at leisure afterwards' (*Letters* 2: 292). Henley, meanwhile, was eager to keep up the collaboration, and Damian Atkinson notes, 'throughout their collaboration, WEH was the prime mover believing their fortunes would be made but RLS was not so naïve'.[9] Fanny seemed to agree with Henley. As the collaborators waited anxiously for reviews of a later, 1884 performance, Fanny wrote to Henley, encouraging him to take on *more* playwriting projects with Stevenson, should the reviews not be positive, and crediting Henley, not Stevenson, with any success the partners would find:

> I am so afraid if the Deacon fails that you will be disheartened. Do everything to make it a success, but be prepared for failure and be prepared, oh *do* be prepared to go on trying again and again. I believe that you have the dramatic instinct, much more than Louis has, and

> I am as convinced as a human being can be that you will ultimately succeed. I feel it in the very marrow of my bones. I do not think Louis should ever have taken a kern of the little that the Deacon has brought in.[10]

This praise for Henley is the more surprising given that, when the letter was written, Louis was just recovering from a severe attack of haemorrhages. Fearing that Henley's high energy was a drain on Stevenson, Fanny sometimes discouraged his presence.[11]

In 1884 the pair were at work on their two subsequent plays, *Beau Austin* and *Admiral Guinea*, while Stevenson was dangerously ill. Fearing that any strain would worsen the frightening pulmonary haemorrhages to which he was prone throughout his life, his doctors forbade him to speak. During the same illness he and Fanny collaboratively composed *The Dynamiter* (1885), suggesting that his collaborations may in fact have provided some of the physical energies he lacked during the most severe portions of his illness. Because of this, when Henley did arrive to collaborate on the two plays, Stevenson's part of the conversation was conducted entirely in his notebook, giving us a unique insight into the regular conversation of the pair as they worked,[12] and showing a pattern that would continue into Stevenson's collaborations with Lloyd Osbourne later on. Stevenson relied on Henley to provide the initial drafts and structures. He would provide the guidance and make all of the final decisions. Working on *Admiral Guinea*, he instructs Henley, 'Notice your Pew here with a mother's eye; he must say nothing disgusting; you must continue to give the brute a certain charm'; but immediately afterwards, perhaps exhausted, he becomes frustrated by Henley's overreliance on him: 'don't ask me about details, but fire ahead in God's name.' On *Beau Austin*, once again, he urges Henley towards speed, not quality: 'Get your version of it out, man; don't delay this', and again suggests that Henley should be working ahead of him while Stevenson will preserve his strength for the revisions: 'I haven't gone beyond what you have; and towards the end I was already dead tired and have not made enough of it. Tomorrow I'll go on with the act.' This evidence of the practice the men used lends some support to Lloyd Osbourne's later use of 'ploughing' as a metaphor for his part in their collaborations (he claimed that he would do the hard work of ploughing the ground so that Stevenson could focus on revisions),[13] although probably both Osbourne and Henley seriously underestimated how much energy Stevenson was spending on his revisions of their work. Although the notebook does demonstrate some of the material in both plays is Stevenson's originally, he clearly intended for Henley to be fast-drafting much of the material, with little regard for its quality. Stevenson would see to the quality afterwards.

Or, perhaps not. The quality of the plays was not considered to be high, and for *Deacon Brodie* especially it proved a big disappointment. Henley wrote to Stevenson in 1882, describing the play's opening at Pullan's Theatre in Bradford to a full house of three thousand audience members. He complained that the casting was poor, the props inadequate, the lines badly delivered. In short, everything possible is wrong with the production, except the writing, and yet, 'It stood the strain superbly.'[14] Reviews of the play were not encouraging. In response to the play's 1884 run at the Prince's Theatre in London, *The Academy* writes, 'There is a great deal of merit in the new drama, but it has likewise defects of so marked a kind that they must be removed if the piece is to have a popular triumph ... the play has both the qualities and the faults which belong to so much of the stage writing of a literary man' ('The Stage', 17),[15] and the Athenaeum calls it a 'powerful but unequal work, standing in need of much revision and alteration to fit it for a general public'.[16] Sidney Colvin wrote frankly to Henley that the main character was 'morally unintelligible, unconvincing, and non-existent', and advising him 'don't make the mistake of despising your critics'.[17] Stevenson himself didn't much like it. In 1883 he writes that it is 'dead as mud' but that 'sanguine Henley, that dog-like optimist, hopes against despair' (*Letters* 4: 139–40). After its failure Stevenson returned to playwriting with Henley in 1884,[18] a decision Stevenson's stepson Lloyd Osbourne describes despairingly in his biography of his stepfather. Osbourne blames the project on Henley's charismatic energy and depicts the playwriting project as childish:

> R.L.S. was no longer to plod along as he had been doing; Henley was to abandon his grinding and ill-paid editorship; together they would combine to write plays – marvellous plays that would run for hundreds of nights and bring in thousands of pounds; plays that would revive the perishing drama, now hopelessly given over to imbeciles, who kept yachts and mistresses on money virtually filched from the public; plays that would be billed on all the hoardings with the electrifying words: 'By Robert Louis Stevenson and William Ernest Henley.'[19]

Yet, Osbourne allows that Stevenson was not perhaps as taken in as he at first suggests. Stevenson 'entered enthusiastically into this collaboration, though, with his underlying Scotch caution'. Osbourne recalls that as Henley read *Beau Austin* 'so movingly, so tenderly . . . [d]eep down within me was a disappointment I tried hard to stifle'.[20] In the end, Osbourne writes, 'R. L. S. lost not only the last flicker of his youth in "Wensleydale", but I believe also any conviction that he might be a popular dramatist.'[21] The passing away of Stevenson's youth, his transition from imaginative bohemian to sober and studied author, coincides in Osbourne's mind with the failure of the dramatic projects that Stevenson and Henley worked on together, projects that Osbourne suggests were doomed from the beginning. Osbourne's reflections here have the benefit of hindsight, however. At the time, Osbourne had been a little more sanguine, writing to his mother in 1885 an enthusiastic description of his youthful outing to see Henry Arthur Jones and Henry Herman's blockbuster melodrama (and another collaboratively written project), *The Silver King*. Osbourne writes, 'If Louis would only write a play with a scene so strong as that which I described he would make a fortune at once',[22] showing that he too was susceptible to dreams of yachts and mistresses.

Scholar David Kurnick has argued that theatrical failures had a major role in defining the domestic space of the nineteenth-century novel.[23] Looking at failed dramas by Thackeray, George Eliot, Henry James and James Joyce (but not Stevenson), Kurnick argues that these failures were essential to the success of the prose work that followed. In much the same way, we can see Stevenson returning to the scene of *Deacon Brodie*'s crime, rehashing themes and topics born in the theatre. Despite the play's failure, Stevenson would eventually revise its ideas to great success with *Jekyll and Hyde*. These themes can be productively read as meditations on collaborative writing: its benefits, but also its pitfalls.

Like *Jekyll and Hyde* would later, *Deacon Brodie* revolves around the vicissitudes of male partnership. Its central conflict the tension between the Brodie and his best friend, Walter Leslie. Brodie has gambled away his sister's dowry, though his sister is engaged to Leslie, and then, Hyde-like, he burgles Leslie's home while drunk: 'I was drunk; I was upon my mettle; and I as good as did it. More than that, blackguardly as it was, I enjoyed the doing.'[24] When Brodie loses control of his criminal associates later in the play, he finds himself at the mercy of the double life he had initially chosen. Like Jekyll, he has lost all ability to direct himself at all. Finally, both *Deacon Brodie* and *Jekyll and Hyde* dwell on the difference between serious crimes and trivial offences. *Deacon Brodie* contrasts the felonious activities of the Deacon with the comparatively minor crimes of black-market brandy and cockfighting. Just as Jekyll creates Hyde in a misguided attempt to rid himself of his dark side, *Deacon Brodie* instructs the reader that a little crime and immorality is the privilege of the middle-class *flâneur*: that, without it, a more dangerous dark side threatens to emerge. Stevenson himself famously frequented brothels as a young man, and biographers have even tried to chase down evidence of a first love that he may have found there.[25] Certainly, in his adolescence he curated an image of himself as an unrepentant rule breaker, though now his various immoralities seem more humanising than evil or scandalous.

Deacon Brodie brings together two themes that will persist in Stevenson's work throughout the entirety of his career. On the one hand, it shows the fraught nature of male/male friendships and partnerships. The Deacon betrays his best friend, Walter Leslie, in favour of criminal associates. *Jekyll and Hyde* is also structured as a meditation on male friendships, as it opens with Jekyll's friend Utterson, who is suspicious, and even jealous of Hyde, thinking Hyde is a new friend, or perhaps even lover. Nearer the end of his career, this same theme will dominate *The Wrecker* (1892), written with Lloyd Osbourne, where the protagonist Loudon Dodd struggles with his relationship with his best friend and business partner, Jim Pinkerton. Significantly, this conflict occurs most pointedly in literature written collaboratively – *Deacon Brodie* is *about* a falling out between two friends, written within a friendship soon to fall apart. At the same time, this same theme is played out within the protagonist himself, a drama most explicitly seen in *Jekyll and Hyde*, but developed through virtually all of Stevenson's fiction.

That Stevenson and Henley were obsessed with the problem of a protagonist in conflict with himself is evident in yet another of their proposed plays, never written. The pair wanted to revisit Sophocles' *Ajax* (*Letters* 4: 37–9), an updated version, Henley writes, that would have had in the titular role 'an elderly Anglo-Indian engineer, who – brave, honest, magnificent – plays the unconscious criminal as one of several directors in a fraudulent bank'.[26] We see the pair revisiting, obsessively, the same old themes: in Sophocles' *Ajax*, the Greek warrior, possessed by rage, tries to kill his compatriots because they have denied him the armour of Achilles. Instead, Athena turns him against livestock, whom he believes are his friends. Here, too, we see friendship, betrayal, a two-sided hero, the struggle for self-control. In the end, the failure of the collaborative endeavour would mean the failure of the friendship. Sidney Colvin explains that 'the practical experiment in play-writing on which Stevenson spent so much effort with little or no result in conjunction with this same friend made the wife regard the friendship as one that brought a dangerous amount of exertion with no corresponding advantages.'[27] The description of *Ajax* above comes from Henley's review of Graham Balfour's 1901 biography of Stevenson (published seven years after Stevenson's death).[28] Like Ajax, Henley strikes out at his former friend, claiming that Balfour (who was Stevenson's cousin) had written too complimentary a piece. Henley rages that the manly, vital Stevenson who was Henley's friend had slowly been replaced by a priggish and self-righteous Stevenson who emerged later in life. He even takes the liberty of changing the spelling of Stevenson's middle name, spelling it Lewis as Stevenson's grandfather had done, insinuating that *his* friend was the more British Lewis, and not the Gallic Louis. Male friendship, betrayal and duality: the same notions that run through *Deacon Brodie*, *Jekyll and Hyde* and *Ajax* return in Henley's petulant review: 'For me there were two Stevensons', he writes: 'the Stevenson who went to America in '87; and the Stevenson who never came back'.[29]

Even though Stevenson and Henley's dramatic career was a failure, theatricality dominates Stevenson's thinking about literature, and with it the sense of art as a communal endeavour. Theatre is an art of collaboration. Indeed, from its imagined classical choral origins, it is impossible to imagine theatre without collaboration, at least in the sense that it requires the collaborative energies of the playwright, the director and the actors. According to Kurnick, 'what happens on stage communicates first and always the fact of collective endeavour'.[30] Besides, theatre (literally) is play, and for Stevenson play is the origin of all literature. In his 1878 essay 'Child's Play', Stevenson puns on his own title, arguing for drama as a rudimentary imagination. Children, he argues, cannot rise to the abstract storytelling of the adult's daydream – instead, their imagination must be embodied, acted out: 'the child, mind you, acts his parts. He does not merely repeat them to himself; he leaps, he runs, and sets the blood agog all over his body.'[31] Stevenson opposes the 'juvenile lyrical drama' of the sung nursery rhyme to the 'novels in the privacy of his own heart' which only the adult, and not the child can understand.[32] The relation of the child to text is less sophisticated, but it is also more immediate.[33] The essay is given more poignancy when we remember that Stevenson as a child was often ill, and constrained to the bed and his own imagination, as he documents in his *A Child's Garden of Verses*. Kurnick argues that, in contrast and response to the communal nature of theatre, Victorian novelists 'routed their representations of social forces through various forms of inwardness',[34] and that furthermore this this inwardness is tinged with melancholy over the loss over a public, communal space. In Stevenson, this conflict between the ideal of the child's acting of the drama and the inward novel written in convalescence takes form in the literary progression from the collaboratively written and collaboratively staged *Deacon Brodie*, which depicts Stevenson's fights and friendship with Henley, to the inward *Jekyll and Hyde*, where the conflict is played out within a single mind.

In his critical writings as well as in his practice, Stevenson supports what Elaine Freedgood has referred to as 'the Victorian antidiegetic tradition'[35]: the idea that that the Victorian ideal was for the author/narrator to disappear from the narration, just as Stevenson imagined happened in the dramatic play of children. Henry James (another failed playwright, according to Kurnick) makes just such a case in 'The Art of Fiction', where he argues for a mimetic world without authorial intrusion.[36] This mimetic as opposed to diegetic ideal links the Victorian novel (or at least a certain imagined ideal of the Victorian novel) firmly to the dramatic. Indeed, the reader will rarely find authorial intrusion or reflection in Stevenson's fiction. Instead, it is concerned with plot, action, and other appearances of reality that might be acted out to the world.

Even more importantly, both *Deacon Brodie* and *Jekyll and Hyde* can be taken to refer to the situation of the actor himself: the man who pretends to be something he is not, who shows a double face to the world. *Deacon Brodie* plays the part of respected businessman and community member, just as readers have seen Jekyll as the Freudian ego, or the mask we present to the outside world. Drama theorist Bert States explains that the actor on stage never disappears entirely behind the mask of character: there is always 'the ghost of a self' that speaks to the audience.[37] *Jekyll and Hyde* and *Deacon Brodie* both dramatise the parabasic possibilities of stage: that the character who speaks to the audience in one moment could suddenly transform into the actor, the entirely other person who might speak in the next moment. Stevenson and Henley hoped that the role of Deacon Brodie would go to the famous actor Henry Irving. In the end the part was played by Henley's brother Teddy, who (like the Deacon himself) embarrassed them all with his drunken violence, a curious and Hyde-like merging of the real and mimetic world (*Letters* 6: 92–3).

It is also worth considering whether Stevenson's writings can truly be said to have been a failure on the stage. Though written as a

Figure 1.2 Actor Richard Mansfield as Jekyll and Hyde (*c.* 1895). Photograph by Henry Van der Weyde (1838–1924; London, England). Pach Brothers. *Richard Mansfield as Dr. Jekyll and Mr. Hyde.* https://www.loc.gov/item/96511898/

novella, *Jekyll and Hyde* has, since its composition, had an impressive theatrical run! C. Alex Pinkston notes the existence of at least '136 cinematic variants on motifs from Stevenson's novel, twenty-four theatrical productions of the story, seven phonograph recordings, and fourteen literary parodies, sequels, or stories inspired by Stevenson's *Strange Case.*'[38] And that sentence was written in 1986. Martin Danahay argues that it is in performance that Stevenson's text realises its full potential: 'Mansfield's performance dramatised the fissure hinted at, but never fully represented, in Stevenson's text' precisely because embodiment is central to the novella's conceit.[39] So, even if we take Osbourne's comments at face value and believe that Stevenson as dramatist was doomed to failure, there is an affinity for his work and the stage that has overshadowed Stevenson's lack of playwriting ability. In fact, in his biography of Stevenson, Stevenson's cousin Graham Balfour notes that in 1887–8, when Stevenson is in New York, 'not only were there two dramatised versions of

Dr. Jekyll and Mr. Hyde [sic] upon the boards, but *Deacon Brodie* was shortly afterwards produced in Philadelphia by an English company',[40] suggesting that popular stagings of the later hit may have helped in some measure to revive Stevenson's earlier theatrical flop. The renewed life Stevenson's fiction of the double self has had since *Deacon Brodie*'s composition in 1880 would inspire the envy of a better playwright, and it does not seem likely to stop anytime soon.

'The Body Snatcher': Collaborator and Hypocrite

Soon after Stevenson and Henley had finished work on *Deacon Brodie*, Stevenson was thinking of other Edinburgh criminals. 'The Body Snatcher' (1884), his Gothic short story based on Burke and Hare, notorious 'resurrection men' of the 1820s, was published in 1884, but Stevenson was writing it in 1881. Stevenson intended 'The Body Snatcher' as an indictment of Dr Knox (the story's Dr K—), who received the stolen bodies from Burke and Hare, in response to other, exculpatory narratives about him.[41] 'The Body Snatcher' also concerns an ill-chosen partnership and opens with its protagonist Fettes, shabby and repentant, staring down his well-heeled one-time associate, Dr Macfarlane, a reminder that a collaborator is another word for a criminal accomplice. As a medical student, Fettes presided over the dissecting *theatre* where he received the bodies to be studied. (This is one of two allusions to the theatre in the story. Young Macfarlane is 'an authority on the stage'.[42]) Like Deacon Brodie, Jekyll and the young Robert Louis Stevenson, Fettes as a young man was given to late nights and drunkenness, and he receives the corpses in a hangover-induced stupor:

> Here, after a night of turbulent pleasures, his hand still tottering, his sight still misty and confused, he would be called out of bed in the black hours before the winter dawn by the unclean and desperate interlopers who supplied the table.[43]

Also like Jekyll and Deacon Brodie (though by no means like Stevenson himself), Fettes is driven to evil not by his immoral parts – his (unidentified) pleasures, his alcoholism – but because this immorality is combined with a bourgeois respectability, an outward conventionality and ambition that is arguably less forgivable than his dark side. Patrick Scott has argued that 'Stevenson's critical strategy in "The Body Snatcher" is to redirect blame for Edinburgh's most famous murders, from criminality to respectability' (115), and Caroline McCracken-Flesher has argued that Dr Jekyll's worst crime is 'hypocrisy'.[44] Certainly, the narrator judges Fettes more harshly for his respected outward appearance than for his inner conflict:

> Cold, light, and selfish in the last resort, he had that modicum of prudence, miscalled morality, which keeps a man from inconvenient drunkenness or punishable theft. He coveted, besides, a measure of consideration from his masters and his fellow-pupils, and he had no desire to fail conspicuously in the external parts of life. Thus he made it his pleasure to gain some distinction in his studies, and day after day rendered unimpeachable eye-service to his employer, Mr K—. For his day of work he indemnified himself by nights of roaring, blackguardly enjoyment; and when that balance had been struck, the organ that he called his conscience declared itself content. (81)

This schism between his two selves, here not supernatural but simply an ordinary variation of character, prevents him from taking responsibility for his own evil actions: Fettes receives the corpses of murder victims for the medical school. Fettes denies the evidence that the bodies are brought by murders. He asserts that 'There was *no understanding* that the subjects were provided by the crime of murder' (81, emphasis mine), and yet, Stevenson tells us, confusingly, there is every understanding: '... putting things together clearly in his private thoughts, he perhaps attributed a meaning too immoral and too categorical to the unguarded counsel of his master' (81). How can one both know and not know? This is the psychological contradiction allegorised in *Jekyll and Hyde*, here presented more realistically. Macfarlane has no such compunctions:

> 'Come now!' sneered the other. 'As if you hadn't suspected it yourself!'
> 'Suspecting is one thing –'
> 'And proof another. Yes, I know; and I'm sorry as you are this should have come here,' tapping the body with his cane. 'The next best thing for me is not to recognise it: and,' he added coolly, 'I don't. You may, if you please. I don't dictate, but I think a man of the world would do as I do . . .' (83)

As in *Deacon Brodie*, such self-denial comes at a cost, which is loss of control: 'there was no limit to his weakness, and that, from concession to concession, he had fallen from the arbiter of Macfarlane's destiny to his paid and helpless accomplice' (87). The same shift of power occurs as well in *Deacon Brodie*'s Act II, where the Deacon quite suddenly finds himself in the debased position of being a part of the gang instead of its leader, subject to arm-twisting and extortion by his former inferior, controlled by the double life he himself had chosen. And, of course, this shift is the fulcrum of *Jekyll and Hyde*.

The idea of the self divided and working at cross-purposes to itself is a frustrating representation of Stevenson's collaborations with Henley. At the time Stevenson writes 'The Body Snatcher', *Deacon Brodie* has been published and awaits its first performance. Stevenson already suspected it would not be a success, and predicted Henley's disappointment, writing to his mother that it would have been 'hissed off the boards' (*Letters* 4: 40). It is impossible to say that Stevenson is Jekyll and Henley Hyde (or perhaps vice versa?) but Stevenson's imagination is not that literal. Yet in all three works this internal conflict is reflected in an external conflict between a man and his bachelor friend, which is alternately either the motivating cause of the internal split or the thing put most at risk by the split protagonist. In her discussion of 'The Body Snatcher', Ruth Richardson speaks of 'the complicit socialisation of maleness; the hypocrisies which so often lie behind worldly success; the damage behind apparent failure; the dark silences that can exist in social relations that pass as bonhomie', an observation that speaks to the centrality of the male homosocial relationship to all three texts.[45]

Both Dr Jekyll and Deacon Brodie are outwardly respectable, but inwardly criminal, and both texts track the shifting loyalty as the protagonist/antagonist betrays and rejects a friend in favour of a criminal associate, and it is by this betrayal that we can track his moral progress. As William Veeder notes, '. . . the Jekyll/Hyde relationship is replicated throughout Jekyll's circle'.[46] The internal schism, in other words, is also reflected through the character's external relations.

There is a robust critical tradition of reading *Jekyll and Hyde* as a fable of male homosexuality, originating in important readings by Wayne Koestenbaum and Elaine Showalter, and with good reason.[47] Jekyll's night-time double life, as Showalter has argued, is suggestive of the double life of the late-century homosexual. That Jekyll's friends believe that Hyde is his lover is so strongly suggested that it is more literal than subtext. While this tension is undeniably present in the text, the novella is about other types of male partnerships as well. Showalter writes, 'In contrast to the way it has been represented in film and popular culture, *Jekyll and Hyde* is a story about communities of men',[48] and Koestenbaum notes that critical reception of the novella has emphasised the absence of women.[49] The story begins with the pairing of Utterson and his companion, Enfield, but soon progresses to describe a number of other male partnerships that are created and then broken. Utterson, desperate over Jekyll's attachment to Hyde and fearing it represents 'disgrace', visits Dr Lanyon, once an intimate of Jekyll's, but now estranged over a scientific disagreement that '"would have estranged Damon and Pythias"',[50] a reference to the legendary Greek friends who were willing to die for one another. Male friendship in *Jekyll and Hyde* is the principal and most important relationship, and at the same time it is precariously fragile.

Koestenbaum, in his discussion of the bachelor circle of *Jekyll and Hyde*, also notes that Jekyll and Hyde's relationship may mirror Stevenson and Henley's, saying that 'collaboration, far from dividing men's strength, promises to double it – as if two men make for a more manly fiction'.[51] Indeed, it seems that sexual tension was an important element in the Stevenson–Henley relationship: Calder says 'Henley was, in a sense, in love with him.'[52] But Koestenbaum's formulation has no room for the violent conflict engendered in that collaboration, or rather, he reads it as merely 'stimulating'.[53] Rather, as Veeder and Beattie have observed, the homosocial world of the novel is filled with tension and Oedipal and 'sibling' rivalries.[54] In this regard, the relations between men, such as Jekyll's relationship to both Utterson and Hyde, mimic the progress of Stevenson's relationship with Henley: erotically charged, yes, but also fundamentally conflictual.

Essays and Dreams: The Double in the Theatre of the Mind

If Stevenson imagined Jekyll and Hyde as the dual actor and character, he also thought of the imagination itself as a stage. His reflections on writing are filled with this comparison, and with descriptions of the writer in conflict with himself. Stevenson's 1888 essay 'A Chapter on Dreams', which contains an account of the composition of *Jekyll and Hyde*, links the creative metaphor of the dream with the creative metaphor of the stage. Stevenson talks about 'that small theatre of the brain which we keep brightly lighted all night long, after the jets are down, and darkness and sleep reign undisturbed in the remainder of the body'. The metaphor is sustained: Stevenson is 'in the boxes', the characters in his dreams are 'actors'. The dream is the theatre of the mind; the theatre is the dream embodied.[55] Stevenson would return to the themes explored in this essay, in 1892, in a letter to F. W. H. Myers, founder of the Society for Psychical Research, of which Stevenson was a member. In this letter, he describes a series of dreams and out-of-body experiences that he believed to be 'of a high psychological interest' (*Letters* 7: 331). (Myers published Stevenson's accounts in the society newsletter.) In the description of dreams that Stevenson gives in 'A Chapter on Dreams' and in the letter to Myers we see an emerging theory of double-authorship, and a sense that collaborative (or conflictive) writing and Stevenson's singly composed pieces are not, in fact, that different.

Stevenson describes the creation of *Jekyll and Hyde* and develops his theory of authorship in 'A Chapter on Dreams', where he distinguishes between two selves:

> Here is a doubt that much concerns my conscience. For myself – what I call I, my conscious ego, the denizen of the pineal gland unless he has changed his residence since Descartes, the man with the conscience and the variable bank-account, the man with the hat and the boots, and the privilege of voting and not carrying his candidate at the general elections – I am sometimes tempted to suppose he is no story-teller at all, but a creature as matter of fact as any cheesemonger or any cheese, and a realist bemired up to the ears in actuality; so that, by that account, the whole of my published fiction should be the single-handed product of some Brownie, some Familiar, some unseen collaborator, whom I keep locked in a back garret, while I get all the praise and he but a share (which I cannot prevent him getting) of the pudding. I am an excellent adviser, something like Moliere's servant; I pull back and I cut down; and I dress the whole in the best words and sentences that I can find and make; I hold the pen, too; and I do the sitting at the table, which is about the worst of it; and when all is done, I make up the manuscript and pay for the registration; so that, on the whole, I have some claim to share, though not so largely as I do, in the profits of our common enterprise.[56]

In this passage describing the genesis of *Jekyll and Hyde*, the collaborator moves from external to internal. Yet a similar structure is at work in both *Deacon Brodie* and 'The Body Snatcher'. Just as true evil in 'The Body-Snatcher' is based in professionalisation and respectability (as indeed it is in *Deacon Brodie*, too), here the moral balance between collaborators is not what it initially seems. The passage is shot through with the language of capitalism: Stevenson holds the 'bank account' and gains the 'profit', while the Brownie repeatedly gets only a meagre 'share'. Stevenson here identifies himself (admittedly with tongue firmly in cheek) as the robber baron who steals more than his due from his mystical worker. It also suggests the author as plagiarist, the sense that the real Stevenson is, in the words of Macfarlane's discussion of nineteenth-century plagiarism, 'merely a rearranger of bits and pieces: an administrator rather than a producer'.[57] The relation between the Dreaming Self and the Brownie is, as Stephen Arata has it, 'at once intimate and estranged' (54).[58] The allegorisation of the collaborator, however, is the more remarkable because Henley had literally collaborated on *Deacon Brodie*, the direct ancestor of the novella.

And yet, 'A Chapter on Dreams' goes further than predicting the duality that generations of readers have found in *Jekyll and Hyde*. In fact, in this highly complex essay, Stevenson describes himself as a whole community of selves. First, there are our memories – our past selves who have now split away from us. The past self is both essential to our identity (because we cannot define ourselves without it), and yet it is no longer part of that identity. In the same way, Stevenson argues, we can understand the dreaming self, whose experiences also create us, though they are not us. (In Stevenson's case, he dreams he participates in the Jacobite rebellion.) It was in *Deacon Brodie* that Stevenson first explored this link between the self of the past and the self of the dream as selves that are other than the conscious self as the Deacon looks back on his life with regret: '. . . I stand upon the grave's edge, all my lost life behind me, like a horror to think upon, like a frenzy, like a dream that is past.'[59] Then there is Stevenson's choice to talk about his own past in the third person, telling us his story is about 'a friend'. Finally, there is the essay's *mise en abyme* structure. Stevenson studied engineering and then law at Edinburgh College. However, in the 'dream-life' of Stevenson's 'friend' he studies medicine. (This describes Fettes, and also Jekyll, but not Stevenson.) So the essay describes dreams dreamed by a medical student, who is dreamed by a college friend of Stevenson's, who turns out to be Stevenson. By characterising authorship as plural in this way, Stevenson challenges the notion of a single and solitary author at all, predicting in his way the dissolution of the idea of the author and its replacement with Michel Foucault's concept of the 'author-function': Foucault notes that first-person references 'stand for a "second self" whose similarity to the author is never fixed and undergoes considerable alteration within the course of a single book'.[60] Recent critics have established that in writing *Jekyll and Hyde* Stevenson was influenced by case studies described in medical journals of the period.[61] Ideas of the mind and of consciousness proliferated near the end of the century, and allowed for greater fluidity and multiplicity of consciousness. Crucially, Stevenson's theory is that the multiplication of the self is in fact *not* pathological. When Jekyll says that he 'learned to recognize the thorough and primitive duality of man; I saw that, of the two natures that contended in the field of my consciousness, even if I could rightly be said to be either, it was only because I was radically both',[62] he is reflecting on his situation *prior* to his experiments. Similarly, Stevenson's descriptions of contending selves in 'A Chapter on Dreams' and his letter to Myers, as frightening as they may be, are not descriptions of mental illness but of the author in his natural state.

Most critics who consider Stevenson's 'A Chapter on Dreams' end up invoking Freud as a matter of course. In particular, Arata and Beattie have identified Stevenson's dream of a terrifying winking dog eating a fly as a species of the uncanny.[63] But Stevenson also describes a markedly Oedipal story that he has dreamed. He splits himself between the disassociated self, which is the author, and the actual self, which is the reader. The entirety of the story, he says, is based around its trick ending, and though he as the dreamer invents the whole story, he claims to remain completely naive to its ending. Stevenson dreams he is a son who quarrels with his father (not himself, although Stevenson often did quarrel with his father). The father and son meet

> in a desolate, sandy country by the sea; and there they quarrelled, and the son, stung by some intolerable insult, struck down the father dead. No suspicion was aroused; the dead man was found and buried, and the dreamer succeeded to the broad estates, and found himself installed under the same roof with his father's widow, for whom no provision had been made. These two lived very much alone, as people may after a bereavement, sat down to table together, shared the long evenings, and grew daily better friends.[64]

As the story continues, the son eventually follows his attractive young stepmother to the murder scene, where she discovers the evidence that he is the murderer. She says nothing, and they go back to their happy life together, until, one morning at breakfast the son breaks under the stress:

> Why did she torture him so? she knew all, she knew he was no enemy to her; why did she not denounce him at once? what signified her whole behaviour? why did she torture him? and yet again, why did she torture him? And when he had done, she fell upon her knees, and with outstretched hands: 'Do you not understand?' she cried. 'I love you!'[65]

Stevenson's claim that he did not know this final twist in the plot of his dream is made dubious because it is essentially the plot of *Oedipus Rex*, and is only plausible because he wrote 'A Chapter on Dreams' eight or nine years before Freud ever mentions Oedipus.

Stevenson, as Glenda Norquay among others has observed, believed the purpose of reading is pleasure. Here he 'interprets his dreams in the role of reader and those dreams offer a reading experience so intense that no subsequent book can equate with the encounter'.[66] But what if, this essay ventures, Stevenson could read Stevenson? Stevenson says:

> I will go bail for the dreamer (having excellent grounds for valuing his candour) that he had no guess whatever at the motive of the woman – the hinge of the whole well-invented plot – until the instant of that highly dramatic declaration. It was not his tale; it was the little people's![67]

Stevenson becomes split into both reader and writer in this idealised, fantasy version of literary transmission. By becoming his own reader, Stevenson is able to replicate a perfect, and unmediated, relationship between writer and reader, one that he experiences with 'a pang of wonder'. This idea of the author as both reader and writer originates in *Jekyll and Hyde*, as Garrett Stewart has found, noting that Jekyll's propensity to enjoy Hyde's crimes puts him in the same situation as the reader of this, or any other narrative, 'taking one's pleasure and enduring one's pain . . . through the agency of another',[68] just as Stevenson is both author and passive recipient of the Oedipal dream from 'A Chapter on Dreams'.

The collaboration enacted in the relationship between reader and writer (imagined inside one mind) becomes the primary topic of the dreams that Stevenson describes in his letter to Myers. What this letter reveals is first, that Stevenson's fixation on the self divided is a recurrent obsession, both in his craft and in his personal life. Second, that this notion of the divided self is inextricable from the writing process, and the identity of the author specifically. And third, that the accustomed treatment of *Jekyll and Hyde* as a story of dualism and polarities – good/evil, rational/irrational, civilised/primitive – does not do justice to the nuance and complexity of Stevenson's thinking about the complexities of the self.

In his letter, Stevenson details four instances of the split self experienced through dreams. He concludes that the other self in each dream is in fact the same other self who dictated the Oedipal dream of 'A Chapter on Dreams'. But in contrast to that essay, where Stevenson's Brownie is secure in his garret, in this letter the dreams are violent, and the relationship between the conscious self and the 'other fellow' contentious. The first dream described is older than the rest: Stevenson says he had it while violently ill at Nice in January of 1884. Fanny had a hard time nursing him during that illness, and was frightened by his bloody haemorrhaging.[69] In pain as he slept, Stevenson believes that his pain is caused by 'a wisp or coil' of something he can only describe as words, which must be brought together to bring him relief. His conscious self realises this idea is absurd and attempts to remain silent, but, Hyde-like, his other self prospers, and in his sleep he grabs his wife 'savagely by the wrist', crying, 'Why do you not put the two ends together and put me out of pain?' (*Letters* 7: 332). It was, he says, 'cruelty', and his description is much like Jekyll under the influence of Hyde: 'Here is action, unnatural and uncharacteristic action, flowing from an idea in which I had no belief and which I had been concealing for hours as a plain mark of aberration. Is it not so with lunatics?' (333). Here, Stevenson is tortured by a string of text, but it as yet has no meaning. It is, he says, 'grotesque and shapeless' (331) without the proper interpreter. The author panics when his meaning cannot be understood. He requires a reader – in this case his wife to 'put [it] together' and thereby end his misery.

The second dream he describes is more recent. In a fever in Sydney (all four dreams in this letter involve illness), Stevenson dreams he is repeating a nonsense word, like 'the nonsense words of Lewis Carroll' (332). However, in his dream logic he is not he, but, rather, Jonathan Swift, who lies dying, and this nonsense word is the dying word of Swift. The dream, Stevenson tells us, is inspired by his reading at the time: a biography of Swift. In repeating Swift's dying word, Stevenson himself becomes confused with Swift, perhaps because he had a sense that he, like Swift, was dying. But then, he tells us, there is the familiar split between the self and the other fellow. Stevenson himself tries to commit Swift's dying word to memory, feeling it is beautiful and important. The 'other fellow' feels that it can be easily found in the biography. Here, as the Oedipal dream, we have Stevenson split between reader and writer, but this time with roles reversed: the self with which he identifies believes he is the writer Jonathan Swift, but the alternate self believes he is a reader of Swift's biography.

That Stevenson thought he was saying the dying word of Jonathan Swift is noteworthy for another reason. Swift, at the end of his life, suffered from aphasia. There were no last words, and if Stevenson was reading his biography he surely knew this. Both of these dreams, as well as the other two described in the letter, are a struggle between words spoken and unspoken: the other fellow wishes to tell Fanny about the wisp of words; Stevenson wishes to withhold it; Stevenson wishes to repeat the dying word of Swift; the other fellow says it is 'the invention of a lunatic'. But in fact it is Swift himself, paralysed, probably insane, who cannot speak at the end of his life, suggesting that to Stevenson's imagination this may be the dying *internal monologue* of Swift – in other words, not Swift's speech, but Swift's dream. For Stevenson, the common experience of realising that an idea from a dream does not make any sense reveals deeper anxieties about the self as writer, failing to make connection with other makers of meaning.

Decentring of authorship becomes a primary concern of Stevenson's exploration of the split self from early works such as (the collaboratively written) *Deacon Brodie* and 'The Body Snatcher' in Stevenson's critical essays and letters, and up through his masterpiece *Strange Case of Dr Jekyll and Mr Hyde*. *Jekyll and Hyde* is only the apex of Stevenson's thinking about the problems of authorship. The exploration of these problems results in Stevenson's definitive rejection of the picture of the author 'as solitary genius' (as in Jack Stillinger's critique of that notion). Instead, *Jekyll and Hyde* when read as a theory of authorship posits the following: first, that writing emerges from a community, specifically in this case, a male homosocial bachelor community; second, that within this community the process of collaboration can be (as it was with Henley) violent and contentious; and third, that this contentiousness is the same whether the collaboration is externalised (as in work with Henley on *Deacon Brodie*), or whether it is moved into the internal, dreaming space.

Jekyll and Hyde holds an important key to understanding Stevenson's emerging theory of authorship as fundamentally collaborative. It represents the self as prism rather than privileging a unified perspective. Thomas writes that 'The end of *Jekyll and Hyde* is the fragmenting of the self into distinct voices, not the bringing together of those pieces into some unified character who speaks with a single voice', and further that 'it enacts the withdrawal of the articulating self from the text – the disappearance of the author'.[70] The extent to which this splitting is binary has been overstated in popular readings of the novella; in fact, Jekyll predicts that 'man will be ultimately known for a mere polity of multifarious, incongruous and independent denizens',[71] a proliferation of authorial subjectivities that is both productive and terrifying, and that reflects the many imagined multiple authors through the story's conception. Emerging as it does from the literal collaborations of Stevenson with Henley and the collaborative space of the stage, the story becomes fantastical when it enters Stevenson's 'theatre of the mind' where the various actors of the dream contend for authorial control.

The history of the text is a history of conflict, literal in the sense of Stevenson's troubled relationship with Henley, psychological in his recreations of his internal or dreaming selves in his letters and essays discussing the novella's creation. These conflicts are not avoidable but essential to the writer's craft, as Stevenson shows that they inhere even in that most important collaboration for the making of literary meaning, that between writer and reader. Shortly after writing *Jekyll and Hyde* Stevenson absolves himself of responsibility for its reception: he writes in a letter 'First, as to a key, I conceive I could not make my allegory better, nay, that I could not fail to weaken it, if I tried. I have said my say as I was best able: others must look for what was meant; the allegorist is one, the commentator is another; I conceive they are two parts' (*Letters* 5: 211). The split that Stevenson imagines in the Oedipal dream (himself as writer, and himself as reader) here gets replicated in the relation between reader and writer as co-creators of meaning. This relationship, too, is one of struggle, as Stevenson shows us in his letter to Myers, where the frustrating reader, Fanny Stevenson, is maddeningly unable to connect the coil of her husband's words and make meaning out of them.

Notes

1. Quoted Worrall, *The Moscow Art Theatre*, p. 27.
2. Hultgren, *Melodramatic Imperial Writing*, p. 98.
3. Booth and Mehew, 'The Main Correspondents: W. E. Henley', *Letters of Robert Louis Stevenson*, vol. 1, p. 54.
4. Hultgren, *Melodramatic Imperial Writing*, p. 127.
5. Caroline McCracken-Flesher, *Doctor Dissected*, p. 102.
6. Booth and Mehew, 'The Main Correspondents: W. E. Henley', vol. 1, p. 60; see also Calder, *Robert Louis Stevenson*, pp. 94–5.
7. Stillinger, *Multiple Authorship*, p. 168.
8. Henley, *The Selected Letters of W. E. Henley*, p. 160.
9. Atkinson, ed., *The Selected Letters of W. E. Henley*, p. 55n.
10. Fanny Stevenson to W. E. Henley, Royal 1884, Edwin J. Beinecke Collection of Robert Louis Stevenson, GEN MSS 664 box 8 folder 199.
11. Calder, *Robert Louis Stevenson*, p. 154.

12. Robert Louis Stevenson, Notebook 36, Edwin J. Beinecke Collection of Robert Louis Stevenson, GEN MSS 664 box 36 folders 835 and 836.
13. Osbourne, *An Intimate Portrait of R. L. S.*, pp. 107–8.
14. Henley, *Selected Letters of W. E. Henley*, p. 113.
15. 'The Stage', (1884), *The Academy* (635), p. 17, ProQuest.
16. 'The Week', (1884). *The Athenaeum* (2958), p. 26, ProQuest.
17. Quoted in Lucas, *The Colvins and Their Friends*, p. 158.
18. Booth and Mehew, 'The Main Correspondents: W. E. Henley', in *Letters*, vol. 1, p. 59.
19. Osbourne, *An Intimate Portrait of R. L. S.*, pp. 55–6.
20. Ibid. p. 56.
21. Ibid. p. 57.
22. Osbourne to Fanny Van de Grift Stevenson, 31 May 1885, Heriot Row, The Robert Louis Stevenson Collection, GEN MSS 684 box 6 folder 92.
23. Kurnick, *Empty Houses*.
24. Robert Louis Stevenson and Henley, *Deacon Brodie*, p. 25.
25. Gibson, *Deacon Brodie: Father to Jekyll and Hyde*, p. 128.
26. W. E. Henley, 'R. L. S.', *The Pall Mall Magazine* 25 (December 1901), p. 512n., British Periodicals, ProQuest.
27. Quoted in Lucas, *The Colvins and Their Friends*, p. 107.
28. Balfour, *The Life of Robert Louis Stevenson*.
29. Henley, 'R. L. S.', p. 506.
30. Kurnick, *Empty Houses*, p. 18.
31. Robert Louis Stevenson, 'Child's Play', p. 356.
32. Ibid. p. 355.
33. Norquay, *Robert Louis Stevenson and Theories of Reading*, p. 105.
34. Kurnick, *Empty Houses*, p. 2.
35. Freedgood, 'How the Victorian Novel Got Realistic, Reactionary, and Great'.
36. James, 'The Art of Fiction'.
37. States, *Great Reckonings in Little Rooms*, p. 125.
38. Pinkston, 'The Stage Premiere of Dr. Jekyll and Mr. Hyde', p. 21. Pinkston cites Harry Geduld's *The Definitive Dr. Jekyll and Mr. Hyde Companion* (New York: Garland, 1983).
39. Danahay, 'Dr. Jekyll's Two Bodies', p. 33.
40. Balfour, *Life of Robert Louis Stevenson*, vol. 2, p. 34.
41. McCracken-Flesher, *Doctor Dissected*.
42. Robert Louis Stevenson, 'The Body Snatcher', p. 82. Subsequent references to this edition will be cited parenthetically.
43. Ibid. p. 80.
44. Scott, 'Anatomizing Professionalism', p. 115; McCracken-Flesher, *Doctor Dissected*.
45. Richardson, 'Robert Louis Stevenson's *The Body Snatcher*', pp. 412–13.
46. Veeder, 'Children of the Night', p. 108.

47. Koestenbaum, 'The Shadow on the Bed'; Showalter, *Sexual Anarchy*. Showalter plays with the significance of the term 'Queer Street' (Showalter, p. 112; *Jekyll and Hyde*, p. 11), a term that *Jekyll and Hyde* actually borrows from *Deacon Brodie*, but it seems unlikely that Stevenson knew the modern use of the term, which Showalter notes dates from about 1900.
48. Showalter, *Sexual Anarchy*, p. 107.
49. Koestenbaum, 'Shadow on the Bed', p. 38.
50. Robert Louis Stevenson, *Strange Case of Dr Jekyll and Mr Hyde*, p. 14.
51. Koestenbaum, 'Shadow on the Bed', pp. 38–9.
52. Calder, *Robert Louis Stevenson*, p. 95; see also Veeder, 'Children of the Night', p. 160n.
53. Koestenbaum, 'Shadow on the Bed', p. 39.
54. Beattie, 'Father and Son' and 'Dreaming, Doubling and Gender', p. 19. Also Veeder, 'Children of the Night', p. 109.
55. Welsh, 'Robert Louis Stevenson and the Theater of the Brain'.
56. Robert Louis Stevenson, 'A Chapter on Dreams', pp. 248–9.
57. Macfarlane, *Original Copy*, p. 4.
58. Arata, 'Stevenson and Fin-de-Siècle Gothic', p. 54.
59. Robert Louis Stevenson and Henley, *Deacon Brodie*, p. 82.
60. Foucault, 'What is an Author?', p. 129.
61. Reid, *Robert Louis Stevenson, Science, and the* Fin de Siècle'; Stiles, *Popular Fiction and Brain Science*; Gish, 'Jekyll and Hyde: The Psychology of Dissociation'; Davis, '"Incongruous Compounds"'; Jackson, 'Twins, Twinship, and Robert Louis Stevenson's *Strange Case of Dr Jekyll and Mr Hyde*'.
62. Robert Louis Stevenson, *Strange Case of Dr Jekyll and Mr Hyde*, p. 59.
63. Arata, 'Stevenson and Fin-de-Siècle Gothic', p. 57; Beattie, 'Dreaming, Doubling, and Gender', p. 11; see also Norquay, *Robert Louis Stevenson and Theories of Reading*.
64. Robert Louis Stevenson, 'A Chapter on Dreams', pp. 241–2.
65. Ibid. p. 245.
66. Norquay, *Robert Louis Stevenson and Theories of Reading*, p. 101.
67. Robert Louis Stevenson, 'A Chapter on Dreams', p. 246.
68. Stewart, *Dear Reader*, p. 376.
69. Calder, *Robert Louis Stevenson*, p. 182.
70. Thomas, 'The Strange Voices in the Strange Case', pp. 73, 75.
71. Robert Louis Stevenson, *Strange Case of Dr Jekyll and Mr Hyde*, p. 59.

Chapter 2

Collaboration and Marriage: *The Dynamiter*

In the 141 years since they met in 1876, there is no figure in Robert Louis Stevenson's life who has been so disparaged as his wife. American Fanny Van de Grift Osbourne met Stevenson while the two were art students at Grez-sur-Loing. Fanny was hoping to get some distance from her philandering then-husband, the prospector Samuel Osbourne. Ten years Louis's senior, with family in tow, she was not the companion that Louis's family or friends imagined for the 25-year-old bohemian. Until quite recently, subsequent assessments had not been much kinder, fuelled by her strong personality, her involvement in the feud between Louis and Henley, and the careful way she guarded access to her ailing husband. But of all of Fanny's perceived flaws, none has more offended the critical establishment than this: she dared to nurse literary ambitions – ambitions that may have exceeded her literary gifts. Furthermore, she was, it is said, interfering, and never reluctant to make her opinions, literary or otherwise, known. The implication, oozing out of W. E. Henley's venomous review of Graham Balfour's 1906 biography of Stevenson and current for another half-century after that, is that, without Fanny's pernicious influence, both Louis and his work would have been more masculine, less conventional, more fun.[1] The anecdote about Stevenson's revision of the *Strange Case of Dr Jekyll and Mr Hyde* (1886) is representative. According to the story, upon reading the first draft Fanny insisted that Louis make it 'more allegorical', causing him to throw it into the fire and begin again. This anecdote has been taken as emblematic of Fanny and Louis's marriage because it brings together many critical assumptions that have been made about Fanny's influence: that it is destructive (the fire), simplistic (the allegory) and probably prudish (critics Elwin and Koestenbaum suggest it was in fact to censor the prurient bits).[2] This chapter will examine Fanny's credited collaborations with Robert Louis Stevenson:

More New Arabian Nights, also titled *The Dynamiter* (1885), and the pair's little-known play, *The Hanging Judge* (1887). The difficulties involved in reading these works as collaborative, the critical tendency to minimise either Fanny's involvement, or the tendency to minimise the works themselves, reveals just how radical and challenging the Stevensons' ideas about collaboration were. In addition, the extra difficulties posed by these, Stevenson's only credited collaborations with a woman, show how notions of gender and authorship complicate our understanding of collaborative writing.

Because of Fanny's adventurous and dramatic life, both in the American West before she met Louis, and later with him in France, America, Scotland and Samoa, she has been a popular subject, both in biographies, such as Margaret Mackay's *The Violent Friend* (1968) and Alexandra Lapierre's *A Romance of Destiny* (1995), and in literature.[3] There has been a movement to recover her as a tortured and underappreciated proto-feminist in works such as Carolyn Kizer's poem 'Fanny', included in the collection *Pro Femina* (collected 2001) and, more recently, Nancy Horan's fictionalised account of the couple's romance, *Under the Wide and Starry Sky* (2014).[4] However, analysis of her literary work and collaborations has been sparse.[5] Whether one admires or criticises her ambitious and forceful personality, there is no denying that her influence on Stevenson and his writings was immense. Although Fanny's influence was pervasive, this chapter will examine only works that bear her name: the framed collection of stories published as *More New Arabian Nights: The Dynamiter*, the play the couple worked on together, entitled *The Hanging Judge*, and Fanny's own ill-fated short story, 'The Nixie' (1888), which prompted a family fight over accusations of plagiarism, and contributed to Stevenson's falling out with Henley. Previous readers have derided or minimised Fanny's influence on Stevenson's work, because of Fanny's perceived lack of talent. In so doing, generations of readers have missed the impact of Stevenson's most long-standing and in many ways most complex collaboration.

Transatlantic Shahrazad: *More New Arabian Nights: The Dynamiter* and Domestic Collaboration

Louis and Fanny had discussed collaborations as early as 1881, when Louis wrote to Sidney Colvin about a proposed story collection entitled *The Black Man and Other Tales*, describing it as 'the new work on which I am engaged with Fanny' (*Letters* 3: 188).

Figure 2.1 Fanny Stevenson at Bournemouth, 1885. Beinecke Rare Book and Manuscript Library.

The collection includes 'Thrawn Janet', 'The Body Snatchers', 'The Shadow on the Bed', which Fanny would later publish, and a story that would become 'The Merry Men' (*Letters* 3: 188n.). But the most extensive work that the couple collaborated on was the collection entitled *More New Arabian Nights*: *The Dynamiter*. The volume was a sequel to Stevenson's popular collection of short stories, *New Arabian Nights* (1882), of which 'The Suicide Club' has become the favourite story. Whereas the earlier collection was predominantly an experimentation with formal aspects of the short story form, in the collaboratively written sequel the two Stevensons tried, for the first time in Louis's career, to move towards a more explicitly political message, though not entirely successfully.

In the earlier collection, *New Arabian Nights*, Stevenson had experimented with loosely structuring his volume after the *Tales from 1001 Nights*. This collection of Persian folktales was massively popular throughout the eighteenth and nineteenth centuries, first in its eighteenth-century French translation by Antoine Galland, and later in the nineteenth century, in more academic translations by Edward

Lane and Richard Burton (Stevenson's was the Galland version). The original folktales feature a series of never-ending stories set into a frame. In the collection's frame, King Shahrayar has been marrying and then immediately beheading the women of his kingdom until Shahrazad, the daughter of his vizier, volunteers to be his next bride. Shahrazad outsmarts the spiteful king by telling him nightly stories, the conclusions of which she endlessly defers.

Stevenson was a fan of the stories, which he identified with the incident-heavy high romance to which he always aspired. In 'A Gossip on Romance' (1882) he discussed the importance of plot over characterisation:

> There is one book, for example, more generally loved than Shakespeare, that captivates in childhood, and still delights in age – I mean the *Arabian Nights* – where you shall look in vain for moral or intellectual interest. No human face or voice greets us among that wooden crowd of kings and genies, sorcerers and beggarmen. Adventure, on the most naked terms, furnished forth the entertainment and is found enough.[6]

Stevenson's allusions to the *Nights* conjure up a certain aesthetic – a literature that eschews realism and chooses play instead, a non-serious relation to the work of representation that characterised both *New Arabian Nights* and *The Dynamiter*.

In the 1850s the *Nights* had been a popular strategy for compiling collections of short stories; the frame narratives provided the context. Both Elizabeth Gaskell, in *Round the Sofa* (collected 1859), and also Wilkie Collins, in *After Dark* (1856), had used the *Nights* in this way.[7] Like those earlier authors, Stevenson's use of the *Nights* is formal rather than thematic. There are a few consistent effects of the form: one is that it creates a tension between frame and story, or between whole and part. Readers may wonder: is the resulting volume a novel or a collection of short stories? Stevenson's *New Arabian Nights*, especially, lacks a developed frame. Instead, it relies on the barely developed character of Prince Florizel, a 'prince of Bohemia'.[8] In line with Stevenson's comments in 'A Gossip on Romance', Florizel does not represent real character so much as he does a stereotype of a certain kind of London bachelor; it is unclear whether Stevenson means more to indulge or ridicule him. (Regardless, he was remarkably popular with late-nineteenth-century reviewers.) In addition, the practice of modelling stories after the *Nights* leads to an overt metafictionality, part of the appeal for an experimenter such as Stevenson:

according to Sandison, the collections represent Stevenson's 'highly self-conscious aesthetic, infusing his texts with their polyphonic diversity'.⁹ Since Shahrazad's stories are made up, so too are the inset stories in collections modelled on the form.

By the 1880s, however, the whole convention was becoming tired – enough so that the *New Arabian Nights* functions as a kind of send-up or spoof on the practice.¹⁰ While the convention of modelling stories after the *Nights* was used frequently before, Stevenson's self-consciousness of the artificiality of this convention, the way in which he puts in in service of indeterminacy and play, is new. At the end of *New Arabian Nights*, Stevenson insists on the fictional nature of the narrative by sending Florizel 'along with the *Arabian Author*, topsy-turvy into space'.¹¹ According to Barry Menikoff, this 'wonderfully postmodern' conclusion would have been disturbing to Stevenson's contemporaries precisely because the admission of the fictionality of the whole endeavour would 'undercut' the stories that came before.¹² Indeed, although the *New Arabian Nights* were popular, some contemporary reviewers did object. W. H. Pollock writes in the *Saturday Review* that 'no reader of intelligence can wish to be reminded that Prince Florizel is merely a device of Mr Stevenson who has "served his turn"', and expressed the wish that 'this last paragraph of Mr Stevenson's first volume could be blacked out like articles supposed to be dangerous in English newspapers sent to Russia'.¹³ The *Nights* and its framing device fostered Stevenson's more playful and adventurous experimentations. In this way they are an ideal model for collaborative experimentation because they call attention to the facts of authorship and narration in a self-conscious way.

The connection between the earlier *New Arabian Nights* and the later *More New Arabian Nights: The Dynamiter* is in Stevenson's reprise of the character of Prince Florizel, now fallen to be a mere cigar merchant, and in his continued use of the *Arabian Nights* structure. In fact, in the second volume it is even more fully realised. *The Dynamiter* has a more consistent through-plot than *New Arabian Nights*, and a more developed frame. In it, Florizel (now known as Theophilus Godall) is the mutual acquaintance who brings together three hapless and effete young men looking for adventure. The stories follow each of the young men as they become involved with a team of Fenian terrorists. The first would-be detective, the socially awkward Challoner, becomes the reluctant escort of a beautiful Mormon fleeing a forced marriage to a mad scientist in 'The Destroying Angel'. The second man, Somerset, becomes involved in tracking down Zero, the principal Fenian dynamiter, while the third, Desborough, is implored to protect 'The Fair Cuban', whose history is given as yet another inset story. As it happens, the narrator of 'The Destroying Angel' and 'Fair Cuban' is one and the same: Clara Luxmore, a wily member of the Fenian team (she narrates the second story in blackface).

The Stevensons' experimental structure now seems quite ordinary, even if it was then ahead of its time, but one thing that remains unsettling is *The Dynamiter*'s farcical tone. The comical take on a prominent issue of the day makes the politics of the text confusing. Recent atrocities such as the Phoenix Park murders in 6 May 1882, in which Lord Frederick Cavendish and Thomas Henry Burke had been brutally murdered with a butcher's knife by the Irish nationalist group the Invincibles, had shocked both the British and the Americans.[14] More recently, the Irish American Fenians, under the leadership of O'Donovan Rossa, had turned to dynamite attacks on London. The Fenian problem did not just pit the English against the Irish. The Fenians operated from the safe haven of the United States, and the English perceived the Americans as slow to take the matter seriously, something they eventually did following 'Dynamite Saturday'.[15] It is for this reason that the historian Niall Whelehan argues that the Fenian movement must be considered from a 'transnational approach'.[16]

The political message of the text is further complicated by another struggle to which the book alludes: growing tensions between America and Spain because of the persistence of slavery in Cuba, and because of would-be Cuban dynamiters attempting to launch filibustering assaults on Cuba from Key West. During 1884 US–Spanish relations were strained by the Spanish occupation of Cuba, especially because the Spanish persisted in using slave labour on the island.[17] The spring of 1884, precisely when Louis and Fanny were hardest at work on *The Dynamiter*, saw the emergence of a Cuban dynamite panic. First, a Cuban separatist, Carlos Aguero, launched a filibuster attempt into Cuba from the United States, just as Narciso López had done decades earlier. Because of tensions over the issue of slavery, Spain worried that the United States would turn a blind eye to attacks originating from their shores, a suspicion that was strengthened by the fact that the United States had, at Spain's request, apprehended Aguero for extradition shortly before he set sail, but had released him after questioning, effectively allowing him to commence his assault. Spain believed his ship to be full of dynamite, which the Americans denied. In the end, Aguero managed to land his ship on Cuba, but with an insignificant twenty-five men.[18] Then, that May, American officials discovered stockpiles of dynamite being shipped to Nassau, where they could be held until they might be ultimately be smuggled into Cuba by rebels.[19]

Nor were these the only Cuban dynamite situations that spring and summer. On 12 June 1884 a Cuban resident of Key West, Federico Gil Marrero, was caught returning from New York to Key West' in possession of a 'fuse, detonating caps, and books of instruction upon the manufacture of dynamite', which he allegedly hoped to assemble in Key West, it being easier to smuggle the raw materials than assembled explosives.[20] New York dynamite manufacturers were reluctant to admit to having sold to any such person, with Atlas Company insisting to the *New York Times* that they 'refuse[d] to sell dynamite to two Spaniards, and that was not very long ago. We have likewise refused to sell for shipment to Key West', citing Spain's extreme restrictions on even legitimate dynamite imports into Cuba (for mining) because of the likelihood it would be used for insurrectionary purposes.[21] That New York dynamite companies would not even do business with suspected Cubans or even with Key Westers indicates the prevalence of the Cuban dynamite fears. Then, in July, R. Rubiera, the New York-based editor of the 'Cuban patriot journal' *El Separatista* was arrested for a suspected shipment of dynamite, also to Key West. Rubiera was released when the shipment proved to be 'common powder' (it is unclear if gunpowder is meant).[22] This was not a British crisis, it was an American one; but in a way the Fenian problem was an American crisis, too, because the rebels in each case were not Irish but Irish American. *The Dynamiter* is likewise a transnational text, co-authored as it is by a Scot and an American with a plot that traverses London, Utah and Cuba.

In addition to its satirical tone, *The Dynamiter* also takes a strangely tolerant view of its criminal characters. Most obviously, there is the sympathetic investigation of the situation of Clara Luxmore – the comfortably upper-class Englishwoman brought by her youth and idealism into a close association with political radicals. But we see the same sympathetic treatment of a young Fenian who sets out to murder Florizel. In 'The Superfluous Mansion', the suicidal young man confesses that he has been led into crime by a radical political sympathy with the downtrodden and against the powerful. As time goes on he loses faith in his terrorist comrades: 'Horrible was the society with which we warred, but our own means were not less horrible.'[23] Somerset understands: 'I held at one time very liberal opinions, and should certainly have joined a secret society if I had been able to find one'

(110). In her reading of *The Dynamiter*, Elizabeth C. Miller argues that, for the late Victorians, political criminals were different from the biological criminal underclass being then described by the criminologist Cesare Lombroso because of their more rational motivations.[24] This explains the wavering devotion to the Fenian cause that we see in the innocent protagonists such as Somerset, and in dynamiters such as Clara Luxmore. Though the Stevensons obviously intend a dark humour in the trivial way that Somerset can put on and throw off sympathy with the dynamiters, this same indecision is reflected in the Stevensons' own conflicted treatment of the political issues involved. To a person, each Fenian is a charming person, sadly misled. Even Zero himself, the principal dynamiter and criminal mastermind of the text, is so likeable that Somerset cannot seem to shake his friendship. It is not that Zero is innately wicked, but that his myopic philosophy has led to a colossal moral blind spot, maddening those who would sympathise with him.

Though (like Clara Luxmore) sympathetic to the oppression of the Irish, Louis was not sympathetic to the violent tactics of the Fenians and other terrorist groups. In January of 1885, while the Stevensons were already well under way on *The Dynamiter*, London was appalled by 'Dynamite Saturday', when the Fenians exploded three simultaneous bombs – one in the House of Commons, one in the crypt of Westminster Hall, and one in the Tower of London.[25] Before the bombings, both Fanny and Louis appear not to have strong feelings about Fenian practices, with Fanny even writing to her mother-in-law in 1884: 'When I think of Gladstone I declare I begin to have some sympathy with the "dynamitards".'[26] After the bombings their attitude changed. Five days later, Louis expressed his wish that the perpetrators be 'lynched' in a letter to his father (*Letters* 5: 73). In a letter to Fanny Sitwell dated spring 1885, Fanny also makes reference to Dynamite Saturday:

> What a dreadful thing these explosions have been. Our Arabian tales have been a good deal knocked over by them, but Louis is remodelling where it is necessary as hard as he can. It is a great advertisement. I cannot tell you how I admire the English policeman . . . I wonder if the dynamiters will come blowing up Louis and me, and our Valentine and our Bogue.[27]

(Valentine was Fanny's maid; Bogue was their dog.) Fanny's letter is unpleasantly narcissistic, pivoting as it does between happiness that the attack will help their publicity and concern that the terrorists will kill her dog, but her alarm would have been typical. Despite the low death count from the Fenian dynamite campaign, it served its purpose in striking terror into the English.[28]

The volume had been largely finished at this point, and Louis was eager for it to appear, which explains Fanny's reference to 'remodelling'. The renewed and terrifying relevance of the Fenian dynamite campaign would have made the pair's farcical and sympathetic treatment of the topic tasteless at best. Dynamite Saturday seems to have forced the Stevensons to come out strongly on one or the other side of the issue. The Stevensons quickly added a preface, dedicating *The Dynamiter* to Police Constable William Cole and Sergeant Robert Cox, two police officers who were injured on Dynamite Saturday, Cole while trying to carry the dynamite out of the House of Commons. In a letter to John Addington Symonds, Stevenson compares the officers to General Gordon, who had in that same year attempted to defend the city of Khartoum in the Sudan even as Gladstone had tried to pull English and Egyptian forces out (*Letters* 5: 81). In the preface, the Stevensons justify their farce by saying 'the authors have touched upon the ugly devil of crime, with which it is your glory to have contended. It were a waste of ink to do so in a serious spirit' (*Dynamiter*, iii). Following on this, the authors (and one imagines it is Louis here) confess

> we have so long coquetted with political crime; not seriously weighing, not acutely following it from cause to consequence; but with a generous, unfounded heat of sentiment, like a schoolboy with the penny tale, applauding what was specious. When it touched ourselves (truly in a vile shape) we proved false to these imaginations; discovered, in a clap, that crime was no less cruel and no less ugly under sounding names: and recoiled from our false deities. (iii)

This disavowal of an earlier flirtation with political crime identifies Stevenson himself with repentant criminals such as Clara Luxmore, or the suicidal terrorist in 'The Superfluous Mansion'. There is a limit, the preface argues, to Stevenson's liberal sympathies and identification with the downtrodden, and that limit is surpassed with the terroristic attacks of the Fenians. But, as Fanny's letter to Fanny Sitwell indicates, the preface itself may be a last-ditch effort to recover a suitable context for the tales after a further atrocity (Dynamite Saturday) had made them politically suspect.

Fanny and Louis wrote *The Dynamiter* at Hyères and finished it at Bournemouth the same year. Louis, the story goes, was desperately ill, and Fanny passed the time by telling him stories. Louis's illness, Fanny thought, was brought about by his collaborations with Henley, with whom he had just finished working on *Beau Austin* and *Admiral Guinea*.[29] In fact, Louis was still fending off Henley's attempts to reinvest him in dramatic collaborations, even as he was ill and had begun his collaboration on *The Dynamiter* with Fanny (*Letters* 5: 21). Henley and Louis finished *Macaire* on 24 January 1885, at the same time as he was in negotiations with the *Pall Mall Gazette* to publish *The Dynamiter* (*Letters* 5: 72) (and also, coincidentally, Dynamite Saturday). If Fanny saw Henley's collaborations as fostering disease, then her own would be healing.

Foucault has said that the *Nights* 'had as their motivation, their theme and pretext, this strategy for defeating death'.[30] It was a feature of the stories that Stevenson had recognised a century earlier. Stevenson wrote to his friend John Meiklejohn in 1880:

> When I suffer in mind, stories are my refuge; I take them like opium; and I consider one who writes them as a sort of doctor of the mind. And frankly, Meiklejohn, it is not Shakespeare we take to, when we are in a hot corner; nor, certainly, George Eliot – no, nor even Balzac. It is Charles Reade, or old Dumas, or the *Arabian Nights*, or the best of Walter Scott; it is stories we want, not the high poetic function which represents the world; we are then like the Asiatic with his *improvisatore* or the middle-agee with his *trouvère*. We want incident, interest, action: to the devil with your philosophy. When we are well again, and have an easy mind, we shall peruse your important work; but what we want now is a drug. (*Letters* 3: 61–2)

Stevenson, in other words, considers stories – at least those stories that are plot driven rather than realist or representational – to be a kind of medical treatment, comparing them to a drug and authors to doctors, so it is fitting that Fanny would tell him stories in the style of the *Nights* during one of his worst illnesses. Fanny's nightly storytelling, meant to amuse and distract her husband, becomes a re-enactment of the life-prolonging storytelling of the *Arabian Nights* frame.

But the *Nights* are not only about staving off death; they are also about marriage. Just as Shahrazad spends the nights telling stories to her husband, so, too, did Fanny Stevenson. The truth is that marriage poses a particular problem for studies of collaboration precisely because we know, or suspect, how often wives have been silent collaborators on their husband's work, and because when two authors share a home there is rarely a written record of who has written what, as there may be with epistolary collaborations. Husbands certainly collaborate on their wives' writings too, but a critical double standard is common; as Bette London has argued, where a wife is presumed to have collaborated on her husband's work, the assumption is that she was working as an assistant or amanuensis, whereas when a husband is found to have collaborated on his wife's, as in the case of Mary Shelley, it 'carries the imputation of . . . incompetence – if not authorial impropriety'.[31] The unacknowledged literary or editorial labour of wives is an open secret of literary history, so pervasive as to be barely worthy of note. In this, Fanny Stevenson, who was an outspoken critic and reader of her husband's work, was no exception. What makes *The Dynamiter* unusual is not the fact of her collaboration, but the extent of it, and even more unusual, that this collaboration is credited. And yet, Fanny remained anxious that her work would not be sufficiently recognised.

In January of 1885 Fanny wrote to her mother-in-law: 'I always have to fight hard for my changes, but in most Henley has borne me out' (*Letters* 5: 71). In a letter dated 20 May 1885 she wrote to Margaret Stevenson again, bragging that 'Sir Percy Shelley, the son of the poet, and his wife, seem quite mad over the Dynamiter', as were family friends the Jenkins. She complains:

> I begin to understand your feelings concerning the 'garden', and you preferring to be thought decently buried; I thought in the beginning that I shouldn't mind being Louis' scapegoat, but it is rather hard to be treated like a comma, and a superfluous one at that; – and then in one paper, which I will send you, the only one in which I am mentioned the critic refers to me as 'undoubtedly Mr Stevenson's sister'. <u>Why</u> pray? Surely there can be nothing in the book that points to sister in particular. Colvin says it is selling everywhere in London, at a great rate. I think I was wise in insisting on launching it at once.[32]

Fanny's anxiety that she might be 'treated like a comma' reveals her deep insecurity that her contribution will not be fully acknowledged, but in this case her husband was quite willing to give her full credit. Perhaps even more surprising is that there is no evidence of any nineteenth-century reader showing surprise or derision at Fanny's co-authorship. Ironically, her literary legacy seems to have been undone by her own ambition, as her insistence on claiming for herself a larger share of the authorship of *The Dynamiter* with the publication of Gosse's 1906 edition served not to enlarge her own reputation, but instead caused *The Dynamiter* itself to fall from the Stevenson canon.

Accustomed as we are to thinking of *The Dynamiter* as strictly minor Stevenson, wading into the nineteenth-century reviews creates a bit of a surprise – Victorian readers thought Stevenson was at the top of his game in this book. *More New Arabian Nights: The Dynamiter* was seen as following on the great success of the *New Arabian Nights*, which had been remarkably popular. If the new book was not considered quite up to the previous one, it was still received as a much anticipated and largely satisfying sequel. (The one complaint that Victorian readers did have was that there was not as much of Prince Florizel/Theophilus Godall as they had hoped.)

Among the nineteenth-century reviews, two stories are almost always referred to the reader's special attention: 'The Destroying Angel' and 'The Fair Cuban'. *The Critic* writes that 'The Mormon story in the present volume and the "Story of the Fair Cuban" are highly imaginative and encourage a hope that the author may someday give us a book containing but a single story.' A reviewer at the *Saturday Review* raved that 'in "The Destroying Angel" and "The Fair Cuban" there are a couple of romantic stories which are equal, if not superior, to anything Mr Stevenson has ever done', and an 1885 review in the New Zealand *Evening Star* reports 'There is nothing, perhaps, in this lot of stories equal to the famous "Suicide Club"; but "The Fair Cuban" and "The Explosive Bomb" will be found, in different ways, almost equally original.'[33] Furthermore, nineteenth-century assessments of these stories were comfortable with both the fact of the collaboration, and with Fanny's role in the process. As important a critic as Henry James wrote Fanny's hand in *The Dynamiter* was 'evidently a light and practiced one'.[34] Twentieth-century readers would be much less approving of those two stories, and about the appropriateness of Fanny's participation in her husband's career.

Most twentieth-century critics who discuss *The Dynamiter* have focused on who wrote what, and Fanny herself seems to have motivated this change in attitude, which ironically has not worked in her favour. In 1906–7 Edmund Gosse published the Pentland Edition of the Works of Robert Louis Stevenson. In his introduction to the work, Gosse quotes Fanny:

> I was to go out . . . for an hour's walk every afternoon, if it were only back and forth in front of our door, and invent a story to repeat when I came in – a sort of Arabian Nights' Entertainment where I was to take the part of Scheherezade [sic] and he the Sultan. There

had been several dynamite outrages in London about this time, the most of them turning into fiascos. It occurred to me to take an impotent dynamite intrigue as the thread to string my stories on. I began with the Mormon tale, and followed it with innumerable others, one for each afternoon. As time passed, my husband gradually regained his health to a degree, became again absorbed in his work, and the stories of Scheherezade were thought of no more.[35]

Only later, when the pair needed money, did they try to recall the stories she had told, but 'We could recall only enough to make a rather thin book, so my husband added one more to the list, "The Explosive Bomb".'[36] Gosse asserts that the Florizel material was Louis's alone, but it was his edition that made concrete the claim that 'The Destroying Angel' and 'The Fair Cuban' were hers, and since then those stories' reputations have suffered accordingly. In 1916 Graham Balfour reiterates that

> husband and wife began to put together the second series of *New Arabian Nights* from the stories which Mrs. Stevenson had made up to while away the hours of illness at Hyères. Stevenson wrote the passages relating to Prince Florizel and collaborated in the remainder; but the only complete story of his invention in the book was 'The Explosive Bomb': by which he designed 'to make dynamite ridiculous, if he could not make it horrible.[37]

Though Balfour's comment is even-handed, more often than not the aim of such investigation is to imply that Robert Louis Stevenson's work was, one way or another, dragged down by his grasping wife. In 1950 Malcolm Elwin was dismissive of Fanny's contributions and talents, though uncertain of where to give credit:

> As he lay in a darkened room, forbidden to speak and fearful of movements, Fanny amused him by making up stories, two of which, 'The Destroying Angel' and 'The Fair Cuban', he adapted in *The Dynamiter*, so affording an excuse to credit Fanny with 'collaboration'.[38]

Perhaps, Elwin's reading suggests, Louis deserves all the credit, and only assigned his wife credit out of a sense of generosity. (Critics will come to the same conclusion about Stevenson's relationship with Lloyd Osbourne.) J. C. Furnas (1951) observes 'the curiously vulgar flavor of Fanny's tales in *The Dynamiter*, which survived even Louis's rehandling'.[39] Margaret Mackay, in her 1968 biography of

Fanny, reports that 'Literary historians have claimed that the title story of "The Dynamiter" alone was her very own.' (There is no such story, but if she means 'Zero's Tale of the Explosive Bomb', then Balfour's account is more credible.) Mackay finds the evidence in the style itself: 'when she laid her hand to fiction it has a coarse texture and synthetic manner that one does not find in those of her husband's works in which she was not a collaborator.'[40] Sandison, in 2003, finds the collection 'brilliant' and 'graceful', excepting '"The Destroying Angel" and "The Story of the Fair Cuban", which are clearly Fanny's work in that they operate in a patently different "key"'.[41] Most recently, scholars in the digital humanities have weighed in on the question, with a team of graduate students at the University of Edinburgh using the practice of stylometry to analyse stories in *The Dynamiter* and compare them to other prose by Fanny and Louis. The technique may be new but the conclusion is familiar:

> 'The Story of the Destroying Angel' and 'The Fair Cuban' are likely to have been written by Fanny. The chapters appear together often enough. The fact they sometimes appear relatively close to the works known to have been written by Robert Louis is due to Robert Louis being a very conscientious writer. His hand in the editing process could have obscured and, ultimately, overpowered Fanny's stylistic features.[42]

What interests me about these conflicting accounts is that in their certainty about their assessments of who wrote what in *The Dynamiter* they show a fundamental disbelief in collaboration. Is collaborative writing even possible? The Stevensons thought it was. But throughout the twentieth century there persists a belief that there will always be some tell on the part of the weaker partner; that the work will cleave in two again for a careful reader. That reader can then comfortably assign those parts of the story perceived as artistic to Louis and those parts that are clunky to Fanny.

I am again reminded of the reported response of collaborative poets Michael Field to Havelock Ellis: 'As to our work, let no man think he can put asunder what god has joined.'[43] The prevailing critical view has been to see Stevenson's collaborations as no better than fraudulent – usually frauds perpetrated on him by his hangers-on. However, critics who work on collaboration such as Lorraine York and Wayne Koestenbaum have rejected this way of seeing collaborative writing, in which 'Authorship itself is not significantly re-theorized or rethought.'[44] Of all of Stevenson's works, *The Dynamiter* is one of his (their) most experimental, as all critics who have worked on it have noted. This bold experimentation extends to a questioning of the nature of authorship itself.

It is critical commonplace to note the absence of women from Stevenson's fiction. In 1888 Henry James observed that 'he needs not a petticoat to inflame him'.[45] The prominence of anti-heroine and supremely unreliable narrator Clara Luxmore is surely a great exception, and the notion that Stevenson could not or would not write from a female point of view has lent credence to the idea that Clara Luxmore and her stories are Fanny's responsibility. (The other exception is the prominent role of the two Kirsties in *Weir of Hermiston* (1896).) In fact, this has led critics and biographers to conclude that Fanny *is* Clara Luxmore: Furnas, in describing Fanny as a liar, notes her statements sometimes sound 'too much like the authoress of certain tales in *The Dynamiter*'.[46]

Both 'The Destroying Angel' and 'The Fair Cuban' are inset into the deepest parts of *The Dynamiter*'s multiple frames. Both stories function as both seduction and deception – Clara, in disguise, spins fictional tales of her own victimisation so that her two young male interlocutors will come to her aid and rescue her. In reality, the point is to involve them in the very terrorist plot they are trying to investigate. In 'The Destroying Angel', Clara tells the inexperienced young Challoner a horror story about her Mormon upbringing and the marriage she is about to be forced into, and in the name of chivalry she begs for his assistance. Challoner is embarrassed to be sceptical:

> What with the lady's animated manner and dramatic conduct of her voice, Challoner had thrilled to every incident with genuine emotion. His fancy, which was not perhaps of a very lively character, applauded both the matter and the style; but the more judicial functions of his mind refused assent. It was an excellent story; and it might be true, but he believed it was not. Miss Fonblanque was a lady, and it was doubtless possible for a lady to wander from the truth; but how was a gentleman to tell her so? (*Dynamiter* 57)

Similarly, in 'The Fair Cuban', Clara Luxmore literally paints herself as Señorita Teresa Valdevia, a Cuban slave of Spanish and African descent, in order to get Harry Desborough to help her smuggle out her supposed treasure: in fact, the box contains a bomb with which she plans to blow up the children's hospital. Unlike Challoner, Desborough is completely taken in, even though the story is more incredible than 'Miss Fonblanque's' Mormon story. At one particularly desperate moment, the narrator is saved by a fortuitous tornado, which appears without warning and wipes out everyone but her. Besides, her narration literally begins 'I am not what I seem' (168).

The Cuban section of *The Dynamiter* exemplifies the novel's troubled treatment of race, which is more in line with Fanny's American than with Louis's Scottish upbringing. Early in the novel, Clara Luxmore insists that the reluctant Challoner deliver a letter to her supposed cousin, giving the password 'Nigger, nigger, never die', to which the counterword will be 'Black face and shining eye' (62). The rhyme, which would not have meant much in Scotland, was a racist children's taunt in the nineteenth-century Midwest, where Fanny had grown up.[47] In a letter to her mother-in-law, Fanny, who had a dark complexion, explains that her classmates had been used to tease her with it when she was a child.[48] Louis was familiar with the phrase too, but more probably from Fanny's childhood than his own; he writes it on top of a letter to his mother in 1882.[49] In one version of 'Nigger, Nigger, Never Die', appallingly recrafted as a hit song in 1897, the minstrel instructs his son, who is being taunted with the phrase, to retort with a third verse that runs 'Irish, Irish flannel mouth Mick, / Look out Irish, don't you heave that brick'. Presumably, the children taunting him are Irish immigrants, and so the song refers to racialised caricatures of the Irish current in British and American periodicals of the time, particularly the caricature of the Irish American terrorist.[50] In bringing together these disparate racisms, even farcically, *The Dynamiter* links Ireland's struggles, American race relations, and the still-current problem of slavery in Cuba.

It is no accident that Luxmore chooses the identity of a Cuban slave as one of her alternate identities. As I have argued above, her assumption of a specifically Cuban disguise is meant to signal her solidarity with Cuban rebels and dynamiters, whose situation as well as tactics bears comparison to the Fenians with whom she works. Like the situation of the Irish dynamiters, this adventure, though nominally international, would not have gone on without significant American involvement. In fact, in both cases it is the impact of a diaspora in America (Irish or Cuban, respectively) trying to enforce their will on their home country. In short, there is good reason why Clara Luxmore decides to dress up as a Cuban slave: it is because in her support of Irish emancipation she would have found common cause with Cuban emancipation, as insurrectionists from both countries were buying dynamite in New York City at the same time. Mrs Luxmore, speaking of her criminally misled daughter, says, 'Some whim about oppressed nationalities – Ireland,

Poland, and the like – has turned her brain' (*Dynamiter* 92), a statement that simultaneously provides a link between Ireland, American race relations and Cuban slavery, and at the same time reveals the naive vagueness of Clara Luxmore's politics. Of course, to our eyes, Clara Luxmore's choice to dress up in black face to draw attention to the plight of Cuban slaves, and, by extension, to the issue of Cuban independence from Spain overall, seems more than ineffective – it is offensive. By the same token, I would argue that the Stevensons' rejection of Clara's sympathy with these political causes is itself facile, dismissing significant issues with a moralistic blanket condemnation of rebellion. However, these struggles predict in some measure what would come later: a global vision but with an American perspective, such as Stevenson would return to (with much greater success and nuance) in *The Wrecker*, and an ongoing concern with resistance to imperialism that would later come to characterise much of his political thought and work at the end of his career.

The Dynamiter connects three author-narrators, Clara, Shahrazad and Fanny. All are female, and all in their own way unreliable. The stories that Clara Luxmore tells in *The Dynamiter* are overtly fictional: even at the moment she is telling them we as readers are expected to understand that they are untrue. Robert Kiely argues that the overt fictionality of Clara Luxmore's stories only shows the extent to which the whole project of *The Dynamiter* is fraudulent, and Sandison writes: 'Fictions are piled on fictions and then detonated as the extravagance of the parody ensures its betrayal.'[51] And yet, like Challoner's reaction ('he thrilled to every incident with genuine emotion'), this fictionality – this belief that we are being deceived, by Clara Luxmore and both Stevensons, is not meant to reduce in any way the pleasure of the story. It is important to realise that the structure of the *Nights* themselves is based upon fictional narrators: because another character with a story to tell is always breaking in, Shahrazad can never complete her stories. In other words, it is precisely these receding fictional narrators that make her stories seemingly infinite. Consequently, an emphasis on the inauthenticity of 'The Destroying Angel' and 'The Fair Cuban' as part of *The Dynamiter* misses the point: that the narrator or author may be fictional is part of the effect. Questions about how much Fanny wrote or collaborated on these stories extends the question of fictionality across the boundary that separates the fictional text from historical reality, but then again, so does the long oral history of the *Nights* themselves: we do not really know who invented those tales, or, in fact, if they are really stories authored by a woman.

A Family Drama: *The Hanging Judge*

In addition to the better-known *Dynamiter*, Fanny and Louis had but one more official collaboration. The 1887 play *The Hanging Judge* was originally planned as another dramatic Stevenson Henley collaboration, but when the men gave the project over, Fanny took it up herself.[52] Just as in the case of *The Dynamiter*, Fanny herself claimed a large share of the credit, and the reputation of the play has suffered accordingly. Apart from Fanny's claims about the authorship of this play, there is little to suggest that it was hers alone, and Stevenson's comments about the play in his letters are unhelpfully restricted to the orders he placed for the printing of proofs, which he does state he intended to correct.

Fanny makes her claim to the authorship of *The Hanging Judge* in the preface to *Kidnapped*, where she writes:

> While my husband and Mr. Henley were engaged in writing plays in Bournemouth they made a number of titles, hoping to use them in the future. Dramatic composition was not what my husband preferred, but the torrent of Mr. Henley's enthusiasm swept him off his feet. However, after several plays had been finished, and his health seriously impaired by his endeavours to keep up with Mr. Henley, play writing was abandoned forever, and my husband returned to his legitimate vocation. Having added one of the titles, The Hanging Judge, to the list of projected plays, now thrown aside, and emboldened by my husband's offer to give me any help needed, I concluded to try and write it myself.[53]

Fanny's dangling participle makes it unclear whether the genesis of the hanging judge idea comes from Fanny (if it were she who had added the idea to the list of projected plays), or whether it was originally on Henley and Stevenson's list. In a letter to Colvin in 1895, Henley will claim it was his idea.[54] Once again, as in *The Dynamiter*, Fanny's version of the events is reinforced by Graham Balfour's 1916 biography of Stevenson. Balfour mentions *The Hanging Judge* as Stevenson's last play, but similarly assigns it primarily to Fanny, writing that Stevenson 'helped his wife' with it.[55] Beattie writes that 'Fanny told Graham Balfour that Louis liked her scenario, rearranged it, and wrote alternate scenes with her, which they then exchanged and rewrote.'[56]

Then again, there is some evidence it was a true collaboration. On 6 December 1887 Fanny writes from Saranac to someone she refers to as 'Preamble' (possibly Sidney Colvin) that it has been finished 'amid much dissension and general acrimony' (*Letters* 6: 73–4), and Lloyd Osbourne also describes it as written by the two 'in collaboration'.[57] Either Fanny has exaggerated her own authorship after the fact, and it was in fact jointly composed by the two of them, or the play is indeed her work, but if so, why was it printed with both of them listed as authors? Did Fanny merely hope that appending her more famous husband's name to her own play would help it gain more attention, as Henley had believed? And yet, this strategy had not worked for Henley before, even with Stevenson's actual collaboration. It seems likely that the play was meant as a private amusement only; two manuscript versions held at the Beinecke were privately printed by the Parliamentary Typing Association and bound in ribbon and plain white paper rather than being sent to publishers (and not very well either, as they misspelled Fanny's name as Fanny Van de Gript Stevenson, instead of Grift).[58]

Regardless, the play has met with a great deal of critical hostility and neglect; more, even, than Stevenson's dramatic failures with Henley. When Edmund Gosse compiled his complete works of Robert Louis Stevenson, Fanny wrote to him suggesting that *The Hanging Judge* be included. Gosse declined, presumably feeling it was of too low a quality, but later relented and printed the play's first published version, as a separate title, in 1914. As Gosse explains it in his introduction to this edition:

> When, in the summer of 1907, I was consulted by my old and valued friend, the late Mrs Robert Louis Stevenson, as to what should, and what should not, be included in the Pentland Edition of her husband's works, which she had asked me to see through the press, she added, dubiously, 'And then there's *The Hanging Judge* – what do you say to that?' ... I expressed a great anxiety to see it, and she accordingly (July 9, 1907), forwarded a typed copy of it to me, leaving it to my judgement whether it should or should not be included in the Pentland Edition. On reading it; I determined that it should not be so included; Mrs Stevenson acquiesced, but left the play with me, in case my view should change.
>
> It has not changed, but as I understand that other copies are in existence, I think it well to have this text privately printed, as it is that which was selected for the press by Mrs Stevenson herself.[59]

As with the *Dynamiter* stories 'The Destroying Angel' and 'The Fair Cuban', it is Fanny's contaminating presence that serves to make it unpalatable. Ian Bell represents the project as so far Fanny's own that he does not even list it as co-authored, but as by Fanny herself. He also takes a dim view of it, writing that Fanny 'squander[ed] Louis' time on it'. In a critical essay on Stevenson's dramatic attempts, John Cairney declines to consider it, calling it 'notable only for being completed'.[60]

The play is a classic nineteenth-century bigamy plot. It concerns Mr Hargrove, the hanging judge of the title, his wife and their daughter, Eleanor. At the moment of her engagement, Eleanor learns that her biological father is her mother's first husband, Gillespie. After Gillespie was transported and presumed dead, Eleanor's mother remarried her first love, Mr Hargrove, who has raised Eleanor as his own. Now, Gillespie is back, with plans to blackmail the family: 'I am a gentleman in delicate circumstances, and my wife – or your wife, we need not quarrel for a pronoun, it is all in the family – your wife or mine, is what you call a bigamist.'[61] Gillespie is again arrested, with planted counterfeit bills, and Hargrove sentences him to death. In a strained moment of dramatic irony, Gillespie's execution occurs at the very same moment as Eleanor's wedding. At the end of the play, Hargrove and his wife die together of guilt over having murdered Gillespie; she of a heart condition and he of poison.

The idea of a hanging judge – a judge inclined to condemn his defendants to death – grew directly out of Stevenson and Henley's work on *Deacon Brodie* (1880). Robert MacQueen, Lord Braxfield (1722–99), the man who had tried and hanged the historical Deacon Brodie, was known for 'great and unnecessary severity', which led to his nickname the 'Hanging Judge'.[62] Henley argues that Stevenson's interest in this figure was inspired by 'a story in Sheridan LeFanu's *Through a Glass Darkly* [sic], a book for which R. L. S. had a profound respect. *I* brought it on the cloth, as a *motif* for a play.'[63] (The story referenced is Le Fanu's 'Mr Justice Harbottle' (1872).) In his essay 'Some Portraits by Raeburn', first published in *Virginibus Puerisque* in 1881, Stevenson describes an encounter with a portrait of Lord Braxfield at an exhibition at the Scottish Academy. In this essay, Stevenson urges sympathy with the notorious and hated judge:

> So sympathetically is the character conceived by the portrait painter, that it is hardly possible to avoid some movement of sympathy on the part of the spectator. And sympathy is a thing to be encouraged, apart from humane considerations, because it supplies us with the materials for wisdom. It is probably more instructive to entertain a sneaking kindness for any unpopular person, and, among the rest, for Lord Braxfield, than to give way to perfect raptures of moral indignation against his abstract vices.[64]

It is an unusual rhetorical move to make, to plead for sympathy and even mercy in the case of a man infamous for having no mercy, a man who, according to William Forbes Gray, was 'coarse and jocular when he ought to have been dignified and circumspect; vindictive when he ought to have been dispassionate; cruel when he ought to have been just'.[65] And yet, the play *The Hanging Judge* functions as an exploration of the justifications that such an executioner might have for his sins. Though Hargrove in the play makes the wrong decision, his moral dilemma is fundamentally sympathetic, following Stevenson's hope in 'Some Portraits by Raeburn' to allow forgiveness even to he who will not forgive. In particular, it seems odd for Stevenson himself, whose morality did not really run to authoritarianism. Nevertheless, the figure of Braxfield was to obsess Stevenson for the rest of his life and career.

Stevenson returns to the notion of the hanging judge in his last, and unfinished, novel *Weir of Hermiston*. In fact, in 1892 he would write to Colvin that he wished he could call that novel simply *Braxfield* (*Letters* 7: 408). (In his diary that same year, he light-heartedly refers to himself as 'looking like Braxfield' as he presides over the mock trial of several of his Samoan servants who were suspected of stealing his pig.)[66] In *Weir of Hermiston*, Archie Weir chafes against the strict upbringing of his father, Adam Weir, a 'hanging judge', in a relationship readers have found reminiscent of Stevenson's own conflicts with his father earlier in life.[67] Belle Strong, who helped with *Weir of Hermiston* as Stevenson's amanuensis, was later to share with Colvin that the ending of that novel was to feature the senior Weir trying his own son, and having to make the decision of whether to hang him – a dramatic moral dilemma even if a legally unlikely plot based, according to Henley, on a dramatic problem in Edward Bulwer-Lytton's *Paul Clifford* (1830).[68] In the end, Colvin wrote, 'the ordeal of taking part in the trial of his own son has been too much for the Lord Justice-Clerk, who dies of the shock', just as in *The Hanging Judge* Mrs Hargrove dies of the shock of watching her second husband condemn her first.[69]

So, although Balfour and Bell describe *The Hanging Judge* as Fanny Stevenson's own work, written merely under advice from her husband, Louis's impact was greater than mere editor. This particular problem – of whether, and in what circumstances, one might sympathise with Braxfield, was of ongoing interest to Louis, and the plot of the play certainly reflected the couple's discussions. As histrionic as the play may be, the scenario was close to home for the couple. Fanny herself had had some trouble with the unlooked-for return of her own husband. Sam Osbourne, who like Gillespie was a rogue, and who, also like Gillespie, had at one point been presumed dead when his party on a gold-prospecting expedition was massacred.[70] Years after their divorce, Sam Osbourne continued to show up, and Jenni Calder notes that Fanny received his visits to their (now-grown) son Lloyd in 1885 with some anxiety.[71] An autobiographical reading of *The Hanging Judge* puts Stevenson himself in the role of the loving, yet authoritative stepfather, and Sam Osbourne as a bad penny that keeps turning up.[72] Only thirty copies were privately printed,[73] and in his order for the printing Stevenson requests specifically 'a somewhat blackguard looking turn out; so as to seem unassuming' (*Letters* 5: 369). The story, perhaps, was too personal, and better suited to intimate family performances, where the principals would be recognised.

Collaboration, Plagiarism and 'The Nixie' Scandal

Just one year later Fanny would have a successful publication, but not without controversy. Fanny's short story 'The Nixie', and the scandal that resulted from its publication, further exposes the complexities that surround collaboration. The story, published in Scribner's in 1888, concerns a wealthy, languid young man who meets, and protects, a strange young woman on the train. When his carriage mate follows him on his hunting trip, the two steal a boat and set off on a trip down the river. Only after the young man is nearly drowned and saved by passers-by does he realise that his companion was, in fact, a nixie, or water spirit. The story is firmly in the fantasy genre, with more in common with late-century works such as Arthur Machen's *The Great God Pan* than with anything Robert Louis Stevenson wrote. Though little has been written about the story itself, much has been written about the circumstances of its creation. 'The Nixie' is famous not for itself, but because it effected the end of the friendship between Stevenson and Henley.

On 9 March 1888 Henley wrote to Stevenson responding to the publication of the story:

> I read *The Nixie* with considerable amazement. It's Katharine's; surely it's Katharine's? The situation, the environment, the principal figure – *voyons*! There are even reminiscences of phrases and imagery, parallel incidents – *que sais-je*? It is all better focused, no

doubt, but I think it has lost at least as much as it has gained; and why there wasn't a double signature is what I've not been able to understand.[74]

Stevenson responded angrily to the accusation of his wife's plagiarism, and the friendship suffered accordingly. According to the story, Stevenson's cousin Katharine de Mattos had shared with Fanny a concept for a story she planned to write. The story was to feature an escaped inmate from an asylum who meets a man on a train. Fanny was taken with the idea, but proposed that the inmate character be a nixie. The two should collaborate! Katharine demurred, and after that accounts differ, but in any case Fanny had her nixie story published in *Scribner's*.

Why Henley took up Katharine's cause is unclear; the consensus has been that Katharine was his *protégée*. There has been much speculation on what Katharine de Mattos wrote, and how complete it was. On one side, Edward Cohen, in his book-length study of the dispute, concludes that 'it has never been proved that Mrs. De Mattos truly wrote her version of the story',[75] but Stevenson himself, after hearing back from Katharine, concludes she did write it and was unable to get it published (*Letters* 6: 146–7) and Beattie reports that de Mattos had read her story to the family.[76] The fact remains that, without de Mattos's manuscript, the extent of Fanny's plagiarism is unknown; nevertheless, we must consider (as de Mattos surely did in her refusal to collaborate on the project in the first place) whether a story in which the main character is a nixie can truly be said to be the same as one in which she is not!

There is, however, one line in Henley's paragraph to which I would like to call attention. He wonders not that Fanny should have written the story, but 'why there wasn't a double signature'. The declaration, so essential to our understanding of the collaborative project, was missing. It seems clear that the reason there was not one is that Katharine de Mattos did not want one – that she did not want to be the author of a supernatural story about a nixie, and she did not want to work with Fanny. Henley's suggestion was probably against Katharine's interest more than it was against Fanny's, who might have been quite willing to have Katharine's name attached. But Henley, still wrapped up in ideas of collaborating with Stevenson, sees the double signature as the ethical solution to the problem. Surely any theory of collaboration must maintain as a minimum standard that collaboration must be consensual: a collaboration this was not. However, Henley's statement reveals much about his true motivations.

Charles Baxter, the pair's closest friend, identifies not 'The Nixie' but the plays as the source of the problem:

> The fact is that these cursed plays have been at the bottom of all the mischief. I have never heard a grumble from Henley with regard to you except in that connection. He relied hopefully on them for money, and thought you little interested in them, and blamed you accordingly . . .[77]

Henley never accused Stevenson of taking too much credit for the plays; rather, he accused him of investing too little. It is an odd accusation because it seems to acknowledge that Henley's contribution on its own, even with Stevenson's celebrity attached, was never enough to make the plays a hit. The day before, Stevenson had written to Baxter, 'The tale of the plays, which I have gone on writing without hope because I thought they kept him up, is of itself something; and I can say he never knew – and never shall know – that I thought those days and months a sacrifice' (*Letters* 6: 134),[78] correcting himself the following day and denying that Henley should be held responsible for Stevenson's ill health during the playwriting debacle (136). Although written in a bitter mood, it is evident that the conflicts about the plays had not subsided for either man. Henley's resentment about 'The Nixie', his attempt to shape that story as collaboratively written, and his resentment that Fanny (whom he had never liked) seemed to be claiming credit she had not earned, covered his resentment over an actual collaboration.

Despite Fanny's best efforts, her collaborations with her more famous husband never gained her the reputation she hoped for. *The Hanging Judge* has never been well received, and was only published as a conciliation to her. 'The Nixie', her ham-handedly proposed collaboration with Katharine de Mattos, has made her famous not as an artist, but as the cause of strife between her husband and his best friend. Only *The Dynamiter* was commercially successful, and it too fell out of favour in the years after Louis's death, and its loss of reputation correlates with Fanny's own claims for her hand in it. Certainly the structure of *The Dynamiter*, making use as it does of inset stories within a frame, lends itself to theories about who was responsible for what, with the result that critics have assigned 'The Destroying Angel' and 'The Fair Cuban' to Fanny, and then rejected them as unworthy. It does seem probable that, as the legend goes, she told these stories, or ones that resembled them, to her husband while he was sick at Hyères, and yet, this does not tell us that they were 'her' stories. In any collaborative writing exercise, one person may indeed have the germ of an idea, but the text will be something different. No more can Katharine de Mattos, who hated the idea of a story about a nixie, be said to be the author of 'The Nixie', though she may have had her idea unfairly poached. Macfarlane argues that attitudes towards plagiarism were shifting in the second half of the nineteenth century as the ideal of writing moved towards an idea of *inventio*, or a rearrangement of other material. Stevenson, as this book seeks to show, was an overt proponent of this shift, as represented by his frequent collaborations and double signatures on his works. Indeed, the vanishing frames and *mise en abyme* structure of *The Dynamiter* functions as an elaborate send-up of just this kind of criticism, in that it features the narrations of the ever-elusive Clara Luxmore, who tells us (repeatedly) 'I am not what I seem.'

Notes

1. Henley, 'R. L. S.'
2. Elwin, *The Strange Case of Robert Louis Stevenson*, pp. 201–2; Koestenbaum, 'Shadow on the Bed'.
3. Mackay, *The Violent Friend*; Lapierre, *Fanny Stevenson: A Romance of Destiny*.
4. Kizer, 'Fanny'; Nancy Horan, *Under the Wide and Starry Sky*.
5. Though not absent – see Beattie, 'Fanny Osbourne Stevenson's Fiction'.
6. Robert Louis Stevenson, 'A Gossip on Romance', p. 61.
7. Murfin, 'Victorian Nights' Entertainments'.
8. Robert Louis Stevenson, *New Arabian Nights*.
9. Sandison, 'A World Made for Liars', p. 141.
10. Murfin, 'Victorian Nights' Entertainments'.
11. Robert Louis Stevenson, *New Arabian Nights*, p. 204.
12. Menikoff, '*New Arabian Nights:* Stevenson's Experiment in Fiction', pp. 343–4.
13. W. H. Pollock, Review of *New Arabian Nights* by Robert Louis Stevenson, *Saturday Review* 19 (August 1882): 250–1, reprinted in Maixner, *Robert Louis Stevenson: The Critical Heritage*, p. 110.
14. Kenna, *War in the Shadows*, p. 67.
15. Shane Kenna, interview by Cathal Brennan and John Dorney.
16. Whelehan, *The Dynamiters*, p. 12.
17. John W. Foster to Frederick Theodore Frelinghuysen, Madrid, 15 December 1883, Papers Relating to the Foreign Relations of the United States, Document 341.

18. 'Latest Intelligence', *The Times* (London, England), 10 April 1884: 5+. *The Times Digital Archive*. Web. 12 October 2018; Frederick Theodore Frelinghuysen to Mr. Reed, Washington D.C., 30 April 1884, Papers Relating to the Foreign Relations of the United States, Document 365.
19. 'Conspirators in the Bahamas', *New York Times* (1857–1922); New York, 22 May 1884: 2; 'Dynamite for Cuba: The Discoveries Made by Agents of the Government', *New York Times* (1857–1922); New York, 24 July 1884: 8.
20. 'Cuban Dynamiter Captured', *New York Times* (1857–1922), 13 June 1884: 1.
21. 'The Sale of Dynamite: Nobody Will Admit Having Supplied Cuban Rebels', *New York Times* (1857–1922), 35 July 1884: 8.
22. 'Dynamite for Cuba', *New York Times*, p. 8.
23. Robert Louis Stevenson and Fanny Stevenson, *More New Arabian Nights: The Dynamiter*, p. 105. Subsequent references to this edition will be cited parenthetically as *Dynamiter*.
24. Miller, *Framed*, p. 187.
25. Whelehan, *The Dynamiters*, p. 2; Kenna, *War in the Shadows* and interview by Brennan and Dorney.
26. Fanny Stevenson to Margaret Isabella Stevenson, 25 May 1884, Edwin J. Beinecke Collection of Robert Louis Stevenson, GEN MSS 664 box 8 folder 211.
27. Lucas, *The Colvins and Their Friends*, pp. 163–4.
28. Kenna, interview by Brennan and Dorney.
29. Balfour, *Life of Robert Louis Stevenson*, vol. 2, p. 5.
30. Foucault, 'What is an Author?', p. 117.
31. London, *Writing Double*, p. 20.
32. Fanny Stevenson to Margaret Isabella Stevenson, 20 May 1885, Bournemouth, 1885.010, Robert Louis Stevenson Museum, St. Helena, California.
33. 'The Dynamiter', *The Critic: A Literary Weekly, Critical and Eclectic* 3 (27 June 1885): 304, ProQuest; 'Two Stories', *Saturday Review of Politics, Literature, Science and Art* 59 (1885): 664, ProQuest; 'Topics of the Day: From Our London Correspondent', *Evening Star* 6950 (Dunedin, New Zealand, 10 July 1885): 4, Papers Past.
34. James, 'Robert Louis Stevenson', p. 1248. Marjorie Stone likewise concludes that the Victorians 'more readily accepted literary couples or collaborators' than 'anxious' twentieth-century critics in her collaborative essay with Corinne Davis on collaboration and the Brownings in Corinne Davies and Marjorie Stone, '"Singing Song for Song"', pp. 159–60.
35. Gosse, Introduction to *More New Arabian Nights: The Dynamiter* by Robert Louis Stevenson and Fanny Stevenson, p. 179.
36. Ibid. p. 179.
37. Balfour, *Life of Robert Louis Stevenson*, vol. 2, p. 5.

38. Elwin, *Strange Case of Robert Louis Stevenson*, p. 186.
39. Furnas, *Voyage to Windward*, p. 195.
40. Mackay, *The Violent Friend*, both quotes p. 193.
41. Sandison, 'A World Made for Liars', p. 149.
42. Chen, Mingyuan et al., '*Deciphering* The Dynamiter'.
43. See Introduction, note 33.
44. York, 'Crowding the Garret', p. 293
45. James, 'Robert Louis Stevenson', p. 1233.
46. Furnas, *Voyage to Windward*, p. 210. Fanny herself compares herself to that dynamiter's mother, saying in a letter to her mother-in-law, 'Mrs. Luxmore says "my husband's obstinacy opposed to my firmness of character", a sentence which well describes Louis and me, only Louis reverses the thing.' Fanny Stevenson to Margaret Isabella Stevenson, Bournemouth, 1885.005, Robert Louis Stevenson Museum, St. Helena, California.
47. Bleakney, 'Folk-lore from Ottawa and Vicinity', p. 166.
48. Fanny Stevenson to Margaret Isabella Stevenson, n.p., November 1884, re-dated by Mehew as Oct./Nov. 1882, Robert Louis Stevenson Museum, St. Helena, California. See also Beattie, 'Fanny Osbourne Stevenson's Fiction'.
49. Fanny Stevenson to Margaret Isabella Stevenson, n.p., November 1882? Letter 32, Robert Louis Stevenson Museum, St. Helena, California.
50. Osborne, William, lyricist, 'Nigger Nigger Never Die', Nellie Sylvester, composer (New York: Primrose and West, 1897), Levy Sheet Music Collection, Box 143 Item 010, Johns Hopkins University, http://levysheetmusic.mse.jhu.edu/catalog/levy:143.010 For discussion of late nineteenth-century caricatures of Irish Americans, see Whelehan, *The Dynamiters*, p. 217. I have not found any evidence of whether or not this third, Irish, verse, was around during Fanny's childhood.
51. Kiely, *Robert Louis Stevenson and the Fiction of Adventure*; Sandison, *Robert Louis Stevenson and the Appearance of Modernism*, p. 109.
52. Bell, *Dreams of Exile*, p. 181.
53. Fanny Stevenson, Preface to *Kidnapped*, p. xi.
54. Lucas, *The Colvins and Their Friends*, p. 247.
55. Balfour, *Life of Robert Louis Stevenson*, vol. 2, p. 4.
56. Beattie, 'Fanny Osbourne Stevenson's Fiction', p. 142.
57. Osbourne to R. and R. Clark, Printers, 17 April 1929, Edwin J. Beinecke Collection of Robert Louis Stevenson, GEN MSS 664 box 17 folder 450.
58. Robert Louis Stevenson and Fanny Van de Grift Stevenson, *The Hanging Judge*, manuscript, Edwin J. Beinecke Collection of Robert Louis Stevenson, GEN MSS 664 box 30 folder 708.
59. Gosse, Introduction to *The Hanging Judge* by Robert Louis Stevenson and Fanny Van de Grift Stevenson, pp. 5–6.
60. Bell, *Dreams of Exile*, p. 195; Cairney, 'Helter-Skeltery', p. 193.

61. Robert Louis Stevenson and Fanny Van de Grift Stevenson, *The Hanging Judge* (Scribner's), p. 251.
62. Roughead, ed., *Trial of Deacon Brodie*, p. 218; William Forbes Gray, *Some Old Scots Judges: Anecdotes and Impressions*, p. 98.
63. Lucas, *The Colvins and Their Friends*, p. 247.
64. Robert Louis Stevenson, 'Some Portraits by Raeburn', p. 228.
65. William Forbes Gray, *Some Old Scots Judges*, p. 107; Roughead is easier on him in *Trial of Deacon Brodie*, p. 218.
66. Fanny Stevenson and Robert Louis Stevenson, *Our Samoan Adventure*, p. 184.
67. Duncan, 'Stevenson and Fiction', p. 21.
68. Lucas, *The Colvins and Their Friends*, p. 245.
69. Colvin, 'Editorial Note', quoted in Kerrigan, Introduction to *Weir of Hermiston* by Robert Louis Stevenson, p. xxxiii.
70. Bell, *Dreams of Exile*, p. 96.
71. Calder, *Robert Louis Stevenson*, p. 217.
72. This would cast Fanny's daughter, Belle Strong, as Eleanor. Hilary Beattie suggests that Stevenson's relationship with Belle, and Fanny's ensuing jealousy, is itself part of the psychological underpinning of *Weir of Hermiston*, which features the protagonist's attraction to two heroines – one older and one younger – another connection to *The Hanging Judge* which also features a Belle Strong-like character in a prominent role. See Beattie, 'Dreaming, Doubling and Gender', p. 24.
73. Robert Louis Stevenson and Fanny Stevenson, *The Hanging Judge*, p. 232.
74. Henley, *Letters*, p. 168; also published in Stevenson, *Letters*, vol. 6, p. 129.
75. Cohen, *The Henley–Stevenson Quarrel*, p. 23.
76. Beattie, 'Fanny Osbourne Stevenson's Fiction', p. 137, and see Cohen, *The Henley-Stevenson Quarrel*, p. 33.
77. Charles Baxter to Robert Louis Stevenson, 5 April 1888, quoted in Cohen, *The Henley–Stevenson Quarrel*, pp. 35–6.
78. Also quoted in Cohen, *The Henley–Stevenson Quarrel*, p. 29.

Chapter 3

Counterpoint: Fanny's and Louis's Pacific Diaries

This chapter continues my examination of Stevenson's collaborations with his wife, Fanny Stevenson, by looking at unpublished collaborations in diaries and holograph manuscripts that the pair have left. I argue that these private family papers reveal an ongoing preoccupation with the sexual exploitation of children in the Pacific Islands at the end of the nineteenth century, as part of the commercial colonial interests in the region. Though the topic pervades the unpublished writings of Stevenson and his family during their travels, it does not make its way into his published travel writings of the period, *In the South Seas* (posthumously published in 1896) nor in his longer Pacific novels, *The Wrecker* (1892) or *The Ebb-Tide* (1894). It is present—but not fully articulated – in his novella *The Beach of Falesá* (1892). In order to understand how consistently Louis observed and wrote about this particular issue, it is necessary to look at his collaborative writing process with members of his family, particularly Fanny.

Louis, and those with whom he collaborated, had a clear sense of a Stevenson brand, defined by a stringent sense of social decorum that pervades his published works. This respectable brand was curated to a large degree by Stevenson's close friend Sidney Colvin, who acted as Stevenson's London representative and managed much of his reputation from England while Stevenson was in the Pacific, and whose more conservative sensibilities had a profound impact on Stevenson's reputation then and now.[1] While Stevenson's writings remained decorous, Fanny's diaries served Louis not only as a place to record travel impressions as material for his later writings but also a place to explore issues that strayed beyond what would be possible to articulate explicitly in his literary works – if he were to maintain his commercial viability, as many around him pressured him to do.

Through a review of Fanny's published diary, *The Cruise of the* Janet Nichol (1914) and holograph manuscripts held in three different archives, this chapter explores the relationship between published works and unpublished manuscripts, revealing that his literary works from this period were not simply a matter of his own artistic genius, but involved the careful, collaborative deliberation of Stevenson's circle. This circle, comprising Fanny Stevenson and Sidney Colvin most prominently, operated on Stevenson's authorial identity in complex and sometimes contradictory ways. While the pair attempted to shape Louis's writings into a form more in line with his reputation, Fanny specifically allowed him greater range of subject matter through her own private writings than he would otherwise have had. We discover through these manuscripts Stevenson's principal project in the South Seas, one beyond the parameters of decorum and commercial pressures, one beyond the published genres in which he had proven successful, a polyphonic anthropological study of the effects of colonialism on the Pacific Islands, a project cut short by his early death. Stevenson was well aware of the variety of forums in which he was writing, and his collaborations with his wife allowed him freedoms that his more branded forums would not.

My previous chapter discussed *The Dynamiter* (1885) and *The Hanging Judge* (1887), the only two works produced during Robert Louis Stevenson's lifetime that bear Fanny Stevenson's name. Paradoxically, previous critics have simultaneously minimised and regretted Fanny's influence on these acknowledged collaborations. As Wayne Koestenbaum argues in *Between Men*, the act of naming collaboration – the shared byline on the work – is an affirmative means of distinguishing a collaborative relationship from one of indebtedness or influence. Even the act of defining collaboration as only those works that have a shared byline, however, reveals just how much we presume authors are influenced by others: their editors, their family and other writers. No work is conceived and created in solitude, and collaborative writing is different from solitary writing only in the degree, and not in the fact, of the collaboration. The solitary author is thus an agreed-upon fiction. Just as Michel Foucault suggests with his idea of the 'author-function' that the model or concept of the author is quite different from the man or the woman him- or herself, so too the fiction of the solitary author hides a community. When the living, breathing, relational person is converted into Foucault's author-function, one of the things that is left out is the collaborative nature of the art.

In 1888 Stevenson and Fanny, accompanied by Fanny's son, Lloyd Osbourne, and Louis's mother, Margaret Stevenson, departed San Francisco on the *Casco* bound for the Pacific Islands, travelling through the Marquesas, the Paumotus and Tahiti. Although the family did not know it at the time, it was an area of the world from which Stevenson would never return. The family took two more significant cruises. They travelled on the *Equator* in 1889, at the end of which trip they decided to purchase land on Samoa. They took another cruise on the *Janet Nicoll* in 1890, before returning to Vailima, their now home on Samoa, where they would live until the end of Stevenson's life in 1894. Records of their cruises on the *Casco* and the *Equator* were published first as letters to the New York *Sun* and *Black and White*, and then posthumously compiled by Sidney Colvin into the travel volume *In the South Seas*. Observations and reflections in *In the South Seas* in turn heavily influenced his fictional Pacific pieces, including *The Wrecker*, *The Beach of Falesá* and *The Ebb-Tide*. Consequently, Stevenson's published and unpublished observations of the region have not just biographical but also literary import; they were, in a sense, the earliest drafts of his fiction and non-fiction writings.

The published non-fiction was heavily influenced not only by his own diaries but also those of his family, and especially his wife Fanny's. Oliver Buckton writes that Stevenson used diaries as a 'quarry' for his writings from the period.[2] Therefore, in Stevenson's fiction and non-fiction from the Pacific Islands, Fanny's influence is pervasive, raising questions about shared experiences, marriage and authorship. Even more markedly, Fanny's own published writings show substantial contributions from her more famous husband. Fanny's experiences of some of this travel were subsequently published in her diary, entitled *The Cruise of the* Janet Nichol, which was initially published in 1914, and which has recently been republished under the editorship of Roslyn Jolly.[3]

Fanny claims in her preface to *The Cruise of the* Janet Nichol that her diary was not intended for publication, and indeed, the diary was not published until twenty years after Louis's death, and a few months after Fanny's own death. She goes on to note that:

> It was, originally, only intended to be a collection of hints to help my husband's memory where his own diary had fallen in arrears; consequently, it frequently happened that incidents given in my diary were re-written (to their great betterment), amplified, and used in his. I have deleted these as far as possible, though not always completely.[4]

This was not her consistent position, however. Fanny and Louis had drastically different ideas about what his Pacific non-fiction should accomplish. Writing to Sidney Colvin from Honolulu on 1 May 1889, Fanny bemoans Stevenson's more rationalistic obsessions, complaining that

> Louis has the most enchanting material than any one [sic] ever had in the whole world for his book, and I am afraid he is going to spoil it all. He has taken into his Scotch Stevenson head, that a stern duty lies before him, and that his book must be a sort of scientific and historical impersonal thing . . .

and later complains to him of Stevenson's deep engagement with Darwin: 'He had got "Darwin on the Coral Insect" – no, Darwin was "Coral Reefs"; somebody else on Melanesian language, books on the origin of the South Sea peoples, and all sorts of scientific pamphlets and papers.'[5]

Louis's idea was that the works would be more political and anthropological. Fanny's idea, on the other hand, was that they would be more personal and full of adventures.[6] Though travel writing of the period has often been read as supporting the work of empire generally (see, for instance, Pratt),[7] Stevenson was committed, however imperfectly, to critiquing what he saw as the destructive influence whites had upon the Pacific, as Rod Edmond, among others, has argued, a project that those around him found to be at odds with the entertaining adventures for which he was known.[8] Jolly quotes Fanny as saying '"Very well," I say, "if you will not, then I shall. I'll gather together all my letters, and publish them with my diaries wherever they will fill up a gap you have wantonly left."'[9] This statement is deceptive, for what Fanny hides here is that she uses Louis's notes to plug the gaps in her own writings, and I have found it is just as often the case that 'incidents given in' Louis's hand, originally, were 'rewritten . . . and used in' hers: Fanny incorporates and lays claim to material that Louis had written. There are two ways in which Louis contributed to his wife's diary. First, he wrote his observations directly into the handwritten document, which we can see clearly by the difference of handwriting in the manuscript. Second, fragments that Louis clearly wrote, that we have in his handwriting, were later rewritten into Fanny's published diary. These fragments do not appear in her original, handwritten diary. Though Fanny states that she wished for her diary to be a hint to her husband's memory, it seems it was often the other way around, with his jotted notes forming the basis for her own published writing. To that end, the pair's diaries document the family's travel in a way more fully understood if they are taken together instead of separately.

The objection will surely be made that Fanny was appropriating, or even plagiarising her more accomplished spouse's writing for her own aggrandisement, as indeed she did in the case of her ill-fated 'collaboration' with Katharine de Mattos on 'The Nixie', discussed in an earlier chapter. And yet, close attention to these portions of shared writing show that they preserved, but concealed, important observations about the family's experiences.

For, in each case where we find Louis's original handwritten work in Fanny's diary the writings treat the same topic – that of the erotic nature of the contact between the Pacific Islanders and the European or American visitors who landed on their shores. The Stevensons were particularly preoccupied with their encounters with the children, young girls especially, who would vie for Louis's attention, and the implications of the relationships this created. Descriptions of such girls occur in in the family's descriptions of the islands of Niue, Manihiki, Penrhyn, Nassau and Atafu: all of them islands visited on the *Janet Nicoll*, none of them islands described in *In the South Seas* when it was later compiled by Sidney Colvin. These encounters are described without shock or judgement, even though across the ocean and around the world the British were increasingly scandalised by such abuses. The Stevensons did not participate in the sexual exploitation of children, but they did describe it as rather ordinary. Ironically, this normalisation occurs not long after Britain has begun avidly policing child sexuality and child prostitution in London, by, for instance, raising the age of consent to sixteen in 1885. While the late Victorians were touchy about the idea of English girls being exploited sexually, prohibitions were slower to catch on when it came to other races.[10] Also, while regulation of prostitution and sexual encounters through contagious disease laws was deemed necessary across Britain's colonial holdings both to protect soldiers from venereal disease and also to bolster British claims of moral and cultural superiority,[11] the islands visited by the Stevensons were not British holdings, even though they were overrun by British, American and European commercial interests. Britain regulated prostitution abroad to protect colonists and colonial interests,[12] but white traders in the Pacific were already seen as a debased population.[13] As such, prostitution was not regulated, nor did any governmental power have an interest in doing so.

Recent criticism on the nineteenth-century diary has interrogated whether the diary is a public or a private document. Lynn Z. Bloom has argued that all diary writing (excepting the day-planner variety) keeps an audience in mind, but other critics have extrapolated that the nature of this audience is neither stable nor unproblematic. Anne-Marie Millim has noted that the genre, like all autobiographical writing, must balance two, sometimes conflicting impulses, 'the desire to remember and be remembered, which coexists with the need for confession and absolution', while Rebecca Steinitz similarly finds a characteristic ambivalence, tension or even anxiety around the question of whether the diary is private or meant to be shared.[14] For instance, the diary may be addressed to a future self, or it may imagine a larger and more dispersed audience, and furthermore, as Millim has argued, the private or public status of a diary is not only a matter of 'authorial intention', but is also up for renegotiation at any later point.[15] Louis's diary would become public – he was already world-famous in the 1890s, and the family's private papers, and Louis's especially, would be sought after and picked over after his death, and yet diaries filled important private roles for the family as well. The need to balance the private self with the persona of the author became a pressing and delicate endeavour.

Although Fanny did not make the decision to publish her *Janet Nichol* papers until the end of her life, and many years after the end of Louis's life, from its conception it conformed to Steinitz's description of the diary as 'an intimate text that circulated'[16] – that is to say, Fanny is explicit in noting that it is to be read by her husband, as in fact his is to be read by her. By extension, it seems clear that Fanny's son Lloyd Osbourne read both Fanny's and Louis's diaries, and they his, both in order to consult on Louis's work, which would be published, but also as a way of reflecting on their shared experiences. Lloyd also kept a diary the year of 1889,[17] although the diary was inscribed as a Christmas gift to M. I. S. (Louis's mother, Margaret Stevenson). She commandeered it for a time, writing the entries from 24 January to 9 February, before returning it to Lloyd to finish, even though she maintained her own diary in this period.[18] We know that the family shared Louis's diary, which was later rewritten into *In the South Seas*. While the family was on Papeete, Tahiti, on 30 September 1888, and Louis is sick, for instance, Margaret Stevenson writes that '. . . Lloyd and I are busy making a typewritten copy of Louis's diary and this fills up the entire mornings'.[19] Letters, too, were a shared endeavour. Stevenson's stepdaughter Isobel Strong was never one of his collaborators, but he did use her as an amanuensis late in life when his health was failing. In an interview she recalls a series of letters to the author J. M. Barrie:

> 'We all had more or less of a hand in the Barrie letters,' said Mrs Stevenson's daughter, Mrs Strong, 'and as I was his amanuensis, I often interpolated of my own accord in a rather jocose mood. You know Mr Stevenson dictated all of his later books to me, and he once wrote Barrie that I 'had a growing conviction that I was the real author of his works.'[20]

The family's investment in copying and preparing Louis's diary and letters shows that these were documents that were always meant to be shared and circulated. That Louis was also inclined to write in his wife's diary shows that her diary, too, was seen as a form of communal family property. The family's diaries serve a purpose neither entirely private nor entirely public. Instead, they presuppose a limited audience encompassing family and possibly close friends. This circumscribed and intimate audience had concerns of accuracy and nostalgia that were substantially different from those of Stevenson's larger public.

The collaborative nature of these diaries, by deflecting traditional assignments of authorship, allowed the family to observe things that would otherwise have remained unsaid. Whereas Fanny's influence on Stevenson's work has been traditionally thought of as suppressive, as discussed in my previous chapter, I find the opposite – that it was principally liberating in giving him an outlet for concerns that he as a public figure could not otherwise share, or even record. For, in looking at Fanny's and Louis's diaries as collaborative documents, we see a different perspective on the Pacific Islands than is ordinarily associated with the famously family-friendly author. Completely private papers could not be thought of, and yet, he and Fanny still seek a way to record the family's experiences in a more intimate and private way. The result is a patchwork of diaries that reflect a more erotically charged Pacific than the one he described in his letters to the New York *Sun*, composed of cobbled-together pages slipped into Fanny's diary and mutually composed reminiscences. By examining how Fanny's diary forms a supplement and a counterpoint to Louis's own, we can better understand how Louis builds multiple perspectives into his published writing, both his travel writing and his fiction, and also how he uses his wife's authorial voice to encapsulate, isolate and sanitise some of the family's observations in the Pacific Islands.

July–August 1889: Butaritari

Stevenson had originally intended to collect his observations into a magnum opus on the Pacific region to be titled *The South Seas*. In her book-length study of Stevenson's Pacific writings, Roslyn Jolly has detailed how Stevenson had hoped to present a more scientific and anthropological study of the region, and how Fanny and Sidney Colvin worked to undermine this new direction in Stevenson's work to try to redirect him back to what they saw as his most commercially successful work – the self-reflective, 'romantic' writer.[21] The larger book *The South Seas* was never realised; instead, we have his last work of travel writing, posthumously published in the slimmer volume *In the South Seas*. Most of the material contained in *In the South Seas* is present in Stevenson's handwritten journal of the period, with one notable exception – when the family reaches the island of Butaritari, Louis allows Fanny to narrate the family's experience with a recitative musical performance. While Fanny's observations are themselves not especially provocative, his decision to include them is. Significantly, her voice joins the conversation in the context of his theories of the Butaritarian style of musical performance, and the greater possibilities it allows as a collaborative, polyphonic and even conflictual art form. In the Butaritari chapter, we see that, far from resenting the intrusion of his wife's voice and ideas, Louis self-consciously invites conflict and struggle into his work as a central part of his artistic practice. In fact, the presence of different voices in Louis's and Fanny's diaries is not a manuscript issue alone, but forms a central part of Louis's aesthetic theories – the very theories that make his writings so experimental and even modern. Fanny's alternate narrative offers a counterpoint to Stevenson's dominant one: a counterpoint that he borrows from to enrich his own singular narrative.

The chapter is entitled 'The Five Days' Festival', and it describes a Butaritarian performance, which Louis calls an 'opera'. Louis invites Fanny to witness the scene in confirmation of his observations of its excellence. Where the notes of the husband are allusive and analytical, Fanny, in keeping with her sense that the Pacific writings should be more personal, is emotionally overwhelmed and transported: 'My blood came hot and cold, tears pricked my eyes, my head whirled, I felt an almost irresistible impulse to join the dancers.'[22] However, it is the passage immediately preceding Fanny's observations that explicitly discusses Louis's thoughts about collaboration. Stevenson describes the performance of a number of soloists, but emphasises rather the effect of the group: 'A varying number of soloists stood up for different songs; and these bore the chief part in the music. But the full force of the companies, even when not singing, contributed continuously to the effect . . .' (*ISS* 189). The combination of competing soloists backed by larger chorus has a rough beauty, and is characterised by discord: 'The voices of the soloists would begin far apart in a rude discord, and gradually draw together to a unison; which, when they had reached, they were joined and drowned by the full chorus' (189). The voices of the soloists in this example are unimportant – it is when they come together with each other and with the full chorus that they reach their artistic potential. By marking discord, and not coordination, as the hallmark of the performance, Stevenson proposes a theory of collaboration that is conflictual

Figure 3.1 Butaritari native dance. This image is from the photograph album entitled 'The Cruise of the Equator' of Robert Louis Stevenson's travels around the Gilbert Islands and Samoa in 1889. The City of Edinburgh Museums and Galleries; Writers' Museum.

rather than harmonious. This idea of the productive nature of discord had always characterised Stevenson's thinking. Even as early as 1882, in his essay 'Talk and Talkers', Stevenson had argued that the highest art of conversation is the debate, writing that: 'The spice of life is battle; the friendliest relations are still a kind of contest; and if we would not forego [*sic*] all that is valuable in our lot, we must continually face some other person, eye to eye, and wrestle a fall whether in love or enmity.'[23] The dialectic that emerged from disagreement kept thought and art from sinking into the banal, or the obvious.

Stevenson compares Butaritarian discord to the musical counterpoints of European opera:

> I was continually reminded of certain quarrelsome concerted scenes in grand operas at home; just so the single voices issue from and fall again into the general volume; just so do the performers separate and crowd together, brandish the raised hand, and roll the eye to heaven – or the gallery. Already this is beyond the Thespian model; the art of this people is already past the embryo; song, dance, drums, quartette and solo – it is the drama full developed although still in miniature. (*ISS* 190)

In invoking the *imbroglio* of European opera – those scenes in which artistry comes out of seeming musical confusion or disagreement – Stevenson identifies struggle and quarrelsomeness as hallmarks of the artistic endeavour. He simultaneously extends and denies this aesthetic to Western art, because he is reminded of operas at home, and yet suggests that Butaritarian intrigue surpasses that. Here, in Stevenson's music criticism, it is specifically the polyphonic characteristics of the Butaritari performance that vindicate it as an advanced artistic form (and thereby certify the civilisation of Butaritari as an artistically advanced civilisation), contrasted with primitive, choral recitation ('the Thespian model'). This kind of argumentative counterpoint characterises Fanny's own conflicting accounts of her assistance to her husband, above. At one moment she defers to his authority, suggesting her writings are merely a 'collection of hints', while at others she seeks to wrest control of the narrative. Stevenson himself invites his own polyphony by opening the narrative for his wife's voice. Jolly notes that 'the relation between husband's and wife's travel-writing was not always collaborative; it could be combative, and even competitive',[24] but combat and competition can themselves be forms of collaboration. Like duelling banjos, the diaries simultaneous existences complement and enrich each other, Louis's prose ornate, reflective, allusive; Fanny's vigorous, spare, energetic.

By comparing a Roman Classical model of stagecraft (the Thespian) to what Stevenson understood as a radically disruptive (to the European listener) polyphonic aesthetic, Stevenson revisits the opening of *In the South Seas* where he speculates on the possibilities created by removing oneself from the stranglehold of Euro/American society: to 'escap[e] out of the shadow of the Roman empire, under whose toppling monuments we were all cradled, whose laws and letters are on every hand of us, constraining and preventing' (*ISS* 9). As Jolly has argued, Stevenson was unusual among travel writers for his time in his willingness to frankly compare European systems, identified with the Roman, with the laws and cultures of the South Pacific, without assuming that the Pacific cultures were savage or innocent. Stevenson's suggestion in the opening chapter that Pacific legal traditions, such as the *tapu*, were equal to or perhaps even superior to Roman ones, challenges the narrative of the time, which characterised such beliefs as superstitious or worse.[25] Here, he asks the same question from an aesthetic perspective. *How* much, Stevenson asks, might our cultural inheritance prevent us from seeing other possibilities for legal systems, or for art? Stevenson had always travelled – to France, New York, San Francisco – finding that it was horizon broadening. He had also always experimented with other perspectives in his work, whether imagining things from the viewpoint of the monstrous as in *Jekyll and Hyde* or of the political criminal as in *The Dynamiter*. The Butaritarian episode is thus characteristic of Stevensonian thinking in that it tries to imagine an aesthetic problem from multiple perspectives, cultural and otherwise. In invoking opera as the model art form, it recalls Stevenson's dramatic experiments with his friend W. E. Henley, which I have discussed in an earlier chapter. In that earlier effort, he attempts to pull the more collaborative model of the stage into the generally more solitary endeavours of the writer. Here the model is even more radical because opera combines not just a variety of authors but also a variety of art forms. And by identifying Rome as the restrictive patriarch, Stevenson makes clear that travel to San Francisco or France, tried before, will not allow him to break free of the unspoken and assumed constraints given by European culture. Europe and America, while they may have varied cultures, all share the same classical ancestry. But the disruptive perspective of this new culture with few shared influences will liberate the creative mind, allowing for a more drastically original perspective.

28 April 1890: Niue

In the year 1890 the Stevensons, who had already been in the Pacific for more than a year, undertook a three-month cruise among the South Sea Islands on the *Janet Nicoll*, which was detailed in Fanny's own diary, now published as *The Cruise of the* Janet Nichol. With a few exceptions, most of the islands visiting on the *Janet Nicoll* were never discussed in Louis's published work – they did not make it into *In the South Seas*, though there is evidence, in the form of draft tables of contents, that he at one point intended to include them.[26] As a result, we have a much stronger sense of the islands visited on the *Janet Nicoll* from Fanny's writings than we do from Louis's. There exist, however, several pages of fragmentary material, split up over Stevenson archives held at Yale University, at the Huntington Library and at the Robert Louis Stevenson Museum. These holograph manuscripts allow us to piece together Louis's observations of these islands and give us hints about what he would have covered if he had completed his planned writings about the islands the *Janet Nicoll* visited. In most cases where we have these fragments, material that Louis originally wrote has been retroactively included in Fanny's diary, often without attribution.

On the 28 April 1890 the family landed at the island of Niue. Stevenson describes this landing in his notes,[27] which also contain material relating to the island of Olosega. Stevenson went on to use material from these notes describing Niue in *In the South Seas*, while Fanny used material from Olosega in *The Cruise of the* Janet Nichol, even though these descriptions are taken from the same sheet of paper. About Niue, Stevenson describes how the culture formerly treated illegitimacy: 'thus a father or a brother would dash his sisters or his daughters illeg . . . down the cliffs. Xtianity has made them much slacker, says the missionary.'[28] This appears to be the source material for the following passage in *In the South Seas*, which is found in the Marquesas section of the book:

> Mr Lawes, the missionary of Savage Island,[29] told me the standard of female chastity had declined there since the coming of the whites. In heathen time, if a girl gave birth to a bastard, her father or brother would dash the infant down the cliffs; and to-day the scandal would be small. (*ISS* 35)

Further down this very same manuscript page, however, he describes the development of the island of Olosega by the Jennings family of

American capitalists: 'he [Jennings the first] blew out a passage to the beach with dynamite; he built the schooners of the island wood, floated them off with barrels, and sold them to the German Firm.'[30] This material would never make it into *In the South Seas*, but Fanny would use it, word for word, in *The Cruise of the* Janet Nichol (*CoJN*, Jolly 78).

While *In the South Seas* only mentions Niue in passing, Fanny describes their landing there extensively in *The Cruise of the* Janet Nichol, and especially describes Louis's encounter with a native girl – an encounter that would later prove troubling to Sidney Colvin. After detailing the family's welcome by the residents of the island, she adds this: 'I was some distance from Louis, who has written the following in my diary' (*CoJN*, Jolly 71). Despite Fanny's claim, in the original handwritten diary, her description is Niue is brief, and is only in her hand. She only reports: 'When Louis came up he said the women embraced him and got his matches and tobacco away from him',[31] with no further mention of this encounter. In her published diary, she continues '(He used this afterward, but as it seems to belong to my diary I thought I might let it stand)' (*CoJN*, Jolly 71), though in fact, Stevenson never did use his material from Niue.

Fanny made significant use of her husband's unpublished notes to colour in her observations when the time came to publish *The Cruise of the* Janet Nichol. Both Fanny's journal and the first of the fragments in Stevenson's hand similarly describe the rough landing of the missionary ship the *John Williams*, which they watched from the safety of their own ship. Both describe arriving on the island, and Fanny borrows Louis's description of the Niuean women: Fanny describes 'the women, whose many-coloured garments we had remarked even from the ship, glowing on the cliff like a bank of flowers' (*CoJN*, Jolly 71), while Louis has 'coloured dresses we had remarked even from the ship, glowing in the clifftop like a bank of flowers'.[32] Remarkably, this borrowing of exact phrasing by Fanny occurs immediately *before* she credits Louis, and indeed there is no such phrasing in her handwritten diary, where she more prosaically describes the men and women in 'their best clothes'.[33] In other words, though Fanny's published diary correctly states that Louis has written some of the material in it, it does not accurately indicate *which* material he has, and which she has written.

If Stevenson had intended to write about Niue, suggested by Fanny's statement that he 'used this later', why did he not? Both Fanny's and Louis's notes on the island run very close together, and suggest that Louis, Fanny and later Colvin were working together to shape public reception of the family's records. Each description we have of Niue from Stevenson describes his reception by the islanders, his present of tobacco, and a girl who steals his matchbook and then condescends to return him a single match. In Louis's manuscript, he describes how 'A bevy of girls followed, hugging and embracing me and going through my pockets; it was the nearest thing to an ugly sight, and still it was pretty; there was no jeering, no roughness; they fawned upon and robbed me, little well-behaved and healthy children with a favourite uncle.'[34] In the continuation of the manuscript, he observes:

> A certain plump, little fellow (more like a Hawaiian), with a coquettish cast of face and carriage of the head, and conspicuous by a splendid scarlet flower stuck in her ear, had visited me with a particular thoroughness, not even respecting (as the others did) my trouser pockets; and I demanded my matches. She shook her head at first; then, from some unknown receptacle, produced my box, drew out a single match, replaced the box, and with a subtle smile and considerable grace of demeanour, something like a courtly hostess, passed me the match.[35]

Once again, Stevenson never used this material, but Fanny includes it word for word in *The Cruise of the* Janet Nichol (*CoJN*, Jolly 71), but with one telling edit: she deletes the phrase 'not even respecting (as the others did) my trouser pockets'. Fanny must have feared that the image of the Niuean girl digging through Louis trouser pockets was unseemly. Indeed it was, and Louis saw it so. In a letter to Charles Baxter he specifically mentions the trouser pockets again (adding '*proh pudor*' – for shame! (*Letters* 6: 388)). When he described the same incident in a letter to Colvin 30 April 1890, he called the manners of the girls 'something between a whore and a child, which a touch would have made revolting but as it was, was simply charming like the Golden Age' (*Letters* 6: 389), a statement which was subsequently censored by Colvin (*Letters* 6: 390 and n.).[36]

It is not new to find Colvin, and to a lesser extent Fanny, at work trying to make Robert Louis Stevenson's corpus adhere to standards of Victorian propriety, nor is it surprising that Colvin would try to obscure this particular observation, which remains distasteful so many years later. What is remarkable in the couple's treatment of the Niue incident, however, is that we see Fanny not censoring but preserving her husband's observations, albeit under her own (less famous, and therefore less scrutinised) name. The family's collaboration is in service of censoring a sexualised depiction of the Pacific Islands, which Fanny simultaneously preserves in intent but softens.

6 May 1890: Manihiki

Two islands that Stevenson intended to describe in *In the South Seas*, but did not, are Manihiki and Penrhyn, both in the Cook Islands. Both are listed in a draft table of contents.[37] About Manihiki, Stevenson proposed the following chapters: 'XXVII Manihiki Architecture – Brand new fellow-countrymen – "The copra eaters" – Charms of Manihiki – A love affair.' Although the Penrhyn section would ultimately be published in the New York *Sun*, as I will discuss below, Stevenson never published his observations of Manihiki. Nevertheless, we do have holograph fragments detailing his observations, written in his hand, and these correspond to the table of contents that he proposed. We can further supplement the Manihiki material with information in Fanny's diary, because once again, as at Niue, Fanny took material that Stevenson must have intended to publish on his own, and published it herself when she first published *The Cruise of the* Janet Nichol in 1914. Although this material is interesting for its discussions of architecture and as source material for *The Ebb-Tide*, it most crucially reiterates the Stevenson family's experiences with the erotic colonial encounter. As in Niue, the Manihiki material features Louis's encounter with an island child (the 'love affair' of the table of contents, above) with observations by both Louis and Fanny that strain the limits of propriety, giving us an important explanation for why Louis and Fanny may have ultimately suppressed these pages.

The Manihiki architecture evidently impressed both Louis and Fanny, as did the attractiveness of the people. On one manuscript page, Stevenson writes 'The pleasantest low island in the world; excellent sheet, excellent homes; the church all carved wood and inlaid pearl shell; sofas and beds in every house: the gayest and most pleasing people.'[38] The church mentioned is given a fuller treatment in Fanny's diary:

> The church, a thatched coral building without flooring, was really beautiful. The seats, with backs, are in rows, each with a fine, narrow mat spread over it. On either side run galleries, the balustrades elaborately carved and stained with yellow, red, and pink dyes. In the middle of one balustrade the word 'Zion' was carved. The pulpit was a mass of carving and inlaid mother-of-pearl; the altar, which ran round it, was covered with fringed mats extremely fine and worked in different colours. (*CoJN*, Jolly 87)

Although Stevenson in the end would not return to Manihiki for *In the South Seas*, the emphasis on the beauty of the architecture, the inlaid mother-of-pearl, and both Louis's and Fanny's observations about the attractiveness of the people (*CoJN*, Jolly 81) recurs in the epilogue to *The Wrecker*, which Stevenson was writing at the time:

> Dear Low: The other day (at Manihiki of all places) I had the pleasure to meet Dodd. We sat some two hours in the neat, little, toy-like church, set with pews after the manner of Europe, and inlaid with mother-of-pearl in the style (I suppose) of the New Jerusalem. The natives, who are decidedly the most attractive inhabitants of this planet, crowded round us in the pew, and fawned upon and patted us; and here it was I put my questions, and Dodd answered me. (545–6)

The balustrade carved with the word 'Zion' from Fanny's diary is here preserved in the author's sense that the church style is that of the 'New Jerusalem', though he is not certain ('I suppose'). The observed superiority of the people of Manihiki to the rest of humanity further reinforces the religious and utopic overtones of the description.

While the architectural details from Manihiki are found in *The Wrecker*, co-written with Lloyd Osbourne, other details from Fanny's diary and the holograph fragments pop up in Stevenson and Osbourne's other co-written novel, *The Ebb-Tide*. Again, in the draft table of contents to *In the South Seas* discussed above, Stevenson proposed a chapter entitled 'The copra eaters', an allusion that connects the dissolute figure of the white South Seas trader to Tennyson's drugged-out sailors. 'The copra eaters' would never be published, at least not under Louis's name, but once again, Fanny would include it in *The Cruise of the* Janet Nichol. Its draft can also be found in Louis's Manihiki fragment, which describes three beachcombers that the couple met:

> They have nothing but copra to eat; but as one obligingly said, 'We have no right to complain. They give us what they have.' The same person said their present way of life 'had an air of loafing on the natives', which he disliked. But they are all fond of their high station as whites; and the ex-marine has fallen under the scorn of his companions for becoming 'Kanakaised', they are in some subjection, we could see; but own themselves well used. They had had no tobacco for some months.[39]

('Kanaka' is a derogatory term for a Pacific Islander.) This passage was later published by Fanny with very little editing in *The Cruise of the* Janet Nichol as such:

One man said his present way of life 'had an air of loafing on the natives' which he disliked, but they all seemed proud of their high position as whites, with the exception of the ex-marine, who had fallen under the scorn of his companions for becoming 'kanaka-ised'. Still, that they were under some subjection, we could see, but owned themselves well used. They do not exactly *like* copra, but, as one said: 'We have no right to complain; they give us what they have.' They had no tobacco for months, which they felt a great privation. (*CoJN*, Jolly 82)

No such passage exists in Fanny's handwriting in the original diary, though she does describe a man she calls 'the passenger', who 'said he felt almost like a loafer doing no work, and living in the charity of the people'.[40] These three beachcombers would become the originals for the dissipated antiheroes of *The Ebb-Tide*. At the beginning of that novel, the American Captain Davis leads his two white British companions in a song-and-dance routine for a boat of native sailors, hoping to sing for his breakfast. The race humiliation is pointed – the natives show a generous sympathy for the starving men, who dance 'even as a poor brown Pyrenean bear dances in the streets of English towns under his master's baton'.[41] The inspiration for this sad and entitled trio, forced to beg from the ship crew that they think they should be commanding, can be traced back to Stevenson's original Manihiki fragment, rewritten (barely) into *The Cruise of the* Janet Nichol.

Further Manihiki fragments at the Silverado Museum in St. Helena, California[42] follow a familiar theme. As at Niue, and as we will see again in Penrhyn, the Stevenson's experience at Manihiki likewise features Louis being 'claimed' by a girl from the island – in this case a four-year-old girl named Fani. According to Fanny, the girl attached herself to Louis, and consequently the people of Manihiki consign the Stevensons to that family, taking them to Fani's house to spend the night, for instance, rather than the house that they had initially been assigned.

The Stevensons' private writings about Fani on Manihiki suggest a thinly disguised awareness of the sexual exploitation of children on the islands. There is no reason to believe that Stevenson participated in any such thing. Nonetheless, it is critical to note the normalisation of child exploitation evident in these passages because it provides us with an explanation why the material from the *Janet Nicoll*, and only that material, was suppressed. Perhaps more significant still is that Fanny later restored much of this material through her own filter. For instance, in Fanny's published diary she reflects 'how decently whites must have behaved here, that this little creature should have come up to Louis in the dark as naturally as a child to its mother' (CoJN, Jolly 91), insinuating that the island of Manihiki has been rather free of child (sexual?) abuse. Again, we find that this observation was not Fanny's originally, though she chose to preserve it, but rather in manuscript pages it was Louis who first observed 'that this little kitten should have come up to me in the dark with her imminent declaration, as natural as a child to its mother'.[43] In the manuscript diary, this is even more jarring, because Fanny when she first describes Fani's approach to Louis explains 'They say all their children are very fond of white men, which is very much to the credit of the white. We have remarked that the beach comber, wherever we find him, is almost invariably good looking.'[44] Fanny further implies that without his American wife, Louis would be sought after as a husband for an island child, if not four-year-old Fani (although perhaps her), then at least one of her sisters. '[Fani's] sisters stayed by him until the whistle sounded . . . No doubt Louis could have eaten copra from that day forth at the father's expense' (CoJN, Jolly 91), another observation borrowed from Louis's notes.[45] Louis himself only nods to the encounter in his published writing. In the section of *In the South Seas* entitled 'Depopulation', he remarks that 'no people in the world are so fond . . . [of] children' and notes:

> Only the other day, in the Marquesas, if a child conceived a distaste to any stranger, I am assured the stranger would be slain. And I shall have to tell in another place an instance of the opposite: how a child in Manihiki having taken a fancy to myself, her adoptive parents at once accepted the situation and loaded me with gifts. (ISS 30)

Besides further demonstrating Stevenson's intention to publish his writings on Manihiki, this passage contains a curious haziness – what 'situation' is it that Stevenson thinks Fani's parents have 'accepted'? The proffered gifts seem more like a dowry. This sentiment appears several times in the family's description of their reception in the islands, where the people who receive them are disappointed or even angry that Louis is already married. It will occur again less than three weeks later, on the island of Atafu, discussed below.

Other phrases that we find in Fanny's *The Cruise of the* Janet Nichol also originate in manuscript notes that Louis had made. For instance, in the published edition of *The Cruise of the* Janet Nichol,

Fanny writes of Fani that she was 'as neat as a little statue, as tight as india-rubber' (Jolly 89), though no such statement occurs in the manuscript version of her diary. We do, however, find it Louis's manuscript fragment: 'Her name was Fani, and Etetera, pronounced to rhyme with et caetera; she was as neat as a little statue, as tight as india rubber [so was her sister/ so was Johnnie Bull]; copra must be good food for children.'[46] (The remainder of the paragraph, in which Fanny describes the racial typology of the Manihikians in particular, also originates in Stevenson's notes, and not in Fanny's diary.) Also reproduced in Fanny's diary is Louis's description of Fani's brother, the aforementioned Johnny Bull as 'another satellite, in the form of a very handsome boy; so that I walked between them with a hand of each; but this flirtation did not go so far.'[47] Fanny describes how Fani's fifteen-year-old brother, 'the lovely "Johnny Bull", who was on board almost as soon as they were, hovered about smiling, and when he saw a chance slipped an arm round Louis's neck' (*CoJN*, Jolly 91). Recent important scholarship by Lee Wallace has interrogated the regulation of same-sex desire in encounters between Europeans and Pacific Islanders, and Oliver Buckton has argued that same-sex desire characterised specifically Stevenson's encounters with the Pacific.[48] While I have found quantitatively more evidence of Louis's concern with sexual encounters between men and young girls, this description of Johnny Bull is an undisguised reminder that sexual desire on the islands was multifaceted, though always asymmetrical in power, whether the imagined relationship is between Stevenson and Fani or Stevenson and Johnny Bull.

9 May 1890: Penrhyn

Stevenson's description of the island of Penrhyn, which the family visited on the *Janet Nicoll*, was published by Sam McClure in the New York *Sun* in 1891 as part of the original arrangement that Stevenson had with McClure to publish a series of letters describing Stevenson's Pacific travels. Although most of these letters to *The Sun* were posthumously compiled in 1896 in *In the South Seas*, the Penrhyn material, as well as material pertaining to his travels to Hawaii, was not.[49] (It was later added back to the South Seas edition of his complete works (1925), and so is available in some but not all available volumes.) Colvin chose to include only the material that follows Stevenson's journal of the *Casco* and *Equator* cruises, held at the Huntington Library; he omitted material from other cruises and travels, including that of the *Janet Nicoll*. It is difficult to know why. Colvin explains 'These [Hawaiian] chapters did not come out at all to his own satisfaction and have accordingly been omitted. So have some others describing a visit to Penrhyn in the course of his third voyage',[50] but if Stevenson ever did say such a thing, we have no record of it, although he did say that the *Janet Nicoll* material 'was rather worse than I have looked for' (*Letters* 7: 85). In fact, Stevenson had always wanted a bigger, not smaller, volume about his travels in the region (*Letters* 7: 26).

Despite its absence from *In the South Seas*, the Penrhyn material proved influential to Stevenson's other writings. Stevenson's description of a white figurehead found on Penrhyn in *The Sun*, matches Fanny's description of the same in *The Cruise of the* Janet Nichol.[51] That figurehead is rewritten as the woman of 'leprous whiteness' who with outstretched arms presides over Attwater's island in Stevenson and Osbourne's *The Ebb-Tide*. In *The Cruise of the* Janet Nichol, Fanny describes the statue as '. . . the figurehead of a wrecked ship, a very haughty lady in a magnificent costume. She held her head proudly in the air and had a fine hooked nose' (*CoJN*, Jolly 95). In *The Sun*, Stevenson uses the same word 'haughty' to describe her, but more specifically brings the description in line with the themes of *In the South Seas* by emphasising the long shadow of Roman culture in the statue's nose and dress: 'a very white and haughty lady, Roman nosed and dressed in the costume of the directory, contumeliously, with head thrown back, she gazed on the house and the crowding natives'.[52] Fanny also describes 'a gentle soft-eyed youth from Edinburgh, now fairly on the way to become a beach-comber' (*CoJN*, Jolly 95), surely the original for Robert Herrick, also of *The Ebb-Tide*.

Material describing Penrhyn includes the letter to *The Sun*, Fanny's *Cruise of* the Janet Nichol, and manuscript fragments held at the Huntington and Beinecke Libraries. The Huntington fragment describing the results of a tidal wave on Penrhyn and the pearling boats that Louis saw there again overlaps with Fanny's diary. Fanny says that a pearling boat has just come in filled with natives:

> the colours are enchanting: the opaline sea, the reds and blues of the men's clothing, running from the brightest to the darkest of shades, the yellow boats wreathed with greenery, the lovely browns of the native skin, with the brilliant sun and the luminous shadows. (*CoJN*, Jolly 95–6)

Louis's fragment preserves the imagery but changes the referents:

> The whole island was in a ferment and all the boats were gay with white sails and light paint; and the men were dressed in any shade of red and blue, they were all garlanded with green upon
>   as gay with kerchiefs?
>   their ~~hands as~~ ~~with~~ wreaths of greenery; and the bustle was set in
>   the verdure of the palms, and the changing opal of the lagoon . . .[53]

The red, the blue and the opaline are still there, but the green garlands have transferred from the boats to the men, and the publication in *The Sun* preserves these changes:

> The boats were gay with white sails and bright paint: the men were clad in red and blue, they were garlanded with green leaves or gay with kerchiefs: and the busy, many-colored scene was framed in the verdure of the palms and the opal of the shallow sea.[54]

Following the pattern from Manihiki, where Fanny liberally borrows from Stevenson's unpublished fragments, we might expect to find these observations were originally Louis's, but in this case Fanny's handwritten diary shows this same constellation of colours. The lines are written much as they are in the published version of her diary. But there is no evidence that at Penrhyn she had poached on her husband's notes to give heft to her own diary, at that time or later. The red, the blue, the green garlands and the opal occur in both spouses' handwritings, and it is impossible to say who first saw or thought of organising the scene by colour in such a way. Is the originality of the lines in the perception, or in its expression? Is it possible that the colours were so striking that Louis and Fanny had the same strong impression, simultaneously, but separately (even the sense of the lagoon as 'opaline')? Or is this moment of visual perception too idiosyncratic to be independently derived? These questions again urge us to consider that in all writing, but in travel writing most especially, the attempt to record accurate impressions for both historical and family use is not a solitary one; that while the Stevensonian voice in *In the South Seas* (for example) is a solitary one, the experiences that he is describing were fundamentally communal and collaborative.

After this picturesque description of the pearling boats, the letter to *The Sun* describes a performance by a group of island girls, one of whom in particular caught Stevenson's attention. 'A girl of 11 or 12 was my especial commandant,' Stevenson writes, and 'Although she . . . ordered me about, and even shook and punched me, it was with no real presumption, only the pretty freedom of a girl that knows herself in favor.'[55] The girl described, and Stevenson's relationship to her, is of a type that connects on the one hand to girls like the match thief on Niue and Fani on Manihiki, but also connects to other girls who had strongly affected Stevenson – girls who were suffering from leprosy on the island of Molokai. The romantic and libertine tropes familiar from Niue and Manihiki give way to Stevenson's more political writing, as he changes mode to describe the incursion of leprosy into Penrhyn, which happened sometime after his visit. The Penrhyn writings are thus connected to Stevenson's larger pessimistic reflections on Pacific depopulation. Comparing Penrhyn to Molokai, where he had also made a strong connection with a group of young girls in 1889, he rages at the possibility that the girl who had so entertained him may be infected. Although it is impossible to know for certain why the Penrhyn material would be published, but not later compiled, the echoes of the Niue and Manihiki writings, clearly once intended for publication but never published, are notable.

17 May 1890: Nassau

The *Janet Nicoll*'s landing on the island of Nassau is described in Fanny's diary, but not in any of Louis's published or unpublished manuscripts. However, Fanny's diary reveals the extent to which the couple saw their travels as shared experiences, as the Nassau entry shows the couple sharing the documentary process in Fanny's journal. Unlike the other islands, Fanny never saw Nassau at all; she bemoans the fact that it is considered too dangerous for her to make the landing (*CoJN*, Jolly 110). Why the landing would be considered too dangerous for Fanny is a bit of a mystery, since she was accustomed to rough conditions, and at any rate it was Louis and not she whose health was delicate. Louis and Lloyd disembark without her. While Fanny claimed her diary was supposed to be a 'support' to Louis's memory – an eyewitness account that he can rely on in later reconstructions, on Nassau she relies on his eyewitness account. Fanny begins by transcribing Louis's observations into her own journal, but eventually allows him to take over. Fanny's absence from her own journal is not tangential but central to the Nassau visit, as it will also be to the family's visit to Atafu, discussed below, because on both islands Louis's arrival without a wife underscores the transactional sexuality that was a commonplace of the family's visits to the islands – a transactional sexuality far more explicit here, in the manuscript diaries, than it ever was in any published travel writing that Stevenson produced.

In the published editions of her diary, Fanny reports that 'When Louis came back he gave me the following account of his visit, starting from the very beginning' (*CoJN*, Jolly 110). The description of the island is then quoted. However, in Fanny's handwritten diary, we see that she begins by transcribing, but then turns the volume over to her husband. 'I begin again from Louis's dictation', the transcription begins, but then the handwriting abruptly changes. Mid-sentence, Louis has taken the book from Fanny's hands and finished the account himself:

> I begin again from Louis' dictation. 'First thing in the morning we saw the whole population gathered on the beach ... A little later, seeing Lloyd come out from under a blanket where he had been changing plates, he made us all die laughing [Fanny's handwriting ends here, and Louis's begins] *with his pantomime of terror; he called everyone 'old man'* . . .[56]

With Fanny remaining on board and only the two men embarking, the erotic nature of the contact between islander and visitor is amplified. Louis is captured by two island wives who 'led me into the shed, where Mrs Jim was [*sic*] piled up pillows at my back, supported me in her arms and proceeded to feed me like an infant with cocoanut pudding. Mrs Jim, meanwhile patted and soothed me.'[57] The women go on to good-naturedly pick his pockets. When the men finally leave the island, Louis records, 'I saw Mrs Joe make a sudden plunge under her skirts, and the next moment her gaudy lava lava was flying in the air for a sign of farewell.'[58] In the published version of the diary (though this is not in the original), Fanny helpfully glosses the scene so: 'When a native woman dons a civilised garment she still retains her native garment, the *lava-lava* twisted round her body' (*CoJN*, Jolly 112). It seems that it is Fanny's absence that provokes the women's flirtatious treatment of Louis, and yet, it is in her diary that he preserves the record of it.

24 May 1890: Atafu

When the *Janet Nicoll* lands at Atafu, Fanny again stays on board the ship, this time complaining of rheumatism (*CoJN*, Jolly, 116) and defers to her husband's description of the island. As on Nassau, the description of the island is notable for the frank flirtations of the island women towards Louis. While onboard the ship, Fanny is visited by Amalaisa, a trader's wife whose fair hair Fanny noted. The trader explains that his wife must be half-German due to 'a great many German sailors about the islands'; Fanny believes her to be an albino. Calling her 'Fani mai felini' (Fanny my friend), Amalaisa pins a lock of hair into Fanny's book. At this point, Louis again takes the diary, and the description of the island is again in his handwriting. Louis narrates that, on arriving on the island, he is ushered towards 'some twelve stalwart dames sitting on a wall' (CoJN, Jolly 118), where a boy, who seems to act as a procurer, tells him 'All these girls he laugh at you' (*sic*). (Fanny later glosses this as 'these ladies smile upon you'.) Louis continues, 'A little later one of the boys asked me: "You want wife?" "I got wife on board," I said. "Wife on board," cried he with unmistakable scorn, "no good!"' Finally, Louis describes Amalaisa's attentions to him. Only after she hears of his wife, Louis explains, does Amalaisa then go on board and transfer her affections to Fanny, but 'the factitious nature of this sentiment . . . didn't prevent its being an immense success' (CoJN, Jolly 118–19). By virtue of her gender, Fanny feels an unspoken sympathy with Amalaisa; this is characteristic of her encounters with native women throughout the family's travels, as Jolly has observed.[59] Uncharacteristic is the romantic nature of the token – a substantial hank of blonde hair that is still preserved in Fanny's diary to this day.

In both landings, Atafu and Nassau, the men go on shore alone. Both encounters suggest the reality of sexual solicitation or trade that attaches to the white man landing on the Pacific Island. Nowhere in any of Stevenson's non-fiction travel writings does this suggestion of sexual trade or negotiation attach to himself in the way that it does in the two entries I have described, preserved not in his own manuscripts, but in Fanny's diary.

The Beach of Falesá

The topic of the sexual trade of children of the island preoccupies Stevenson in his private papers not for publication, as I have shown. It enters his published writings in only one place: one of his most complex and controversial works, his novella *The Beach of Falesá*. Indeed, Stevenson's work in *The Beach of Falesá* reveals a similar give and take around sexuality and commerce in the Pacific;

however, the extent to which this novel is about children has been obscured by contemporary habits of reading. According to Barry Menikoff, *Falesá*, which is deeply critical of white people's exploitation of Pacific Islanders, 'ran counter to some of the most deeply held political, sexual, and religious convictions of those responsible for its publication'. Consequently, of all Stevenson's texts, it was 'the most mutilated and corrupted'.[60] In *The Beach of Falesá*, the trader Wiltshire, the text's unreliable narrator, marries the native Uma with a false marriage certificate. By the conclusion of the novella, the immoral and mendacious narrator is in some measure redeemed when this exploitative relationship proves to be a true companionate marriage. Difficulties in reading the text abound because, as Katherine Bailey Linehan has noted, Stevenson 'hides behind the narrative mask of a heavily racist first-person narrator and subtly contrives to make that protagonist simultaneously the vehicle and object of social criticism', making it difficult to untangle the biting social criticism of the novella from the bigoted and jingoistic narrative voice.[61] Colley finds that Stevenson's position concerning the impact of white culture in the islands in the novella is characterised by complexity and ambiguity.[62] Nevertheless, most critics concur that the story, on balance, strongly condemns the influence of empire and commercialisation in the Pacific Islands.[63]

Stevenson based his novella on a true story he recounts in *In the South Seas* in the chapter entitled 'Husband and Wife'. There, he reports the rumour of a woman whose marriage certificate, 'when she proudly showed it, proved to run thus, that she was "married for one night", and her gracious partner was at liberty to "send her to hell" the next morning' (*ISS* 200). In the version of this published in *The Sun*, Stevenson had written 'All these *children* were legitimately married. It is true that the certificate of one, when she proudly showed it, proved to run thus . . .'[64] In *In the South Seas*, this is replaced with the less controversial 'All these *women* were legitimately married . . .' (emphases mine). Menikoff notes that 'The prospect of children engaging in sexual intercourse was undoubtedly too unnerving for a late-Victorian publisher.'[65] And yet, this is the undisguised topic of *The Beach of Falesá*, a fact that critics of the novella have either failed to note, or have found not worthy of remark. This includes Menikoff's discussion of the novella, because his observation about 'children engaging in sexual intercourse' is in reference to the article in *The Sun* about Stevenson's actual observations; he does not then apply it to the novella. Menikoff goes on to say that while Stevenson compares native wives to children, 'they are not children; they are married and bearing babies to their husbands.'[66] His conclusion is that this analogy is part of the patronising treatment that characterises the attitudes of white traders. There is, however, another possibility, which is that Uma is described as child-like because she is a child.

There is so much evidence in *The Beach of Falesá* that Uma is in fact a child that Stevenson does not seem to have been at pains to conceal it. John Wiltshire describes Uma as being 'like a child' and like a baby. She is 'like a child dodging a blow'[67]; she runs away from him 'like a child or a kind dog' (125); she 'shook with sobbing like a little child' (142); she has the look of a baby (119); she tries on clothes from traders 'like a baby' (141), and Wiltshire says 'she was a woman, and my wife, and a kind of baby besides' (143). Though she is proud in public, Wiltshire comments that 'She played kitten with me now that we were alone' (125), a statement that is reminiscent of Stevenson's description of four-year-old Fani on Manihiki, when he is surprised 'that this little kitten should have come up to me in the dark with her imminent declaration, as natural as a child to its mother'.[68] Wiltshire's pet name for her throughout the novella is 'little wifie' (142 and throughout). Uma is a 'brown bit of a girl' (142). She is also physically distinct from the mature women on the island. While Case complains that they are 'a trifle broad in the beam' (119), Uma in contradistinction is 'very young and very slender for an island maid' (119). That her slenderness is due to her age is made clear in Wiltshire's final comments: years after the time during which the novella is set, she is 'a powerful big woman now, and could throw a London bobby over her shoulder. But that's natural in kanakas too; and there's no manner of doubt that she's an A one wife' (186). When Case and Wiltshire decide that Wiltshire should take a wife, it is because they have seen a parade of children walking by:

> ... all the children in the town came trotting after with their shaven heads and their brown bodies, and raising a thin kind of cheer in our wake, like crowing poultry.
> 'By the by,' says Case, 'we must get you a wife.'
> 'That's so,' said I, 'I had forgotten.' (119)

It is the children marching by that reminds both Case and Wiltshire that Wiltshire should select a mate, a suggestion that this is not shocking to them but merely conventional. Jolly has found that Stevenson was inspired not only by his experiences but also by Pierre Loti's *The*

Marriage of Loti (1880), an account that features another European man marrying (in this case) a fourteen-year-old island girl.[69] Interestingly, Loti's other semi-autobiographical work about a Japanese alliance of different ages and races, *Madame Chrysanthème* (1893), would go on to inspire Puccini's creation of *Madame Butterfly* thus explaining a certain family resemblance between Uma and Cio-Cio-San in character and situation.[70]

Then, too, there is the question of the consensual nature of their arrangement. Critics have generally taken at face value the idea that Uma is fooled by the marriage certificate, and that there is therefore a certain dark burlesque in her exploitation – she is, in this reading, a presumably grown woman who is tricked because she is illiterate, and because she wants the form of a marriage to a white trader, even one as sleazy as Wiltshire. For instance, Seamus O'Malley, who finds the scene 'darkly comic', notes that 'Ironically they only need this fraudulent ceremony because the missionaries have convinced the native women that they have to be married before having sexual relations.'[71] And yet, there is ample evidence that Uma has little agency in her own disposal. When Wiltshire first admires her, Case says, 'You can have your pick of the lot for a plug of tobacco' (*Falesá*, 120), and only after Wiltshire recoils does he correct himself: 'O, no, don't you misunderstand me – Uma's on the square.' On their wedding night, she falls before him on the floor and cries out 'I belong you all-e-same pig!' (126). When Wiltshire later discusses Uma's history with her, he is troubled by her stories of entanglements with a young local man and with Case himself – entanglements that reveal the economic and political necessities of her various alliances (143–6), and thus expose the exploitative nature of his own relationship with her.

Nevertheless, it is the false marriage certificate, and not Uma's age or reluctance, that has been given as the reason for the censorship of this important work. The matter of the false marriage certificate in *The Beach of Falesá* proved a particular sticking point for publication, and was left out of the serial version in the *Illustrated London News* and was changed to a duration of one week in some subsequent editions,[72] and the fixation on the propriety of this one point of scandal in the text seems 'hardly worth the battle; the bowdlerised material is so unexceptional'.[73] Beyond this one historically controversial line, Menikoff in his edition seeks to restore the 'array of dialects and idioms' ranging from sailor's slang to Beach-la-mar, the hybrid Anglicised language of island trade.[74]

The work that Menikoff has done to restore Stevenson's original intentions to *The Beach of Falesá* shows just how difficult ideas of authorship and authority become within the literary marketplace, and thus is itself controversial. According to Vanessa Smith, Menikoff's project of restoring the original text falls into some of the same problems that it seeks to rectify, for while 'Menikoff draws attention to the subtle ways in which editors and publishers, aiming for the production of a smoothly literate text, ironed out disruptive elements', in seeking to reverse the intrusions of editorial voices Menikoff's work falls itself into a Romantic conception of authorship: 'motivated by a belief in the integrity of authorial creation that leads him back to the original, the signatory hand'.[75] Writing in *The Beach of Falesá*, Smith insists, is transactional, and fits in with Stevenson's abiding interest in the liminal, and the contact zone.[76] In other words, Menikoff's edition, which above all seeks to restore the polyphonic nature of Stevenson's original text, with its use of hybrid language such as Beach-la-mar, demeans the polyphonic nature of its composition. While this hybridity is important to Stevenson's writings, and Smith's point is supported by McGann's cautions about authorial intent and volume editing (see Introduction), this sort of after-the-fact censorship does not fit the model of the collaborative because of the lack of dialogue and consensus.

1890–1894: Tahiti and Samoa

In January 1890, a few months before they departed on their *Janet Nicoll* cruise, the family purchased the Vailima estate on Samoa. This was to be their home until Stevenson died in 1894. While there, both Lloyd and Joe Strong would be implicated in sexual scandals. Isobel Strong (Fanny's daughter) and her husband, Joe, accompanied the family for much but not all of their Pacific travel. He was an artist (a painter and photographer) for the Hawaiian court, and for a time he and Stevenson had worked together on a collaborative photojournalistic project entitled 'A Samoan Scrapbook'.[77] However, Louis and Strong's friendship soon disintegrated, and a contributing factor was Strong's infidelities. (Strong's alcoholism was another.) Fanny writes in her diary in December of 1892 that Strong had been 'living with a native woman of Apia as his wife ever since he came here – an old affair begun when he was here before. Also, he had been engaged in an intrigue with Faauma [a servant at Vailima].'[78]

Lloyd's romantic life on the island also caused familial and cultural conflict. Fanny wrote to Colvin that she had a young attendant, Miss Zosephina, who disappeared suddenly, 'whereupon her mother demanded compensation from me, declaring that Lloyd had levanted with her'.⁷⁹ When Lloyd was produced, with alibi, the girl's family redirected their accusation to Ah Fu, a Chinese cook whom the Stevensons employed, and to whom they were loyal, demanding he be arrested. Though he describes Tahiti, and not Samoa, Lloyd discusses the possible implications of this change in perpetrator in his *Casco* diary, unpleasantly:

> To sleep with a European without deriving pecuniary advantage is thought improper, though I have known of several girls refusing money; to sleep with a 'tinto' or Chinaman is the lowest and most degrading offence against decency and honour, and it is one of the friendly jests of Tahiti to accuse a girl of being found with a Chinaman. She flushes up, and her 'ita' has that angry, sullen note of a jealous and sullen people.⁸⁰

Fanny intervened on Ah Fu's behalf, and a local magistrate sided with the Stevensons. Fanny claims not to know what happened to Zosephina, and when she finally returns, 'looking haggard and battered, and as though she had drunk for a week', Fanny takes this as evidence of the moral inferiority of the Samoans: 'They are a very different people from the Marquesans, the Tahitians, or even the Low Islanders, all of whom I liked, and many of whom I loved.'⁸¹ A letter from Stevenson to his cousin Graham Balfour three years later suggests that Lloyd in fact may have been involved, despite Fanny denying it here. Swearing his cousin to secrecy, Stevenson describes a young woman who is spending time at the family estate, even caring for Stevenson himself when he is sick. Booth and Mehew's footnotes identify her as 'Sosofina, the daughter of Fono at Tanugamanono'. Eventually, Fanny decided the relationship had gone too far, and demanded that Lloyd either marry the girl or dismiss her. 'It appeared the gallant would not wed the dame, neither would he quarrel with her, and the result has been that a new chief's house has been built in Tanugamanono' (*Letters* 8: 8–9). Louis's letter was dictated to Isobel Strong, so the scandal really was an affair that concerned, and was known by, the entire Stevenson family. As to Zosephina's age, Fanny does not specify, though she does, disturbingly, tell us in her very same 1890 letter about Zosephina that 'ten here is equal to fourteen in England'.⁸² Gordon Hirsch notes that 'Katherine Durham Osbourne, who married Lloyd in 1896, was surprised to discover when she visited Vailima that Lloyd already had a Samoan wife.'⁸³ Thus, according to Hirsch, the topic of relationships between

Figure 3.2 'Samoan Girl: Sosophina'. Photograph by Lloyd Osbourne, 1889. This image is from the photograph album entitled 'The Cruise of the Equator' of Robert Louis Stevenson's travels around the Gilbert Islands and Samoa in 1889. The City of Edinburgh Museums and Galleries; Writers' Museum.

white men and native women or girls finds its way into Osbourne's subsequent fiction more insistently than it does in Stevenson's. There is a level of sexual explicitness that is pervasive in the notes of the Stevenson family that nevertheless does not appear in any writings that the Stevenson's allowed to be publicly shared.

Further reading of Lloyd Osbourne's diary of the period finds him preoccupied with the sexual habits of the Pacific women, and his own sexual adventures there: 'The women of the South Seas think of nothing but one thing, and the name is tapu in English.'[84] He adds:

> Of all countries in the world I think Tahiti faces social problems with the most success. Here there are practically no prostitutes, for every unmarried girl is allowed unlimited freedom, and is practically encouraged in what we call immorality. The parents of most of the Papeete girls possess the most respectable of parents, and the father

of my little sweetheart was said to be rich. Every girl is supposed to have lovers; there is no shame in having natural children, and as the love of adopting infants is inherent in the Tahitians, there is no trouble of getting rid of their children.[85]

The *Casco* was in Tahiti in 1888, two years before he was accused of 'levanting' with Zosephina or Sosophina in Samoa, so it appears that he had at least two relationships there. It is not surprising that Lloyd, who was twenty in 1888, would have sought out romantic adventures while travelling the Pacific. Certainly, he could not have hid them from his mother and stepfather under the circumstances, and it is unlikely that this diary was private from them. Still, I have not found any reference to the Tahitian sweetheart referred to here. That she is described as his 'little sweetheart' is suggestively troubling in light of children such as Fani and of Fanny's oblique reference to Zosephina's age.

The fantastical nature of Tahiti comes with but one reservation, which is that Osbourne already suspects it may be somewhat more mercenary than it seems:

> To a young man there can be no place in the world so delightful as Tahiti, but he must have some pretentions to the rank of gentleman. Captains of ships, naval officers and ordinary gents have a pleasant time, but to a common sailor or a workman it is by no means the same entrancing fairyland.[86]

Osbourne's sense of Tahiti specifically as sexual paradise, *le mirage tahitien*, dates back to the observations of Bougainville published in 1771; not surprisingly this view has been corrected by twentieth- and twenty-first-century historians who have found the welcoming reception that Europeans met on Tahiti was the defensive strategy of a people afraid of being overtaken by visitors, and not a reflection of Tahitian women's innate warmth or elastic sexual morality.[87] Louis's own descriptions of Tahiti, which he had discussed including in *In the South Seas*, are not available or were never written: the section of his *Casco* diary entitled 'Tahiti' because it was apparently written there instead contains retrospective material on the Marquesas included in *In the South Seas* as 'The Story of a Plantation'.

A more realistic picture than that offered by Osbourne of the sexual pressures put on girls and young women appears in the startling raw autobiography of Fanny and Louis's Samoan friend Laulii Willis. The wife of Canadian-born architect Alexander Willis, Laulii Willis had lived in San Francisco, and was unique in being able to write in English, making her the only Samoan female voice, and one of the only Samoan voices, that we have access to from the period. As part of its evangelical mission, the London Missionary Society, which was the dominant missionary society in the region, established 'training colleges, schools for boys, for girls and "promising young women", and schools for half-caste children' in order to create native pastors to further minister to the region.[88] A pupil in one of these schools, Willis was a strictly brought-up Protestant, although she regretfully confesses in her text that she owed her English-language literacy to the Catholics. Willis writes that only children with white blood are taught to read and write by the Protestants, a neglect of duty which she regrets is driving Samoans to the Catholic Church.[89] Willis's autobiography covers her childhood, horrifyingly and violently impacted by Samoan civil wars, her adolescence in the Protestant mission, and finally her travels to San Francisco as the nervous and self-conscious Samoan bride of Alexander Willis.

In its best sections, Willis's text is fast-paced, full of incident, and quite explicit about the perils white colonialism posed for adolescent Samoan women in particular. In one long and remarkable section of the text, which is alone important enough to make the autobiography worthy of more note, Willis describes being pursued by a white man named Hunt. Willis (aged fourteen) is walking home with her first husband, Selia, a young Samoan man, when the pair are invited into a bar by the predator. As Protestants involved with the mission, the two are not allowed to drink, but Selia is persuaded. Once Selia is drunk, Hunt turns his attention to various gambits to isolate Willis – giving Selia cash, for example, and sending him for more beer. In the section's degrading climax, Selia agrees to sell Willis to Hunt in exchange for a fancy coat. Even as Willis resists his advances, Hunt thinks that Samoan women are little more than prostitutes there for his purchase. Willis, on the other hand, is determined not to be seen this way. In order to distinguish herself from women like the deceived Gilbert woman who was rewritten into Uma in *The Beach of Falesá*, Willis includes a reproduction of her marriage certificate in her autobiography, ensuring that the American women who pick up her book will have no confusion about the validity of her marriage to Alexander Willis!

In order to write her autobiography, Willis collaborated with her husband as well as with an American editor, William H. Barnes, author of such page-turners as the *Historical Record of the Grand Encampment of California, I.O.O.F. (Independent Order of Odd Fellows) from its Organization to the Year 1906*. Fanny is sceptical of these intrusions into her story, writing 'The carpenter, Mr Willis, husband of Laulii, who wrote the story of her life (very well when she was allowed to her own expressions), came with the plans for our house', and later:

> In the afternoon Mr Willis the carpenter rode up: he is the husband of the Samoan girl Laulii, who dictated a very curious book of her reminiscences to her husband and a very stupid American. When Laulii's own words were given, the book was charming, but became vulgar and commonplace as soon as another pen interpreted for her.[90]

Although Fanny herself had frequently collaborated with her husband on his work, and although the pair had extensively influenced each other's diaries, here she is sceptical of the imposition of Willis's less talented spouse into her narrative. Ironically, Fanny's accusations against Alexander Willis and William H. Barnes echo what some critics have said about Fanny's own influence on Robert Louis Stevenson's work.

Besides *The Beach of Falesá*, and the encounter that inspired it, the commercial attitude towards sexual encounters with islanders remains relatively absent from Stevenson's body of published work. But it nevertheless pervades Stevenson's handwritten notes, it dominates Lloyd's records of his experiences, and most importantly, Fanny documents it, whether in her own written records or by storing Louis's observations in her comparatively less accessible diaries. This is a topic that the Stevenson clan was thinking a lot about, and Willis's autobiography is therefore doubly relevant – it uniquely describes the transactional relations between Pacific Islander women and white traders from the woman's perspective, and it problematises the question of collaborative writing among spouses. By positing that a genius or primary author, naturally talented in literature (Laulii Willis), is under the control of two socially dominant hack writer/editors (Alexander Willis and Barnes), Fanny Stevenson's critique of the Willis marriage mirrors (and reverses) issues in the Stevenson marriage, and in other partnerships in which Stevenson was engaged. Fanny may feel that Willis and Barnes took advantage of Willis's talent, but the fact remains that there is no possibility of an unmediated Samoan text from Willis. Willis herself, as an English-speaking Protestant Samoan missionary, is a product of a hybrid culture made possible by cultural imperialism in the region, and the hybrid and even corrupted collaborative composition is in fact the precondition for the production of her text.

My next chapter will discuss Stevenson's partnership with his stepson, Lloyd Osbourne, a partnership that will prove to be as unpopular with his publishers as his equitable marriage sometimes was with his friends. Despite the criticism of those around him, Stevenson invited this conflict-heavy *imbroglio* into his creative practice throughout his career.

Notes

1. See, for instance, Booth and Mehew, 'The Main Correspondents: Sidney Colvin and Frances Sitwill', *Letters of Robert Louis Stevenson* vol. 1, p. 52.
2. Buckton, *Cruising with Robert Louis Stevenson*, p. 159.
3. Although the ship the family sailed on was called the *Janet Nicoll*, Fanny misspelled it in her publication. I will be working with three versions of Fanny Stevenson's *The Cruise of the* Janet Nichol in this chapter. The authoritative scholarly version was edited by Roslyn Jolly in 2004. Subsequent references to this edition will be cited parenthetically as *CoJN*, Jolly, to distinguish it from the Scribner's edition of the diary published in 1914, during Fanny's lifetime, to which I will also refer. I also consult Fanny's handwritten diary upon which the published versions are based, held at the Robert Louis Stevenson Museum in St. Helena, California.
4. Fanny Stevenson, *Cruise of the* Janet Nichol, Scribner's, p. v.
5. Fanny Stevenson to Sidney Colvin, 1 May 1889, Honolulu, and Fanny Stevenson to Sidney Colvin, January 1890, Apia; both letters in Edwin J. Beinecke Collection of Robert Louis Stevenson, GEN MSS 664 box 8 folder 192–3.
6. Roslyn Jolly, Introduction to *The Cruise of the* Janet Nichol.
7. Pratt, *Imperial Eyes: Travel Writing and Transculturation*.
8. Edmond, *Representing the South Pacific*.
9. Jolly, introduction to *The Cruise of the* Janet Nichol, p. 40.
10. Walkowitz, *City of Dreadful Delight*, p. 82. Walkowitz does go on to link the scandal emerging from the 'Maiden Tribute' (an 1885 exposé on child prostitution in London, which W. H. Stead published in the *Pall Mall Gazette*) to 'Repercussions . . . throughout the Empire, in the form of age-of-consent (marriage) laws, and, eventually, official prohibitions against liaisons with "native" women' (p. 83).
11. Levine, *Prostitution, Race, and Politics*, pp. 1–4.
12. Ibid. p. 178.
13. Ann Colley, for instance, discusses the way missionaries contributed to the 'stereotype of the trader as a wild, irresponsible liar, cheat, and womanizer', Colley, *Robert Louis Stevenson and the Colonial Imagination*, p. 18.

14. Bloom, '"I Write for Myself and Strangers"'; Millim, *The Victorian Diary: Authorship and Emotional Labour*, p. 14; Steinitz, *Time, Space, and Gender in the Nineteenth-Century British Diary*.
15. Millim, *The Victorian Diary*, p. 2.
16. Steinitz, *Time, Space, and Gender*, p. 83.
17. Lloyd Osbourne, [Diary], Edwin J. Beinecke Collection of Robert Louis Stevenson, GEN MSS 664 box 51 folder 1113.
18. Margaret Isabella Stevenson, Diaries, Edwin J. Beinecke Collection of Robert Louis Stevenson, GEN MSS 664 Box 54.
19. Margaret Stevenson, *From Saranac to the Marquesas and Beyond*, p. 173,
20. Gelett Burgess, 'An Interview with Mrs. Robert Louis Stevenson', *The Bookman* (September 1898): 23, reprinted at http://www.unz.org/Pub/Bookman-1898sep-00023
21. Jolly, *Robert Louis Stevenson in the Pacific*.
22. Robert Louis Stevenson, *In the South Seas*, p. 191. Subsequent references to this edition will be cited parenthetically as *ISS*.
23. Robert Louis Stevenson, 'Talk and Talkers', p. 266.
24. Jolly, introduction to *The Cruise of the* Janet Nichol, p. 39.
25. Jolly, *Robert Louis Stevenson in the Pacific*.
26. Robert Louis Stevenson, *In the South Seas* mss, Edwin J. Beinecke Collection of Robert Louis Stevenson, GEN MSS 664 box 31 folder 753.
27. One page of Stevenson's notes on Niue is held at the Robert Louis Stevenson Museum in St. Helena (Silverado 1974.005.0016a). The second page, containing both Niue and Olosega material, is at the Huntington Library: Robert Louis Stevenson, 'Fragment of a journal kept during the cruise of the "Janet Nicoll," among the South Sea islands', 28 April 1890; 3 and 9 May 1890, Nuieue, Olosenga and Penrhyn, Huntington Library in San Marino, California (HM 20537), 2 pages.
28. Huntington Library, HM 20537. This page is ripped and only partially legible at the top.
29. Another name for Niue.
30. Robert Louis Stevenson, 'Fragment of a Journal', Huntington, p. 1.
31. Fanny Stevenson, Diary, mss, Robert Louis Stevenson Museum, 28 April 1890.
32. Robert Louis Stevenson, notes on Niue, Robert Louis Stevenson Museum.
33. Fanny Stevenson, Diary, mss, Robert Louis Stevenson Museum, 28 April 1890.
34. Robert Louis Stevenson, notes on Niue, Robert Louis Stevenson Museum.
35. Robert Louis Stevenson, 'Fragment of a Journal', Huntington, 1.
36. Pratt discusses the travel writing of the Romantic-era Scot, Mungo Park. Park, too, describes a highly eroticised encounter wherein African women 'inspected every part of my apparel, searched my pockets, and

obliged me to unbutton my waistcoat', which suggests that it may have been a travel writing convention. *Imperial Eyes*, p. 82.
37. Robert Louis Stevenson, *In the South Sea* mss, Edwin J. Beinecke Collection of Robert Louis Stevenson, GEN MSS 664 box 31 folder 753.
38. Robert Louis Stevenson, 'Mahiki notes', Edwin J. Beinecke Collection of Robert Louis Stevenson, GEN MSS 664 box 32 folder 780.
39. Robert Louis Stevenson, 'Mahiki notes'.
40. Fanny Stevenson, Diary, mss, Robert Louis Stevenson Museum, 6 May 1890.
41. Robert Louis Stevenson and Lloyd Osbourne, *The Ebb-Tide*, p. 27. Subsequent references to this edition will be cited parenthetically as *Ebb-Tide*.
42. Robert Louis Stevenson, notes on Manihiki, Robert Louis Stevenson Museum, Silverado 1974.005.0016, pages a–e.
43. Robert Louis Stevenson, notes on Manihiki, Robert Louis Stevenson Museum, c.
44. Fanny Stevenson, Diary, mss, Robert Louis Stevenson Museum, 6 May 1890.
45. Robert Louis Stevenson, notes on Manihiki, Robert Louis Stevenson Museum, d.
46. Robert Louis Stevenson, notes on Manihiki, Robert Louis Stevenson Museum, b.
47. Robert Louis Stevenson, notes on Manihiki, Robert Louis Stevenson Museum, c.
48. Lee Wallace, *Sexual Encounter*; Buckton, *Cruising with Robert Louis Stevenson*, pp. 12–17.
49. Buckton points out that the Penrhyn material was also not published in *Black and White* (Ibid. p. 165). Only the Penrhyn and Hawaii materials were so excluded. Stevenson's description of Tutuila, to which he voyaged on the *Nukonono*, was published in the *Auckland Star*, but likewise not included in *In the South Seas* (see Booth and Mehew, *Letters of Robert Louis Stevenson*, vol. 7, pp. 96n. and 226n.), and only republished years after Stevenson's death. While not consistently sexual in nature, it is arguable more so than other works collected in *In the South Seas*. He describes a sort of lover's lane of the island – a cliff hike that men will coax their girlfriends on in order to seduce them, and describes the salty language of an old woman, who invites Stevenson's guides 'over to her house that night to sleep with her daughter. Doubtless a high spirited pleasantry in the island fashion.' Robert Louis Stevenson, 'Tutuila', pp. 133–6, 146.
50. Sidney Colvin, editorial note to *In the South Seas* in *In the South Seas and A Footnote to History* (New York: Scribner's, 1905), p. x.
51. See also Buckton, *Cruising with Robert Louis Stevenson*, p. 166.
52. Robert Louis Stevenson, 'The South Seas: Life under the Equator. Letters from a Leisurely Traveller', *The Sun* 14 (24 May 1891): 23,

Chronicling American Newspapers, Library of Congress, http://chroniclingamerica.loc.gov/lccn/sn83030272/1891-05-24/ed-1/seq-23/
53. Robert Louis Stevenson, 'Fragment of a Journal', Huntington, p. 2.
54. Robert Louis Stevenson, 'The South Seas: Life under the Equator', p. 23.
55. Ibid. p. 23. This section corresponds with Stevenson's manuscript description of the girls singing on Penrhyn: Robert Louis Stevenson, '*In the South Seas* fragment, holograph, corrected', Robert Louis Stevenson Collection, GEN MSS 684, box 9 folder 164, Beinecke.
56. Fanny Stevenson, Diary, mss, Robert Louis Stevenson Museum, 17 May 1890.
57. Ibid.
58. Ibid.
59. Jolly, 'Women's Trading in Fanny Stevenson's *The Cruise of the "Janet Nichol*."'
60. Menikoff, *Robert Louis Stevenson and 'The Beach of Falesá'*, pp. 4, 5.
61. Linehan, 'Taking up with Kanakas', p. 407.
62. Colley, *R. L. Stevenson and the Colonial Imagination*, pp. 39–44.
63. See Linehan, 'Taking Up with Kanakas'; Rod Edmond, *Representing the South Pacific*; Julia Reid, *Robert Louis Stevenson, Science, and the* Fin de Siècle'; Patrick Brantlinger, *Rule of Darkness*; Vanessa Smith, *Literary Culture and the Pacific*; and Fuller, *Dark Paradise*, pp. 119–31.
64. Cited in Menikoff, *Robert Louis Stevenson and 'The Beach of Falesá'*, p. 86.
65. Ibid. p. 86.
66. Ibid. pp. 85–6.
67. Robert Louis Stevenson, *The Beach of Falesá*, p. 119. Subsequent references to this edition will be cited parenthetically as *Falesá*.
68. Robert Louis Stevenson, notes on Manihiki, Robert Louis Stevenson Museum, c.
69. Jolly, 'South Sea Gothic: Pierre Loti and Robert Louis Stevenson'.
70. Copper, 'Nineteenth-Century Spectacle', p. 44; see also Jolly, 'Stevenson's "Sterling Domestic Fiction"'.
71. O'Malley, 'R. L. Stevenson's "The Beach of Falesá" and the Conjuring-Tricks of Capital'.
72. Menikoff, *Robert Louis Stevenson and 'The Beach of Falesá'*, pp. 84–9.
73. Ibid. p. 84.
74. Ibid. p. 58.
75. Vanessa Smith, *Literary Culture and the Pacific*, pp. 167, 168.
76. See also Colley, 'Robert Louis Stevenson's South Seas Crossings'.
77. See Manfredi, 'Pacific Phantasmagorias'.
78. Fanny Stevenson and Robert Louis Stevenson, *Our Samoan Adventure*, p. 185.
79. Lucas, *The Colvins and Their Friends*, p. 229.
80. Lloyd Osbourne, *Casco* Diary, 1888–89, Robert Louis Stevenson Silverado Museum, St. Helena, California, page gg. Used by permission.

81. Lucas, *The Colvins and Their Friends*, p. 229.
82. Ibid. pp. 228–9.
83. Hirsch, 'The Fiction of Lloyd Osbourne', p. 71n.; see also Mackay, *The Violent Friend*, p. 450.
84. Lloyd Osbourne, *Casco* Diary, p. 77.
85. Ibid. p. gg.
86. Ibid. p. hh.
87. Pearson, 'European Intimidation and the Myth of Tahiti'; Bolyanatz, *Pacific Romanticism*; Vanessa Smith, *Intimate Strangers*.
88. Colley, *R. L. Stevenson and the Colonial Imagination*, p. 20.
89. Willis, *The Story of Laulii, a Daughter of Samoa*, p. 129.
90. Fanny Stevenson and Robert Louis Stevenson, *Our Samoan Adventure*, pp. 12, 25.

Chapter 4

Disjecta Membra: Collaboration and the Body of the Text in *The Wrong Box* and *The Master of Ballantrae*

By far, Robert Louis Stevenson's longest-running, and most productive, partnership was with his stepson, American Lloyd Osbourne, with whom he wrote three separate novels: *The Wrong Box* (1889), *The Wrecker* (1892) and *The Ebb-Tide* (1894). The extent to which these novels reflect equal contributions of both men varies. All three novels have been critically undervalued in the Stevenson canon, although *The Ebb-Tide*, the last and least collaborative, has recently undergone substantial reconsideration. It is in this, Stevenson's longest partnership, that he most fully explores the potential of collaboration as an innovative and experimental approach to writing fiction, an approach that was to influence even those works which were not written collaboratively. This chapter will examine Stevenson and Osbourne's first novel together, *The Wrong Box*. *The Wrong Box* stands apart among Stevenson's collaborative works because it is the only work for which we have extensive manuscript material that makes clear the process that the authors used. While Stevenson and Osbourne were writing the pulpy *The Wrong Box*, Stevenson was hard at work alone on a more literary project. The interchange between these two concurrent novels has gone previously unrecognised. This collaborative process Stevenson and Osbourne developed would impact not only its immediate product, *The Wrong Box*, but also that novel's fraternal twin, *The Master of Ballantrae* (1889).

Even more than Stevenson's other collaborative works, the three novels Stevenson wrote with Osbourne are characterised by a metafictional reflection on the nature of collaboration, its perils, and the ways in which Stevenson saw it informing and motivating his creative practice. When twenty-five-year-old Robert Louis Stevenson married thirty-five-year-old Fanny Vandegrift Osbourne, she had two children: seventeen-year-old Isobel and twelve-year-old Lloyd. (A third child, Hervey, had died shortly before they met.) The young stepfather quickly developed a strong attachment to the boy and later became his literary mentor. Just as we have seen in relation to Fanny and Louis's work on *The Dynamiter* (1885), the critical tradition has been to regret Osbourne's involvement in Stevenson's creative practice as uniformly destructive. Critics and fans alike have suggested that Osbourne was no better than a parasite, profiting off of his fortunate connection to the famous author. If critics have, historically, been hard on Fanny Stevenson, they have been merciless to Osbourne. For instance, in a hyperbolic preface appended to *The Wrong Box* manuscript at the Beinecke Rare Book and Manuscript Library at Yale University, G. Hills wrote that Stevenson worked with Osbourne in the unrealistic hope that the young man would someday become self-sufficient, but that 'every hemorrhage [Stevenson] suffered was but the loss of petrol from a frail machine overloaded with his relations by marriage and for their sakes driven beyond all limit' (5), as if Stevenson were a child or a mentally incompetent person, rather than an established thirty-eight-year-old professional, at the time of the collaboration.[1]

I find this account unsatisfactory. Not only does it deny Stevenson artistic agency for his own work, it also fails to take into account his persistent experimentation with the creative process and reinventions of the authorial role. Instead, in his collaboration with Osbourne, Stevenson experimented with a more social and dialogic definition of authorship, though he would never quite cede control of the creative process. The struggle engendered in this process becomes a defining thematic element of his novels from the end of the 1880s until his death in 1894.

Planned Stevenson–Osbourne Collaborations

The Wrong Box, *The Wrecker* and *The Ebb-Tide* are the three works that Stevenson and Osbourne published together, but they represent only a fraction of the collaborative work they contemplated. The extent of the planned works shows that for Stevenson these collaborations were not a side project but an ever-growing part of his literary career. Osbourne typed notes or plot structures for four stories or novels: the offensively titled *The White Nigger*, *The Goldenson*

Figure 4.1 Robert Louis Stevenson (right), Lloyd Osbourne (centre) and Joe Strong (right). Untitled, from the photograph album entitled 'The Cruise of the Casco' of Robert Louis Stevenson's travels around Hawaii and French Polynesia in 1888. The City of Edinburgh Museums and Galleries; Writers' Museum.

Mystery, *Fighting the Ring* and *The Last of the Yeomen*.[2] Fragments of *The Goldenson Mystery*, *Fighting the Ring* and *The Last of the Yeomen* run to three or four chapters, while *The White Nigger* is limited to a cast of characters and an outline, although it was one of the more extensive works planned. *The White Nigger* was a story of the Bibighar Massacre during the Indian Mutiny in 1857. Stevenson describes it to Colvin in a letter dated 9 April 1888, calling it a 'Howler' (*Letters* 6: 152). The main character, Christopher St Ives, is in love with Honoria Norman, the niece of a British brigadier. After the brigadier opposes their courtship, St Ives decides to join the mutineers. Later in the novel, Honoria becomes one of the captives of Cawnpore. She begs St Ives to save her brother, an indigo planter; however, it is too late, as he has already drowned. St Ives is left to reflect on his conflicting loyalties. Osbourne notes: 'After all, only another oppressor, should make no difference.'[3] There are some echoes of other Stevenson works here, most notably the protagonist's name, St Ives, which he would reuse in his posthumous unfinished novel of the same name. Then, too, Stevenson and Henley had considered writing a play, *Ajax*, set in India. Presumably that play, based on the Sophocles play of the same name, would also have concerned a hero who turns against his countrymen. Finally, the willingness to understand (but not ultimately sympathise with) the mentality of the terrorist or traitor to the crown is, as I have discussed early, one of the main projects of *The Dynamiter*, co-written with Fanny, and St Ives's attempt to look coolly on British deaths in the name of a greater good is reminiscent of Clara Luxmore's similar attempts.

A less ambitious proposed collaboration was *The Goldenson Mystery*, a murder mystery taking place in Chinatown, San Francisco, for which we have a fragment similarly typed by Osbourne. This story or novel opens with a clerk finding a banker dead in his parlour, gagged, mutilated and 'trussed like a pig and seared with red-hot irons'.[4] Most of the existing manuscript is taken up with the description of the body, and Osbourne was apparently at pains to outdo himself for gruesomeness. For instance, detectives find an amputated hand at the scene, 'clean parted at the wrist, but with the fingers smashed and beaten into a jelly'.[5] (It does not belong to the corpse – that is the mystery.) Neither *The White Nigger* nor *The Goldenson Mystery* manuscripts contain any notes by Stevenson, so the extent of his input is uncertain, but was likely minimal. Probably the pair had discussed the projects, and Osbourne had worked up a few things for Stevenson's approval.

Fighting the Ring, which I consider more fully in my chapter on *The Wrecker* because I find that it informs that novel, tells the story of a company trying to fight a larger syndicate's monopoly on copper mines. Writing to Fanny on 6 April 1888 Stevenson regrets that they seem unlikely to place this proposed work in the sensational paper the *Ledger* as they had planned, but still have hopes for *The Gaol Bird*, another proposed collaboration mentioned in Graham Balfour's biography of Stevenson (*Letters* 6: 148).[6] Finally, the nine-page *Last of the Yeomen* is a fable-like satire on the English aristocracy. Sir Arthur de Winton, the modern scion of an aristocratic family, has always heard of the famed loyalty of his ancestor's squire, John Hobbs, so it comes as a surprise when his own life is saved by the slightly vulgar descendant of that very same squire. Thus the young aristocrat is burdened by the service of an unwanted vassal.

When ungrateful de Winton sends Hobbs as his representative to sue for his inheritance, de Winton's uncle prefers to leave all the money to Hobbs, who possesses a middle-class vigour opposed to the enervated aristocracy represented by de Winton.

An undated note appended to all of these manuscripts and signed by Katherine D. Osbourne, Lloyd's ex-wife, gives entire credit for the works to Stevenson.[7] Considering Katharine Osbourne's plans to sell the stories for as much as possible, as well as her bad blood with both Stevenson and Osbourne (she has written a scurrilous biography of Stevenson[8]), her claim of Stevenson's authorship is not to be relied upon. Since only Osbourne, and never Stevenson, typed manuscripts, the fragments are clearly Osbourne's, though evidently inspired by collaborative discussions. Regardless, they show that the three novels which we have from Osbourne and Stevenson represent only a small fraction of the work they had once planned to do together.

Some critics, notably Victoria Ford Smith, have even credited Lloyd with a sort of collaboration on Stevenson's earlier works, noting that Stevenson's account of the composition of *Treasure Island* in his essay 'My First Book' reveals it to be based on a map that he had drawn while playing with (then juvenile) Lloyd Osbourne.[9] Although I do not agree with Smith's conclusion that *Treasure Island* is therefore a collaboration with Osbourne, there is much that is useful in her discussion of the possibilities of unequal collaboration, possibilities obscured by our sense that collaborative writing requires equal power relations and equal contribution from both partners. In particular, Smith argues that the Victorian child collaborator gave, or was perceived to give, authors access to 'those codes and behaviors of play imagined to be the exclusive territory of the young'.[10] Stevenson, in other words, was not above using the ideas of his unequal collaborators as the raw material from which to draw inspiration, and to say that he collaborated is not to say that he ceded authority in so doing.

Because, in the end, the collaboration would be unequal. After Stevenson's death, Osbourne would go on to be a prolific, though hardly famous writer, turning his hand to both short stories and novels themed around topics that include the South Pacific and the trend for 'motormania'. Gordon Hirsch, in his study of Osbourne's subsequent fiction, finds it to be creditable, if not much more, though it reveals a 'generally disturbing classism'.[11] To say that Stevenson needed to collaborate to create these works does not require us to assign to Osbourne any specific percentage of the texts (a thing impossible to do with any certainty, even in the very best case of *The Wrong Box*), but rather to acknowledge that the work of authorship was undertaken only in relation to another.

The Wrong Box

Fragments and maps notwithstanding, the first official and published collaboration we have from Robert Louis Stevenson and his stepson Lloyd Osbourne was their dark comedy *The Wrong Box*, which they composed while the family was living in Saranac, New York, in 1888. Lloyd Osbourne was nineteen at the time; the initial draft, which Osbourne begun alone, was entitled *A Game of Bluff*. In a letter to Henry James, Stevenson recalls how 'from the next room, the bell of Lloyd's type-writer makes an agreeable music, as it patters off (at a rate which astonishes this experienced novelist) the early chapters of a humorous romance' (*Letters* 6: 15). According to Fanny Stevenson, when the family needed money for the ship fare to the Pacific, Stevenson suggested that, if he collaborated on a revision, the pair could 'make it go'.[12] When the newspaperman Sam McClure, the editor of the New York *Sun* and *Black and White* (and later the original for the character of Jim Pinkerton in *The Wrecker*), came to Saranac to consult Stevenson about his projected letters to the *Sun* from the Pacific, he sounded a note of caution: 'It was a good story for a young man to have written; but I told Stevenson that I doubted the wisdom of his putting his name to it as a joint author. This annoyed him, and he afterward wrote me that he couldn't take advice about such matters.'[13] McClure was right, in a sense, because of all of Stevenson's works it remains among the least thought of, by both readers and scholars. As an example of collaborative process, however, it is invaluable.

The Wrong Box narrates the struggles of two cousins, Morris and Michael Finsbury, to protect their rights to a tontine; an investment scheme wherein (in the words of the novel),

> A number of sprightly youths (the more the merrier) put up a certain sum of money, which is then funded in a pool under trustees; coming on for a century later, the proceeds are fluttered for a moment in the face of the last survivor, who is probably deaf, so that he cannot even hear of his success – and who is certainly dying, so that he might just as well have lost.[14]

At the outset of the novel, only two participants in the tontine survive: brothers Joseph and Masterman Finsbury. When Morris Finsbury misidentifies a corpse as his uncle Joseph (who has entailed all his means to Morris), he has to hide the body to prevent all the proceeds of the tontine from falling to Joseph's equally elderly brother (and Michael's father), Masterman. Further complicating things (or at least giving Morris a dubious moral justification) is that Morris believes Masterman, too, is dead, and that Michael is hiding this fact. Confusion ensues, as the corpse is shoved in a rain butt, is accidentally shipped to a bohemian artist, is hidden in the chamber of a piano, and is eventually stolen by a highwayman. The novel met with mixed reviews,[15] but it has always found its fans – in fact, most readers have loved or hated it with little middle ground. For instance, while Jenni Calder says there 'can be few who can find much to say it its favour',[16] groups of fans met for years through the twentieth century for a meal celebrating the novel at the Athenaeum.[17] Rudyard Kipling claimed that he could 'take seventy-five percent marks in written or *viva-voce* examination of *The Wrong Box*', thus proving himself to be the ultimate Stevenson fan, although it is not clear whether he means that only a true fanatic would read it.[18] Its dry humour is appealing though a bit arch, making it a popular read among dandies. Max Beerbohm, for instance, the famous humourist and dandy, valued Stevenson the stylist over Stevenson the historical novelist, and therefore found it

> *too* exquisite. That the poor dear weak gentleman allowed himself to be diverted from his true function in writing by the elderly prigs who surrounded him, is a real tragedy. But perhaps one wouldn't revel so much in his fantasies if they were not so few.[19]

The novel has an urbane, Wildean homoeroticism that has led Oliver Buckton to discuss it in terms of the disruptive powers of both closeted male intimacy and of narrative.[20]

The novel's disruption of conventional moralities by anti-establishment young men is part of a critique of capitalistic and speculative excess that allows us to understand its 'hero', the lawyer Michael Finsbury, who might otherwise be a difficult character to support. After promising to help his client William Dent Pitman rid himself of the incriminating body, Michael concocts an outrageous plan involving disguises and fake identities, but then becomes too drunk to see it through, leaving his client desperate with 'rage and despair' at the critical moment (*Wrong Box*, 95). Then, when he does go through with the plan, it involves hiding the piano that contains the corpse in the apartment of another client, Gideon Forsyth, who is therefore at risk of incrimination. Michael is hardly a model of lawyerly propriety. At the end of the novel, he ends up the heir of the tontine, although Richard Ambrosini describes him as having 'a congenial inability to provide a moral solution to any human experience'.[21] This leaves the reader wondering at the moral universe that deems such a character to be the most deserving recipient of the novel's 'happy' ending. Stevenson compares Michael Finsbury to his other dandyish, bohemian hero from *New Arabian Nights* (1882), calling him 'the comic Prince Florizel' (*Letters* 6: 260). Before undertaking the collaboration, he had claimed that Osbourne had drawn much of his inspiration from that Stevenson text (*Letters* 6: 65). It is only in contrast to Morris Finsbury's mendacity that we can understand Michael Finsbury as a hero – in his drunken, protracted adolescence he represents ideals of play, mischief and leisure, completely innocent of the kind of capitalism that would make one disregard one's family for money, because he is lacks the seriousness, professionalism or greed to execute such a plan.

Michael, whom Osbourne based on Stevenson's long-time friend and drinking partner Charles Baxter (*Letters* 6: 71), is an unapologetic drunk whose defiance of Morris's attempts to swindle him is more accidental than deliberate. Baxter did not find the depiction flattering. Reflecting on his reception of the novel in a letter slipped in with the manuscript on 3 November 1915, he notes:

> Rather a curious coincidence occurred in connection with this advance copy of The Wrong Box.
>
> I received it in my office, 11 South Charlotte St. Edinburgh, by the morning post and commenced its perusal in the afternoon train, by which I went to Inchyra Grange, near Polmont, where I was then staying. It gradually dawned on me, that Michael Finsbury was no other than a rather ill-natured caricature of myself, and my feelings toward the author were for the moment decidedly strained.[22]

(Since Stevenson had referred to Michael as Baxter when the novel was still Osbourne's alone, it seems that Michael Finsbury was *Osbourne's* version of his stepfather's friend, not Stevenson's own.)

There has been more work done to disentangle the compositional process of *The Wrong Box* than any other collaborative Stevenson work, but because of the compositional process the pair used, only some of the material can be assigned with any certainty. In Osbourne's own account of the book's creation he takes most of the credit for the composition:

> Mr Lloyd Osbourne gives this interesting account of the mode of collaboration. '"The Wrong Box"', he says, 'was more mine as a whole than either "The Wrecker" or "The Ebb Tide". It was actually finished and ready for the press before there was any though of [Stevenson's] collaboration. There was, in consequence, far less give and take between us in this book than in the others.'[23]

This is supported in Stevenson's letters. In December 1887 Stevenson refers to Osbourne having completed a draft of the novel (*Letters* 6: 65), and even begun on a revision (*Letters* 6: 71), and this is before Stevenson undertakes the collaboration. It is not until March of 1888 that Stevenson first mentions the collaboration, writing to Henley that

> Lloyd's story was so damned funny and absurd that I lost my heart to it, and am now about half through my version. Lots of the lad's stuff stands; he has a genuine talent of a kind, and a fine idea of fun. The collaborated work is to be called *A Game of Bluff*! It is the merest farce, an Arabian Night on the scale of a novel; and I have laughed consumedly as I wrote. (*Letters* 6: 125)

Stevenson here acknowledges that he is rewriting the novel, but how extensively?

The strong evidence for Osbourne's more predominant contribution to the novel has caused readers to treat it with some cynicism, suspecting that Stevenson's name may hide the fact that *The Wrong Box* is, fundamentally, an Osbourne work. The possibility that Stevenson's input was minimal caused a squabble in the *Times Literary Supplement* in 1970, when novelist Graham Greene wrote a letter to the editor alleging that its publisher, Scribner's, was hiding corrected manuscript proofs which they had declined to reissue, as they had promised Stevenson they would do.[24] Editor David Randall, responding to Greene's letter two weeks later, recalled showing Greene the manuscripts, saying

> I showed him, only they had their original titles *A Game of Bluff* by Lloyd Osbourne and Robert Louis Stevenson. Their chief scholarly interest, if I recall accurately, was to show that Lloyd Osbourne had a lot more to do with the book than he is usually given credit for.[25]

Randall responds to an implication that Scribner's was not without prejudice in hiding the manuscripts. Just as Katherine Osbourne (above) had claimed Stevenson as a primary author for fragments clearly written only by Osbourne when she wished to sell them, Scribner's may have worried that, if the true extent of Osbourne's authorship were known, the manuscript would lose all value. Randall suggests another motive for Scribner's failure to reissue a corrected novel: 'The truth is that they did not think much of it when they reluctantly published it in 1889, and sixty years has not changed their minds.'[26]

Not all who have studied the origins of *The Wrong Box* have concluded that it is Osbourne's work in balance, however. Ernest Mehew, in his scholarly edition of *The Wrong Box*, has carefully accounted for the manuscript history of the text. Mehew concludes that Stevenson's revisions were sufficiently heavy that 'the form and the manner of the final version is almost entirely his',[27] though he does allow that the plot and characters were Osbourne's, a conclusion that fits well with Osbourne's claim that the structure of the book is his own, and the style Stevenson's. Scribner's, for obvious reasons, insisted that Stevenson's name appear first on the title page of the American edition as a precondition of their contract (*Letters* 6: 282),[28] although the pair in fact submitted the manuscript with Osbourne's name coming first. Stevenson required that Scribner's would list Osbourne's name first on the English edition, an agreement that the publishing house did not honour (*Letters* 6: 282n.). Mehew also notes a practical consideration for the collaboration – by collaborating with the American Lloyd Osbourne, Stevenson could protect his work with American copyright, an issue that was still relevant until the International Copyright Act of 1891.[29]

How is it possible, with so much commentary by both authors and their family, and with an actual manuscript written by both men, that there could still be disagreement about the extent of Osbourne's contributions to *The Wrong Box*?

The original manuscript is in three volumes, with the bulk of the manuscript pages in Stevenson's hand, interspersed with twenty-three typewritten pages from Osbourne, which have nonetheless been heavily revised by Stevenson. Stevenson almost always rewrote a fair-hand manuscript to submit to publishers, which he did not do in this case. Because Osbourne exclusively used a typewriter, and Stevenson wrote only in long-hand, there can be (one would think) no confusion about exactly who wrote what. But because of the very nature of collaboration and of the way that Stevenson chose to engage in it, this documentary evidence in the end can ultimately never tell us precisely where we should give credit to Osbourne and where to Stevenson, nor did the authors mean to have their work disentangled in this way. Nevertheless, it does provide ample evidence of how they worked together. Just as Stevenson had done earlier working with W. E. Henley on *Beau Austin*, and as he would later do with Osbourne on *The Wrecker*, Stevenson relied on his more junior collaborator to provide the early drafts of the works, and he valued speed over quality in his partner.

One significant limitation imposed by the supposedly 'original' manuscript of *The Wrong Box* is that it does not contain all of Osbourne's original draft. Although Richard Ambrosini concludes that Osbourne wrote only twenty-three pages, and that these Stevenson revised,[30] that conflicts with statements by both Osbourne and Stevenson attesting to the presence of a complete (or near-complete) Osbourne draft. Moreover, Osbourne numbered his pages, so we can see that the pages that we do have from him are discontinuous: his pages twelve and fifteen are included, for instance (numbered by Stevenson as twenty and twenty-five respectively), but the intervening pages are Stevenson's.[31] The pre-existence of an entire typed draft constrained Stevenson's revisions in a way that he was not constrained in any other collaboration. As Osbourne recalls, 'Louis had to follow the text very closely, being unable to break away without jeopardizing the succeeding chapters.'[32]

Furthermore, the lines of the text are continuous from one page to another, even if in some cases Stevenson has had to finish his sentence on the top of Osbourne's pages. However closely Stevenson followed the discarded manuscript pages, he would have been constrained by the length of the page. Stevenson has annotated Osbourne's pages, making minor edits and here and there rewriting a paragraph, but more notably deleted, often crossing out as much as half a page. However, in the case of even some quite large deletions (though by no means all), Stevenson has rewritten them in his own hand, sometimes staying fairly close to the original. For instance, in chapter four, where Wickham is 'playing billy' with the crate labels, Stevenson has crossed out the following lines, written by Osbourne, in their entirety:

> Mr Wickham was delighted at being left alone with the luggage, and took advantage of the opportunity to shew [*sic*] Michael what a dashing fellow he was. When he joined the lawyer in the smoking carriage his face was much flushed, and his cigar, which had gone out, was nearly bitten in two with excitement.

> 'What a lark!' he cried gleefully, 'I've sent those cousins of yours a packing case as large as a stable. I've distributed grouse amongst a number of deserving people. I've mixed up all the labels, and as there was a case of Warren's blacking, and a safety bicycle, and a barrel of oysters, and a yacht's binnacle there will be the devil to pay when they are all delivered. It's all in the most fearful mess, and I only hope we shan't be lynched before we get to London.'
>
> 'You had better take care, my young friend,' remarked Michael. 'I am getting tired of hauling you out of your scrapes; my reputation is beginning to suffer.'[33]

Despite boxing out and deleting all of this material, Stevenson's rewrite stays fairly close to the original:

> Smitten with the desire to shine in Michael's eyes and show himself a person of original humour and resource, the young gentleman (who was a magistrate, more by token, in his native country) was no sooner alone in the van than he fell upon the labels with the zeal of a reformer; and when he rejoined the lawyer at Bishopstoke, his face was flushed with his exertions, and his cigar, which he had suffered to go out, was almost bitten in two.
>
> 'By George, but this has been a lark!' he cried. 'I've sent the wrong thing to everybody in England. Those cousins of yours have a packing case as big as a house. I've muddled the whole business up to that extent, Finsbury, that if it were to get out, it's my belief we should be lynched.'
>
> It was useless to be serious with Wickham. 'Take care,' said Michael. 'I am getting tired of your perpetual scrapes; my reputation is beginning to suffer.'[34]

While this is admittedly heavily revised, Stevenson preserved many details, and much of the phrasing of the original. If this sample is characteristic of how Stevenson treated Osbourne's missing manuscript pages, it suggests that just because a page is in Stevenson's hand does not mean that he deserves all the credit. Other material written in Stevenson's hand may have been, and probably was, similarly copied from Osbourne's manuscript, but we do not have Osbourne's original manuscript pages in every case. We do not really know how much he relied on Osbourne's original manuscript and how much he changed. What we have from Osbourne's typewriter we may be certain is Osbourne's work. However, the work in Stevenson's hand, which is the majority, cannot be clearly assigned. Of the three collaborations that Stevenson and Osbourne worked on together, it is safe to say that *The Wrong Box* is the one that most reflects Osbourne, but we cannot parcel out contributions more exactly than that.

I have argued in a previous chapter that Fanny Stevenson's attempts to lay claim to a greater part of *The Dynamiter* have hurt that novel's reputation. Something similar is at stake in *The Wrong Box*. Hirsch, for instance, overtly links a critical distaste for *The Wrong Box* to a long history of critical and biographical distaste for its secondary author, pointing out that while 'Stevenson was widely liked and admired, Osbourne remains decidedly less so.'[35] Ambrosini argues that putting aside *The Master of Ballantrae* (which Stevenson was concurrently writing) to 'indulge a nineteen-year old college dropout' might be 'the most heinous of his many sins against the sanctity of authorship'.[36] (Since Ambrosini concludes that the novel is on balance the work of Stevenson, he admits it into the Stevenson canon for its biting critique of the publishing industry.) Hills's preface to the manuscript, which I again take as representative of the anti-Osbourne attitude popular among critics of the last century, seeks to claim both that Osbourne had little to do with *The Wrong Box* (Hills in fact credits Stevenson with even the original idea) but also that he is completely responsible for its amateurishness. Surely, if Osbourne has not had much hand in the three novels here considered, he cannot at the same time be blamed for any literary weaknesses.

Still, the typewritten Lloyd Osbourne manuscript *A Game of Bluff* evidently did need some extra help to make it marketable, and in this novel, which centres on a peripatetic corpse, the authors envisioned Osbourne's manuscript as a certain amount of dead material. The idea of text as corpse, or living body, exceeds the boundaries of the text, bleeding out into the authors' understanding of the circumstances of its creation. Gosse quotes Osbourne's description of Stevenson's contribution: 'He breathed into it, of course, his own incomparable power, humour, and vivacity, and forced the thing to live as it had never before.'[37] This animating metaphor gives further nuance to Fanny's statement that Stevenson's contribution is to 'make it go'. Stevenson's mother is quoted as saying that Stevenson had put '"a little more pepper" into it. That is all Mr Stevenson had to do with it.'[38] In Osbourne's own version, Stevenson, on reading *A Game of Bluff*, says, 'It made my fingers itch as I read it. Why, I could take up that book, and in one quick, easy rewriting could make it *sing*!'[39] Before Stevenson's collaboration, then, the novel exists as merely dead, bland and static matter.

At the same time, Osbourne and Stevenson's frank admission that the novel's purpose is to raise funds as quickly as possible is reflected in Morris's callous reduction of his uncle's corpse to economic investment. Everyone, Morris feels, can be purchased. 'Did you never hear of venal doctors?' Morris asks his brother, John: 'They're as common of blackberries; you can pick 'em up for three pound a head' (*Wrong Box* 19). When Morris, his brother John and their uncle Joseph are in the railway accident, and the presumed corpse of Uncle Joseph is found, 'there was no sentiment in the face of Morris' (25) before he decides to perpetrate his ruse. Needless to say, a man whose response to the death of his uncle in a railway accident is to hide the body to protect his inheritance is a man who has taken commercialism to its amoral extreme. Beattie finds that it depicts Stevenson's own attempt to 'come to terms with the horror of his father's decline and death (and his own guilt over profiting from it)'.[40] No wonder Gordon Hirsch has found that the tontine came to symbolise, for the Victorians, the 'substitution of a cash nexus for values of family and community'.[41] Family is reduced to exchange value; an equivalence that is further emphasised by Morris's inability to even distinguish the corpse of his uncle from the corpse of a complete stranger. Both Uncle Joseph and the unfortunate victim are followers of Sir Faraday Bond, whose prescriptions for diet and dress are, in the novel, immensely popular among the elderly. As a result, the two old men are indistinguishable from each other, because they have the same white hair and wear the same costume, and because, gruesomely, the anonymous old man has lost his face in the accident.

In transit, the corpse of the frail elderly man is mixed up with its imagined opposite: a nude and manly statue of Hercules. (Here is one place that we can, based on the manuscript, confidently assign credit to Osbourne.) As lovers Gideon Forsyth and Julia Hazeltine trepidatiously unpack the statue, they discover two substantial and athletic legs, and then, 'what seemed to be a third. This resolved itself however into a knotted club resting upon a pedestal' (*Wrong Box* 53). This sentence, and the whole erotic tone of the lovers unpacking the statue, is Osbourne's work. Where Osbourne originally wrote 'In spite of a protesting cry from Julia, he [Gideon] threw himself on his knees and helped her pull out the packing',[42] Stevenson revised it to have the lovers, more properly, 'kneeling side by side'. The substitution of statue for corpse echoes the earlier substitution of one old man corpse for another old man corpse. In the callous society of the novel, one body, or one box, is as good as another.

When Morris takes a coal axe to the statue of Hercules in the next chapter, he reduces it to 'no more than a medley of disjected members:

the quadragenarian torso prone against the pedestal: the lascivious countenance leering down the kitchen stair; the legs, the arms, the hands, and even the fingers, scattered broadcast on the lobby floor.'[43] Stevenson's phrase 'disjected members', besides seeming to refer back to Hercules' intimidating 'member', comes from a phrase from Horace, *disjecta membra*, or in English 'scattered fragments', and Horace uses it specifically about texts – to refer to surviving fragments of poems. The phrase itself certainly comes from Stevenson, because in the manuscript the page is in his hand, but the phrase itself is a revision. Stevenson had originally written (or rewritten from an earlier Osbourne draft) that the statue has been reduced to 'no more than a scattered [*sic*] of marble curiosities'.[44] The revision makes the statue's dismemberment more violent, but also more textual. Morris's destruction of the statue shows a shocking disrespect for artistic form. I read 'disjected members' as a cynical observation about the results of collaborative composition on textual bodies. The disjected members of the statue call back to the actual corpse, who has been literally defaced by the railway accident, and then erased, stripped of his identity by a novel that never provides him with an identity. They also, however, call back to Stevenson and Osbourne's own manuscript, and Osbourne's twenty-three typed pages of *A Game of Bluff*, now themselves disjected and scattered throughout Stevenson's rewritten draft of *The Wrong Box*. Either way, the reduction of uncle, statue or manuscript to profit is relentless and absolute.

Later, the text again comments on its own collaborative composition when it reflects on the differing experience levels of its two authors. Harker, the hapless young driver of a carrier's cart, is learning to play the pennywhistle, an instrument that the authors joke is particularly awful when played by a beginner. Lloyd Osbourne himself did play the pennywhistle (Stevenson did, too), and Stevenson had had to endure listening to his young stepson learn it (*Letters* 6: 277, 278).[45] Harker, a character much the same age as Osbourne was when he took the instrument up, is playing, rather significantly, a song called 'The Ploughboy', which was written by William Shield for his opera *The Farmer*, and then subsequently (in 1946) made more famous by Benjamin Britten. The song tells of a 'flaxen-headed ploughboy' (Harker is described as 'tow-headed') who fantasises about greater things.[46] A superior player who is, in reality, a highwayman intent on stealing the carriage approaches him. After Harker has heard the robber's professional playing, the result of hard work and long practice, the man suggests that it is the boy who has the true talent: 'That's one style of play: yours is the other, and I like it best. But I began when I was a boy, you see, before my taste was formed. When you're my age, you'll play that thing like a cornet-à-piston' (*Wrong Box* 139–40). Harker is eager to believe that an innate talent could stand him in competition with, or make him even better than, a master player who had had years of practice. Of course, it is a con:

> . . . when it became clear to Harker that he, the blushing débutant, was actually giving a lesson to this full-grown flutist, and the flutist, under his care, was not very brilliantly progressing – how am I to tell what floods of glory brightened the autumnal countryside? how, unless the reader were an amateur himself, describe the heights of idiotic vanity to which the carrier climbed? (*Wrong Box* 140)

Was this lesson in humility invented by Osbourne, poking a little self-deprecating fun at himself, or was it Stevenson's fictional correction of the younger man? The passage occurs past the point of the manuscript for which we have any of Osbourne's typed pages, so there is no way to know. It correlates nicely, however, with Osbourne's own reminiscences of how he felt when Stevenson offered to collaborate on the project with him: 'I was transported with joy. What would be writer of nineteen would not have been? It was my vindication; the proof I had not been living in a fool's paradise, and had indeed talent, and a future.'[47] The two amateurs – real and fictional – have similar experiences, Harker seeing 'floods of glory' and Osbourne 'transported with joy'; Harker's 'idiotic vanity' and Osbourne's 'fool's paradise'.

The contrast between the artist and the amateur remains the dominant motif through the rest of the novel. The final chapters of the text are littered with titles of imaginary works by hack writers, particularly railway novels – pulpy works meant to be read on the train. Oliver Buckton points out that the idea of the railway novel is central to *The Wrong Box*, from the first sentence, where Stevenson and Osbourne self-deprecatingly anticipate that the reader will enjoy this text 'in an hour . . . in a railway train' (*Wrong Box* 7), to the motivating crisis of the plot – the railway crash that produces the corpse. (And, as we have seen, that is where Charles Baxter was reading it before his awkward encounter.) The railway novel thus 'invokes not only the transient, casual relationship between text and reader common to such consumers but also the tolerance they had for sensational or shocking subject matter.'⁴⁸ Character Gideon Forsyth is responsible for the anonymously authored failed railway novel, *Who Put Back the Clock?*, which 'appeared for several days upon the railway bookstalls and then vanished entirely from the face of the earth' (114), now sadly represented by only three remaining volumes. In a pinch, Forsyth tries to model himself after the hero of that novel, asking 'What would Robert Skill have done?' (121). Forsyth is not the only character whose mental state is dictated by titles of railway novels. When Morris Finsbury feels he is close to being caught, he pictures his situation as the plot of a series of imaginary novels: 'Anxiety the First: *Where is the Body: or, the Mystery of Bent Pittman?*', 'Anxiety the Second: *The Fraud of the Tontine; or, Is my Uncle Dead?*', 'Anxiety the Third: *The Cottage at Browndean; or, The Underpaid Accomplice*' (148) and finally the punctuation-rich 'Anxiety the Fourth: *The Leather Business; or, The Shutters at Last: a Tale of the City*' (148). That the characters live out, in their imaginations, the twists and turns of the railway novel highlights the absurd twists, turns and hijinks of *The Wrong Box* itself, where 'nearly every crime of the traditional police novel is invoked'.⁴⁹ After all, there is no difference between the fictional detective Robert Skill and the fictional lover Gideon Forsyth, or the fictional bumbling criminal Morris Finsbury. On the departure platform at Waterloo Station we find 'the backs of Mr Haggard's novels, with which (upon a week-day) the bookstall shines emblazoned, discreetly hid behind dingy shutters' (161). Though Stevenson and Osbourne take the occasion for a dig at adventure writer H. Rider Haggard, he is not the most ephemeral of the late-Victorian pulp writers – his books are still in print, unlike the fictional *Who Put Back the Clock?* These references, by their sheer profusion, point to the imagined ephemerality of the text of *The Wrong Box* within the mercenary market for popular fiction, demonstrating the authors' tongue-in-cheek cynicism about the novel's importance and its longevity. Although *The Wrong Box* is still considered as among the famous author's most minor works, Stevenson's name, as they must have known, has given the text permanence and kept it in circulation at least in editions of his Complete Works, and there was even a 1966 movie of the novel starring Michael Caine as Michael Finsbury and Peter Sellers in a minor role. Nevertheless, this persistence probably relies more on Stevenson's fame than the text itself. *A Game of Bluff* by new young author Lloyd Osbourne would probably have ended up like *Who Put Back the Clock?*

These frequent references to commercial hack writing reflect Stevenson's self-consciousness about this work, which is also reflected in Stevenson and Osbourne's defensive and apologetic preface:

> 'Nothing like a little judicious levity,' says Michael Finsbury in the text; nor can any better excuse be found for the volume in the reader's hand. The authors can but add that one of them is old enough to be ashamed of himself and the other young enough to learn better. (*Wrong Box* 5)

How far should the skilled author go in producing work for the popular market, and what kind of responsibility did Stevenson have for guaranteeing the literary quality of his productions? Even Osbourne, accidentally or deliberately alluding to his original title, *A Game of Bluff*, wrote that Stevenson was 'bluffing Scribner's into a small fortune' for *The Wrong Box* (*Letters* 6:258 n. 3),[50] reinforcing the nature of this text as a sort of con. Stevenson's awareness that he had a keen commercial sense for what would 'go' is a common theme in his essays, most especially in 'A Chapter on Dreams' (1888), where he had claimed that his dreaming self, and not just his conscious self, was attuned to the whims and preferences of the marketplace. As Glenda Norquay has found, Stevenson struggled throughout his career with questions of commercialism and literary merit; Norquay analyses Stevenson's recurring obsession with the figure of the writer as whore, arguing that he combined ideas of the dangerous pleasures of the text with, specifically, an 'emphasis on commercial transaction in this imagery of seduction'.[51] Norquay's discussion of the writer as whore inflects Stevenson's preface, where he describes himself as 'ashamed' of *The Wrong Box*. And Richard Ambrosini has elsewhere argued that Stevenson's idea of professionalism in fiction was incompatible with the emerging academy that accompanied the rise of modernism, precipitating his ejection from the literary canon in the early twentieth century. Stevenson's consistent marketability, in other words, was a black mark against him for readers looking for a more literary, less easily palatable reading experience.[52] One of his greatest professional gifts – his sense of the market – might compromise his work, and his reputation. At the same time, Stevenson was unwilling to let the light diversion of *The Wrong Box* define him. In Richard Ambrosini's reading, Stevenson's bitter evisceration of the popular press in *The Wrong Box* is the first sign of 'the darkening of his imagination' that would lead to the composition of *The Master of Ballantrae*, *The Wrecker* and *The Ebb-Tide*.[53] The moral questions that Stevenson and Osbourne unashamedly refuse in *The Wrong Box* are taken up with tragic seriousness in *The Master of Ballantrae*.

The Master of Ballantrae

Stevenson could justify the diversion of *The Wrong Box* because he was simultaneously at work on a serious novel, *The Master of Ballantrae*. He often spoke of *The Wrong Box* and *The Master of Ballantrae* together, implying that the one excused the other. On 5 February 1889 Stevenson wrote to Edward Burlingame at Scribner's:

> As soon as I am through with The Master, I shall finish The Game of Bluff – now rechristened The Wrong Box. This I wish to sell, cash down. It is of course copyright in the States; and I offer it to you for five thousand dollars. (*Letters* 6: 245)

Then, writing to Charles Baxter on 8 March 1889, 'Since I have been here, I have been toiling like a galley slave; three numbers of The Master to rewrite, five chapters of The Wrong Box to write and rewrite' (*Letters* 6: 263). *The Wrong Box* was intended to turn a quick profit; the *Master* was meant to be the literary work. Where *The Wrong Box*, which is set in London, shows an urban, modern sensibility, *The Master of Ballantrae* is about the Scottish historical past of the Jacobite rebellion, which Stevenson had treated so successfully three years earlier with *Kidnapped* (1886), and to which he would return in 1894 with the sequel to *Kidnapped*, *Catriona* (also known as *David Balfour*). In fact, although the Scottish historical remained a dominant mode for Stevenson throughout his life and career, in no case did he ever subject any Scottish or historical novel to collaborative treatment. Roslyn Jolly, comparing Mrs Oliphant's review of *The Wrong Box* (discussed below) to her review of *The Master of Ballantrae*, notes that

> After confidence in Stevenson's name had been damaged by a collaboration or experiment the public found unwelcome, readerly satisfaction was generally restored when he returned – writing as a single author – to what most considered his 'proper' imaginative territory: Scotland and romance.[54]

His most traditional, and thus most popular and acceptable, style received the most traditional treatment.

Although *The Wrong Box* and *The Master of Ballantrae* could not be more different stylistically or in their settings, in their plots the two books are remarkably similar. *The Master of Ballantrae* tells the story of a noble Scottish family and their strategy to preserve their estate. The older brother, James, goes to fight with Prince Charles, while the younger, Henry, stays on the estate and remains loyal to the king. By this means the father hopes to preserve the family estate regardless of the outcome of the rebellion. When the prince is routed, it causes lifelong acrimony between the amoral, charismatic heir and the stiff and uncomfortable younger brother who seems to have appropriated his rights. Both *The Wrong Box* and *The Master of Ballantrae* depict a struggle for an inheritance, the ways in which what might begin as mere materialistic acquisitiveness becomes over time entrenched into righteousness and resentment, and the resulting deterioration of humanity and family loyalty. Where Morris and Michael Finsbury struggle to be the recipients of the tontine in *The Wrong Box*, in *The Master* the brothers struggle for control of the estate and, more immediately, of the money associated with it. The novels similarly feature a struggle between two distinct personality types: in *The Wrong Box* uptight criminal Morris is harassed by Michael Finsbury's reckless disregard for propriety, whereas in *The Master* the tense and conscientious Henry is relentlessly tweaked by his shameless and reckless brother.

There is, moreover, a concern with the dead who will not stay dead. The corpse in *The Wrong Box* keeps popping up at the most inconvenient times, and the characters find out that their Uncle Joseph, whom they thought was dead, is actually roaming the countryside and boring people in pubs with long-winded stories. In *The Master*, James Durie is presumed dead not once, but three times. First, the family believes that he has died with the defeat of the Jacobites at Culloden. Then, when the brothers clash in a violent duel, Henry runs James through with his sword and leaves him on the ground, bleeding out and with no heartbeat. When Alison Durie and Mackellar return in the night to see to the body, they find it vanished, leaving Henry to conclude 'nothing can kill that man. He is not mortal. He is bound upon my back to all eternity.'[55] This is followed by yet a third death, and reanimation: the Master is buried alive by his servant Secundra Dass, who has trained him in the Indian art of 'swallow[ing] his tongue' (*Master* 217). When Henry hears of his older brother's alleged death and burial, the report is not good enough for him, and he sets out to find the burial place, determined to have the corpse: '"Why," says my lord, "this is a matter of succession: my son's title may be called in doubt; and the man being supposed to be dead of nobody can tell what, a great deal of suspicion would be naturally roused"' (209). Henry, at this moment, falsely believes that King George has restored James's claim to the estate, but, even so, his fears do not seem reasonable – in the cut-throat world of *The Master of Ballantrae*, no governmental officials ever appear to enforce laws of primogeniture. This fear seems more appropriate to the legal wrangling of *The Wrong Box*, where Morris Finsbury, having gone to a great deal of trouble to hide the corpse he presumes is Uncle Joseph, suddenly realises with horror that he needs a corpse if he is to inherit the leather business. And if Hilary Beattie links the concern with death and inheritances in *The Wrong Box* to Stevenson's Oedipal struggles with the death of his own father, surely these themes are even more explicitly confronted in *The Master* where the remaining brother inherits even the wife meant for his older brother. We have the same story told in two modes – once as comedy, and once as tragedy.

The Master of Ballantrae reflects its own concerns with textual bodies and *disjecta membra* in that it makes use of an editor (the family steward, Mackellar) who compiles the scattered fragments of the text into a unified novel. Like the eighteenth-century novels with which it shares a mood, Stevenson had planned to use a found manuscript frame. He even tried to set up a fiction with Charles Baxter wherein Baxter would pretend to have received the mysterious manuscript in his law office, and he asked Baxter to claim that the family agent of the Durisdeers had delivered the manuscript in the form of a set of memoranda to Baxter's predecessor in 1794, 'with the understanding they will be sealed until 1862, when a century will have elapsed since the affair in the wilderness (my lord's death)' and asking 'Will my doer collaborate thus much in my new novel?' (*Letters* 6: 99). In the end, he rejected the plan as 'too like Scott' (*Letters* 8: 290).

One significant difference between *The Master of Ballantrae* and *The Wrong Box*, however, is that the former has the seeds of a developing political argument, which the latter lacks. Political readings of the text have focused on the divisions within Scotland, with James representing a dashing Highlander aesthetic, and on the status of the text as historical fiction.[56] But, the text, which spans Scotland, India and North America, is far too international to speak of Scotland alone. Tara Ghoshal Wallace reads the final horrific scene of *The Master of Ballantrae*, in which we see Secundra Dass trying to revive James Durie, as one that, in its yoking together of Indian, Scottish and American (including Native American) characters and settings, 'enacts . . . the opportunities, disruptions, and dangers of imperial adventurism during the eighteenth century', finding that *The Master of Ballantrae* is first and foremost 'a text in which imperial adventuring originates in shoddy motives and results in death'.[57] This scene of violent imperialism is one that will recur in the climactic confrontations that end both *The Ebb-Tide* and *The Wrecker*.

Looking at Stevenson's politics as they develop thorough his career, we can see some of the same issues he addressed in *The Dynamiter* presented with greater sophistication. In *The Dynamiter*, imperial critique had been played as farce. Even as the Prince of Bohemia chides the rebel Clara Luxmore for her willingness – as a woman and a mother! – to blow up little children in the middle of London, the mode is comic. Though *The Dynamiter* is almost (not quite) as international a text as *The Master of Ballantrae*, there the critique of the British role in international affairs is ventured but, in the final moment, denied. In *The Wrong Box* too, which was inspired by the aesthetics of *New Arabian Nights*, even a corpse is a comic object. But in *The Master of Ballantrae*, particularly in its imperial unearthing of James's (not quite) corpse, we see Stevenson experimenting with a new mode – that of imperial horror. This particular view of imperial violence is developed here in regards to Scotland but will later be extended to the violence that Stevenson perceives in the Pacific because, according to John Kucich, he 'was motivated to make [this critique], in the first place, because the imperial abuses he observed in the South Seas resonated so strongly with his tragic view of Scottish history.'[58] While *The Master of Ballantrae* attempts to query the role of aristocratic inheritance in a world increasingly shaped by the effects of British imperialism, *The Wrong Box* only cares about itself.

This is not to say that *The Master of Ballantrae* does not engage in the formal experimentation that characterised Stevensonian writing since his experiments in *New Arabian Nights*. The novel is narrated by the steward of the Durrisdeer estate, Mackellar, who vaunts his Master's degree from Edinburgh University as a credential (*Master* 20), making him yet a third 'Master' of Ballantrae. Mackellar's scholarly narration leads to, as Penny Fielding has argued, a juxtaposition of the authoritative written text over the untrustworthy oral tale:[59] the villain James Durie, whose perspective opposes Mackellar's, has the charismatic gift of the gab. And yet because the novel is written as history – it is presented as a found text 100 years after the event – Mackellar's documentary account controls the narrative. Mackellar's narration is inset throughout with other, often dubious, first-person narrations, which he editorialises for the reader. The first such narrative is that of the Chevalier de Burke, an Irishman fighting for the Jacobite cause. The Chevalier has accompanied James from the Battle of Culloden to the high seas, where the two fall in with a band of pirates that terrorises the North Atlantic. Mackellar solicits the Chevalier's memoirs to support his own narrative by providing a first-person account of James's adventures while away from the family. The Chevalier, to Mackellar's chagrin, sends an extensive memoir in the hopes of finding a 'publisher for the whole' (33). Mackellar's opinion of the literary merits of this memoir are not high, and he warns us of their unreliability by contrasting the written document with the oral performance. The first Lord Durrisdeer hears a sanitised version of the adventures in which his son turns pirate, but we readers get other information: 'I put in my first extract here, so that it may stand in place of what the Chevalier told us over our wine in the hall of Durrisdeer; but you are to suppose it was not the brutal fact, but a very varnished version that he offered to my lord' (33). As Nathalie Jaëck has argued, Mackellar 'highlights his own unreliability by editing others' texts', particularly as he 'randomly and rashly expurgates [the Chevalier's] text, which thus begins in the middle of nowhere, hooked onto the main text by frustrating suspension marks . . .' This, Jaëck finds, is of a piece with Stevenson's propensity, throughout his career, 'to dismember, to scatter the text'.[60] In Alan Sandison's characterisation, 'Stevenson subtly and sophisticatedly "plays" with metafictional processes and the deconstructive effects of absent or illegitimate authority.'[61] Textual proliferation calls into question the unity and also the accuracy of the manuscript.

Another crucial inset text comes at the climactic conclusion of the novel. Henry Durie has taken his family to Albany, New York, to live unmolested by his diabolical brother, but James, accompanied by Mackellar as witness, has followed the family across the Atlantic. Now, as James travels the countryside trying to rediscover treasure he had buried on his last American visit, he is accompanied by a team of contract killers hired by Henry to murder him. Stevenson had been in difficulties for how to report the climactic scenes of the novel while remaining true to his narrator Mackellar. The Albany section of the novel could not easily be recounted by his prim and anxious narrator, or at least Stevenson thought it couldn't: 'How, with a narrator like Mackellar, should I transact the melodrama in the wilderness? How, with his style, so full of disabilities, attack a passage which must be either altogether seizing or altogether silly and absurd?'[62] He considered converting the half-written novel to the third person, but decided against it. Instead, Mackellar pieces together the facts from a tracker called Mountain. This narrative, like the Chevalier's, is censored and must be supplemented with others (*Master* 206). Mackellar tells us

> Here follows a narrative which I have compiled out of three sources, not very consistent in all points:
> *First*, a written statement by Mountain, in which everything criminal is cleverly smuggled out of view;
> *Second*, two conversations with Secundra Dass; and
> *Third*, many conversations with Mountain himself, in which he was pleased to be entirely plain; for the truth is he regarded me as an accomplice. (*Master* 194)

Mackellar purportedly gives Mountain's text as an inset narrative in the novel, but in fact, as his presentation of the document shows, it comes to us heavily edited, compiled of inconsistent narrations of which Mackellar himself has presumed to be the judge.

Mackellar's method in revising Mountain's insufficient text is similar to that Stevenson was concurrently engaged in with Osbourne on *The Wrong Box*. In Stevenson's collaborative endeavours, both with Henley and now with Osbourne, his creative practice was to begin with a draft written by the other, presumably weaker partner. In all cases, that early draft was found to be lacking, and required the revision of Stevenson as the senior partner to 'make it go'. In the case of *The Wrong Box* it is the *disjecta membra* of Osbourne's typewritten draft which Stevenson must dismember and then reconstruct. In *The Master of Ballantrae*, this creative practice is literally re-enacted by our master narrator, Mackellar. In this instance he takes the written document of Mountain as his first draft, but finding it both inconsistent and lacking veracity, Mackellar dismembers it and reorders it with supplementary material he derives from conversations with Mountain and Secundra Dass, James's Indian henchman, who is himself a biased and deceptive witness. Presumably, this reordered narrative is influenced by Mackellar's own highly biased reporting, with the result that, as Alison Lumsden notes, this, 'more than any of Stevenson's other fictions, leaves readers with no stable ground beneath their feet', concluding with 'only fragmentation and uncertainty as the narrative "splinters off" into indeterminacy'.[63] As Ian Duncan has pointed out, having the 'narration of a family steward or servant . . . subject to an ironical editorial pressure' is not original to Stevenson but had earlier been practised in *The Moonstone* and *Wuthering Heights,* and Mackellar himself has a certain family resemblance both to Wilkie Collins's Gabriel Betteredge and to Emily Brontë's Nelly Dean.[64] But the practice is given a new relevance when we consider Stevenson himself as a manager of textual fragments whose artistic practice often involved revising the drafts and ideas of others.

The Master of Ballantrae metatextually documents the struggle for power of Mackellar's, and Stevenson's own, editorial authority against the challenges posed by alternate authors and perspectives. Mackellar fights throughout the text for authorial, and authoritative, control of his narrative. His biases are overt. Within the first few pages he has told us that 'Mr Henry had the chief part of my affection' (*Master* 20), and that from the beginning of the narrative when James is believed dead at Culloden, 'the burden of [my thought] was an unnatural jealousy of the dead man for Mr Henry's sake' (23). Mackellar's particularity for Henry is not a formality but is in fact the motivating fact of the entire narrative, a necessary *apologia* for Henry, which Mackellar promises to undertake as faithfully as 'a witness in a court' (19). The narrative's principal purpose is to justify Henry's crime and to make the reader sympathise with him against his more charismatic brother. Stevenson wrote to Henry James that the novel 'leads up to the death of the elder brother at the hands of the younger in a perfectly cold-blooded murder of which I wish (and mean) the reader to approve' (*Letters* 6: 105). Yet later, when he is taken in by James's 'glamour' on the ship sailing to America, Mackellar will confess that too: 'I am perhaps, the more a dupe of his dissimulation, but I believed (and I still believe) that he regarded me with genuine kindness. Singular and sad fact! so soon as this change began, my animosity abated' (*Master* 168). These violently swinging loyalties are prefigured by Mackellar's vision onboard the *Nonesuch* of James sitting across the deck from Mackellar during rough winds: 'Now his head would be in the zenith and his shadow fall quite below the *Nonesuch* on the farther side; and now he would swing down till he was underneath my feet, and the line of the sea leaped high above him lie the ceiling of a room' (160), creating a nauseating disorientation for an absolutist, and landlubber, like Mackellar. Mackellar wonders: is he, as so many lesser minds have been, merely seduced by an attractive but dangerous indeterminacy and moral relativism? Or might there be, as James Durie argues, two sides to a story? 'O! there are double words for everything: the word that swells, the word that belittles; you cannot fight me with a word!' (167–8). The frequent references in both the novel and its paratexts to James as Satan himself calls to mind Milton's *apologia* for God in *Paradise Lost*. At sea with Mackellar, James echoes Milton's Satan when he laments that his vaunting ambition combined with his loss of position together conspire to damn him: 'A bad man, am I? Ah! But I was born for a good tyrant!' (167). But as in *Paradise Lost*, *The Master of Ballantrae* is shadowed by the possibilities of its own counter-readings, and readers and critics have not universally absolved Henry as Stevenson (supposedly) wished them to.

The reason Henry so desperately needs Mackellar to defend him is because he both has the motive and commits the crimes. It is he who marries his brother's fiancée, who is threatened by the return of the true heir, who drives a sword through his brother's chest, and who finally hires a contract killer to do away with him once and for all. It may be Henry and not James who has committed the largest injustices. Douglas Gifford takes James's part, finding Mackellar utterly unreliable, and venturing that James is 'wild' and a 'spendthrift', but an otherwise relatively innocent victim of Henry's own calumny.[65] He goes on to compare the dualism of Henry and James to a similar dualism of David Balfour and the more dashing Alan Breck in *Kidnapped*, a comparison suggested by the fact that Alan Breck appears in *The Master of Ballantrae* in a minor role. Whereas in *Kidnapped* David, the uptight moralist, becomes the moral centre of that novel,[66] Henry's moral authority as the prudent, conscientious figure is less clear. Mackellar would have us believe that it is precisely because Henry is so uptight, and generally unlikeable, that he is so misunderstood, and would have us suspect James's glib and serpent-like charm. In another critical counter-reading of the novel, Richard Ambrosini eviscerates Mackellar's narrative credibility, calling him 'an avaricious and sex-phobic Scottish Calvinist whose supposed objectivity is warped by his hatred for women and his jealousy of a dashing and handsome young aristocrat', and suggests instead that Mackellar stands for 'everything Stevenson most detested in his own culture'.[67] Considering, too, that Stevenson in his youth was neither thrifty nor chaste, it is difficult to imagine him presenting such a character's condemnations of James's financial and sexual indiscretions without irony.

A side-by-side reading of *The Wrong Box* also supports a counter-reading of *The Master of Ballantrae*. *The Wrong Box* also narrates a dualistic struggle between a neurotic character (Morris Finsbury) and his free-wheeling, wild antagonist, Michael, which John Kucich identifies as the struggle between the bourgeois and the bohemian sides of Stevenson's own personality.[68] But in *The Wrong Box* it the neurotic character who is the villain, and we see that along with righteousness and moralising comes greed, pettiness, and ill-humour, flaws that characterise Henry Durie as much as they do Morris. Mackellar's sense that Henry commits his crimes not because he is innately evil but because he is pushed too far by his enemy is precisely the kind of casuistry that Morris engages in throughout *The Wrong Box* as he justifies his decision to hide his uncle's corpse by reasoning that Michael is probably similarly hiding Masterman's body (he is not). The characters of Henry and Morris are also alike in their grudges and resentments. Morris complains to Michael: 'I believe it to be malice . . . You always hated and despised me from a boy' (*Master* 17), while Henry angrily alleges that his father has always preferred James (12) in a character-defining moment in *The Master*. Ambrosini even associates Mackellar's uptight, censorious editorship with Sidney Colvin's attitudes towards Stevenson's own letters, and relies in his analysis on Colvin's suppression of the original preface where Charles Baxter was to have found Mackellar's manuscript.[69] Since Baxter, as the original for Michael, was the opposite of the moralising Mackellar, his involvement in the narrative of *The Master of Ballantrae* heightens the polarities between the character types that we see in both novels.

Without the art of narrative to paint the Master as a Satanic figure, there is a limited case against him. James's sins are sins of character, not actions, and his moral status is ambiguous. In 1887, Stevenson wrote of him that 'the Master is all I know of the devil' (*Letters* 6: 87), but in a fragment for the preface written in 1893–4, he wrote that 'for the Master I had no original, which is perhaps another way of confessing that the original was no other than myself'.[70] Mackellar complains about the Master as a reader, alleging that he cannot find the moral in the texts he prefers (Richardson's *Clarissa*, but also biblical tales), but 'they were to him a source of entertainment only, like the scraping of a fiddle in a change-house' (*Master* 156), and yet this sounds like Stevenson's own literary ideals in his literary criticism. For instance, his argument about the limitations of morality in 'A Gossip on Romance' (1882) directly defends what Mackellar posits as the Master's incomplete readings:

> Conduct is three parts of life, they say; but I think they put it high. There is a vast deal in life and letters both which is not immoral, but simply a-moral; which either does not regard the human will at all, or deals with it in obvious and healthy relations; where the interest turns, not upon what a man shall choose to do, but on how he manages to do it; not on the passionate slips and hesitations of the conscience, but on the problems of the body and of the practical

intelligence, in clean, open-air adventure, the shock of arms or the diplomacy of life. With such material as this it is impossible to build a play, for the serious theatre exists solely on moral grounds, and is a standing proof of the dissemination of the human conscience. But it is possible to build, upon this ground, the most joyous of verses, and the most lively, beautiful and buoyant tales.[71]

However, although Stevenson's ideas of literary play as he explored them in *The Wrong Box*, in his experimental fiction such as *New Arabian Nights* and *The Dynamiter*, and in his essays do not accord with Mackellar's authoritative search for textual certainty, the author and the narrator are alike in one important respect. Mackellar is a reviser, taking the memoirs of the Chevalier de Burke and of Mountain, or indeed the facts of the tragedy themselves, and attempting to manage a diversity of more and less reliable voices and ideas, turning them to account, or 'mak[ing] them go'.

Notes

1. G. Hills, Prefatory notes appended to the mss of *The Wrong Box*, April 1940, Edwin J. Beinecke Collection of Robert Louis Stevenson, GEN MSS 664 Box 112.
2. Osbourne and Robert Louis Stevenson, all documents under 'Fighting the Ring', Edwin J. Beinecke Collection of Robert Louis Stevenson, GEN MSS 664 box 29 folder 686.
3. Osbourne and Robert Louis Stevenson, 'The White Nigger', p. 3, in 'Fighting the Ring', Beinecke.
4. Osbourne and Robert Louis Stevenson, *The Goldenson Mystery*, p. 2, in 'Fighting the Ring', Beinecke.
5. Ibid. p. 5.
6. Balfour, *Life of Robert Louis Stevenson*, vol. 2, p. 40.
7. Katherine D. Osbourne, note attached to mss, 'Fighting the Ring', Beinecke.
8. Katherine D. Osbourne, 'Some Aspects of Robert Louis Stevenson', *Edwin J. Beinecke Collection of Robert Louis Stevenson*, GEN MSS 664 box 51 folder 1112.
9. Victoria Ford Smith, 'Toy Presses and Treasure Maps'; see also Buckton, *Cruising with Robert Louis Stevenson*, p. 248.
10. Victoria Ford Smith, 'Toy Presses and Treasure Maps', p. 28.
11. Hirsch, 'The Fiction of Lloyd Osbourne', p. 55.
12. Edmund Gosse, Introduction to *The Wrong Box* by Robert Louis Stevenson and Lloyd Osbourne, p. 225. In a prefatory note to the manuscript of *The Wrong Box* held at the Beinecke, G. Hills argues that Fanny's

notion that the family needed money for the *Casco* was not only wrong, but 'an attempt to sublimate her shame for the part her son played in the invalid's life' (p. 4). I quote from Hills to demonstrate the scepticism with which critics have considered the Stevenson–Osbourne partnership (not to mention the Louis–Fanny partnership). See note 1 of this chapter.
13. McClure, *My Autobiography*, p. 188.
14. Robert Louis Stevenson and Lloyd Osbourne, *The Wrong Box*, p. 7. Subsequent references to this edition will be cited parenthetically as *Wrong Box*.
15. Mehew, Introduction to *The Wrong Box*, p. xxxiv.
16. Calder, *Robert Louis Stevenson*, p. 279.
17. Bell, *Dreams of Exile*, p. 192.
18. Kipling, *Something of Myself*, p. 100.
19. Max Beerbohm quoted in Riewald, *Max Beerbohm's Mischievous Wit*.
20. Buckton, *Cruising with Robert Louis Stevenson*, pp. 48–54.
21. Ambrosini, 'Stevenson's Self-Portrait', p. 164.
22. Charles Baxter, note accompanying mss of *The Wrong Box*, 3 November 1915, *Edwin J. Beinecke Collection of Robert Louis Stevenson*, GEN MSS 664 Box 112.
23. Gosse, introduction to *The Wrong Box* by Robert Louis Stevenson and Lloyd Osbourne, p. 225.
24. Graham Greene, letter to the editor, 'The Wrong Box', *Times Literary Supplement* 70 (30 October 1970): 1276.
25. David Randall, letter to the editor, 'The Wrong Box', *Times Literary Supplement* 70 (13 November 1970): 1328. Greene and Randall seem to be referring to two different things here – Greene to corrected proof sheets that Scribner's had received too late to incorporate in the final manuscript (see Mehew, Introduction, p. xiii), and Randall to the actual, earlier manuscript. The proof sheets, which are a much later version, bear the title *The Wrong Box*, not the title *Game of Bluff*, and because they are very lightly edited they would not plausibly show anything at all about Osbourne's contributions.
26. Ibid. p. 1328.
27. Mehew, Introduction to *The Wrong Box*, p. xx.
28. See also Ibid. p. xii.
29. Ibid. p. xxii; and Hinchcliffe and Kerrigan, eds, *The Ebb-Tide* by Robert Louis Stevenson, pp. 157–8.
30. Ambrosini, 'Stevenson's Self-Portrait', p. 151.
31. Robert Louis Stevenson and Osbourne, manuscript of *The Wrong Box*, *Edwin J. Beinecke Collection of Robert Louis Stevenson*, GEN MSS 664 Box 112–14. 112 contains chapters 1–5.
32. Quoted in Balfour, *Life of Robert Louis Stevenson*, vol. 2, p. 42.
33. Robert Louis Stevenson and Lloyd Osbourne, manuscript of *The Wrong Box*, Box 112 p. 43A.
34. Ibid. p. 43.

35. Hirsch, 'The Stevenson–Osbourne Collaboration', p. 162.
36. Ambrosini, 'Stevenson's Self-Portrait', p. 151.
37. Gosse, Introduction to *The Wrong Box*, p. 225.
38. Quoted in Mehew, Introduction to *The Wrong Box*, p. xx.
39. Lloyd Osbourne, *An Intimate Portrait*, p. 80, emphasis in original.
40. Beattie, 'Father and Son', p. 352.
41. Hirsch, 'Tontines, Tontine Insurance, and Commercial Culture', p. 83.
42. Osbourne and Robert Louis Stevenson, manuscript to *The Wrong Box*, Box 112, Beinecke, p. 48.
43. Beattie, who reads *The Wrong Box* as reflective of Stevenson's own Oedipal crisis on the occasion of his father's death, finds in this scene an 'underlying parricidal anger', 'Father and Son', p. 352.
44. Osbourne and Robert Louis Stevenson, manuscript to *The Wrong Box*, Box 113, Beinecke, p. 59.
45. Also cited in Mehew, Introduction to *The Wrong Box*, p. xxxi.
46. Stevenson again references 'The Ploughboy' in *In the South Seas* (1896), although it is he himself playing the song and not Osbourne. King Tembinok's cook, whom Stevenson has got in trouble with the king, is skulking around threateningly while Stevenson plays 'The Ploughboy' on the flageolet (*ISS*, pp. 231–2).
47. Lloyd Osbourne, *An Intimate Portrait*, p. 80.
48. Buckton, *Cruising with Robert Louis Stevenson*, p. 44.
49. Hirsch, 'Tontines', p. 90.
50. Also quoted in Mehew, Introduction to *The Wrong Box*, p. xii.
51. Norquay, *Robert Louis Stevenson and Theories of Reading*, p. 83.
52. Ambrosini, 'R. L. Stevenson and the Ethical Value of Writing for the Market', pp. 25–6.
53. Ambrosini, 'Stevenson's Self-Portrait', p. 164.
54. Jolly, *Robert Louis Stevenson in the Pacific*, p. 158.
55. Robert Louis Stevenson, *The Master of Ballantrae*, p. 118. Future references to this edition will be cited parenthetically as *Master*.
56. See, for instance, Martin, *The Mighty Scot*.
57. Tara Ghoshal Wallace, *Imperial Characters*, pp. 17, 33. See also Reid, *Robert Louis Stevenson, Science, and the* Fin de Siècle.
58. Kucich, *Imperial Masochism*, p. 33.
59. Fielding, *Writing and Orality*.
60. Jaëck, 'The Greenhouse vs. the Glasshouse', pp. 52, 48.
61. Sandison, *Robert Louis Stevenson and the Appearance of Modernism*, p. 274.
62. Robert Louis Stevenson, 'Note to "The Master of Ballantrae"', in *Master of Ballantrae*, p. 226.
63. Lumsden, 'Stevenson, Scott, and Scottish History', p. 77.
64. Duncan, 'Stevenson and Fiction', p. 21; Gifford, 'Stevenson and Scottish Fiction', p. 74.
65. Gifford, 'Stevenson and Scottish Fiction', pp. 82, 83.

66. Ibid. p. 66.
67. Ambrosini, '"The Man was at My Mercy"', p. 176. For another reading that sees Mackellar, and by extension Henry, as the villains of the text, see Alan Sandison, *Robert Louis Stevenson and the Appearance of Modernism*, pp. 270–316.
68. Kucich, *Imperial Masochism*, p. 41.
69. Ambrosini, '"The Man was at My Mercy"', pp. 179–82.
70. 'Preface to *The Master of Ballantrae*', Huntington Library, HM 20535, reprinted in Poole, ed. *The Master of Ballantrae*, p. 227.
71. Robert Louis Stevenson, 'A Gossip on Romance', p. 57.

Chapter 5

'A kind of partnership business': *The Wrecker* and *The Ebb-Tide*

When Robert Louis Stevenson undertook *The Wrong Box* with his stepson Lloyd Osbourne in 1889, there is every evidence that he did so as a favour, hoping to teach the nineteen-year-old the art of writing and help establish him as an author. Stevenson's own work on *The Master of Ballantrae* (1889) consumed more of his attention. However, when the pair set to work on their next project, the sprawling, ambitious novel *The Wrecker* (1892), Stevenson gave the project the attention befitting his more serious works. The collaboration was not easy, however, and in a letter to his cousin Stevenson details his growing frustration and emphasises Osbourne's subordinate role, complaining that '[t]he great difficulty of collaboration is that you can't explain what you mean' (*Letters* 8: 364). Despite these difficulties, Stevenson was unwilling to give up on the partnership, and after *The Wrecker*, the pair undertook *The Ebb-Tide* (1894). By then the process seems to have failed; Stevenson confessed that the bulk of the work on that novel was his alone. It is my claim that Stevenson's growing dissatisfaction with the collaborative process forms part of the argument of *The Wrecker*, a novel all about partnerships between men and the difficulties those partnerships produce. The protagonist, Loudon Dodd, an aspiring artist, forms a friendship and business partnership with opportunistic Jim Pinkerton. Dodd's story is echoed in the story of Norris Carthew, who like Dodd, is led into morally dubious enterprises and ultimate ruin by an ill-chosen partnership. *The Wrecker* is a novel about partnerships and the compromises they require – of ethics, art and self-interest, written at a moment when Stevenson himself was the most challenged by his own difficult partnership with Osbourne. The process of collaboration, which initially provided Stevenson with inspiration, began to determine formal characteristics of the work in ways that he had not foreseen. Where *The Wrong Box* was begun in a merely playful spirit, and *The Ebb-Tide* finished with a bad faith cynicism about the possibilities of collaboration, I contend that it is *The Wrecker* that stands as Stevenson's most thoroughly collaborative novel, and the one that demonstrates the powers, but also the difficulties, of this mode of writing.

The Wrecker

The Wrecker critiques excesses of capitalism and speculation, while *The Ebb-Tide* turns a similar cynical evaluation of the colonial. *The Wrecker* was planned as one of three tales that Stevenson and Osbourne would write together. Another, *The Pearl Fisher*, became *The Ebb-Tide*, and a third, *The Beachcombers*, never materialised. Unlike with *The Wrong Box* (which Osbourne had begun alone), there was never a thought of putting Osbourne's name first (*Letters* 6: 330). Regardless of whether one considers Osbourne and Stevenson's undertaking on *The Wrong Box* to be a success (as Osbourne did) or a failure (as did Stevenson's publishers), it undoubtedly affected the pair's work on, and the critical response to, *The Wrecker*, which was published serially in Scribner's between August 1891 and July 1892 (*Letters* 6: 340n.) In April 1893 Stevenson wrote to Edward L. Burlingame at Scribner's, complaining that his royalties from American sales were not what he expected based on the book's success in England (*Letters* 8: 56). On 13 June 1893 Charles Scribner wrote back:

> It would be difficult in a letter to attempt to account for any difference in the sale of 'The Wrecker' in England and here but there are one or two suggestions which I think only fair to mention. In the first place the co-operation with Mr Osbourne has not been well received here; 'The Wrong Box' in not an entire success and perhaps created a prejudice against 'The Wrecker.'[1]

Despite the prejudices of publishers and readers, however, *The Wrecker* proved to be one of Stevenson's most innovative and complex works.

The Wrecker, which is Stevenson's longest novel, is also his most Dickensian in that it veers from comedy to violence with a mystery that revolves around characters in disguise. Rivka Galchen describes it as 'part mystery novel, part adventure novel, part mock Künstlerroman', and notes that it was a favourite with Jorge Luis Borges.[2] Stevenson's thought was to present the popular mystery, but embedded in the context of the longer Victorian novel of manners.³ It narrowly surpasses *The Master of Ballantrae* as Stevenson's most globe-trotting novel, travelling almost as much as Stevenson himself – from Michigan, to Scotland, to Barbizon, France (where Stevenson had studied art and met Fanny), San Francisco, Honolulu, Sydney and Midway Island. Though it is international in scope, it is also Stevenson's most American novel, in that it has both an American co-author and also Stevenson's only American protagonist.

The structure of *The Wrecker* is unusual. Stephen Arata describes it as 'the closest thing to a loose baggy monster that Stevenson ever produced', and Caroline McCracken-Flesher describes it as 'a deliberately wandering tale ... Full of incident, it appears, as Stevenson knew, weak on plot.'⁴ In an early table of contents that Stevenson sent to Edward L. Burlingame he identifies the main plot as beginning after chapter ten ('In Which the Crew Vanish'): '(Here the mystery begins and the story proper) up to here, the book is written: 150 pp. of my MS)' (*Letters* 6: 339). At the time of writing this letter Stevenson had written ten chapters and 150 manuscript pages but had not begun the story! He continues, 'I am a little anxious to have it tried serially, as it tests the interest of the mystery' (*Letters* 6: 340). For readers following Stevenson's proposed serialisation, that would have meant waiting for the fourth instalment to discover what the mystery even was.

The novel begins in Michigan, where the main character, Loudon Dodd, grows up. Dodd abandons his father's plan that he study the stock market, deciding instead to pursue a career as a sculptor in France. There he befriends Jim Pinkerton, a would-be journalist, and is eventually persuaded by him to move to San Francisco, where the pair embark on a number of dubious financial schemes. Eventually, Dodd and Pinkerton hear of a wrecked ship called *The Flying Scud*, lying off Midway Island. A mysterious Captain Trent is bidding well over the ship's worth at auction. Hypothesising that this means the ship is full of opium, they bid aggressively and buy it, and Dodd hires a sea captain named Nares and leaves for the Pacific on a salvage mission. When he gets there, the amount of opium is small – not nearly enough for Dodd and Pinkerton to recoup their investment, and this leads to disagreement between the partners. Here (about halfway through the novel), the mystery plot begins as Dodd finds a photograph on board *The Flying Scud* of the captain and crew, who do not match their descriptions. Dodd decides to pursue the mystery by trying to find the first mate, one Goddedaal, but discovers that this is an assumed name for a young high-born Englishman named Norris Carthew. The remainder of the novel is Carthew's narrative.

Carthew explains that he joined up with a dippy partner, Tommy Hadden (a partnership that mirrors that of Dodd and Pinkerton – Phillips calls him an 'exaggerated form of Pinkerton'[5]), and the two had hired a ship, *The Currency Lass*,[6] for an ill-planned business venture in the Pacific. They made more money than expected when they bilked a desperate man in a copra trade, but the rotten *Currency Lass* went under and the crew ended up castaways. *The Flying Scud* appears, ready to rescue them, but the captain of that ship demands all of their (newly gotten) money. Enraged, the crew of *The Currency Lass* murdered the crew of *The Flying Scud* and assumed their identities, so that the false captain now wishes to buy back the ship that exists as evidence of his crimes.

Stevenson and Osbourne had based much of *The Wrecker* on the true story of *The Wandering Minstrel*, which he had learned from John Cameron, the first mate of that ship.[7] (Cameron subsequently published his recollections of the events in a 1928 autobiography.) In 1888 the barque *The Wandering Minstrel*, which claimed to be on a shark-fishing mission, but was almost certainly on an illegal undertaking instead, wrecked in the lagoon of Midway Island, the same island that was fatal to *The Flying Scud* in Stevenson's *The Wrecker*. After spending months marooned on Midway, during which time Cameron and two others left on one of the boats, the remaining crew was eventually rescued by the British schooner *Norma*, but the captain of that ship demanded extortionate fees for the rescue.[8]

Stevenson's main character, Loudon Dodd, is, like the prototypical Stevensonian hero, a man at odds with himself. Dodd's father, who wishes to make a venture capitalist of his son, sends him to the Muskegon Commercial Academy to study investing. There, students gamble on the real market with pretend money, and Dodd, already sceptical of this sort of business, compares it to 'that academy where Oliver met Charlie Bates' (*Wrecker* 21), and, when successful, says he has come 'athwart the hawse of Jay Gould', gilded age railroad speculator and robber baron. Although Dodd, and the novel as a whole, often critique the heartlessness of the market, he nevertheless has a mercenary outlook and a preoccupation with wealth. Reminiscing about his time at the commercial academy, he reflects, 'To remain rich, then, became my problem; or, in other words, to do a safe conservative line of business. I am looking for that line still . . .' (24), showing an ironic lack of self-reflection because the novel has him continuously undertake new risky speculations. Dodd has, or believes he has, the soul of an artist, so he rejects his investments to go to Barbizon, France, to study sculpture instead, where he turns his hand to making the *Genius of Muskegon*, a statue that will represent his home town. Stevenson based the character of Dodd on his friend the artist Will H. Low, to whom he addressed the novel's epilogue (*Letters* 7: 132), but in his struggle between the artist's calling and commercialism Dodd has obvious parallels in Stevenson himself. Like Dodd, Stevenson had also struggled with his father, who wished him to go into first engineering and then law.

Our first introduction to Dodd is in the preface, occurring after the events of the novel, when he lands a yacht on the Marquesas. 'I am sure I don't know how you make this pay,' observes an Englishman on the island, noting the yacht's large size and ostentatious trimmings. Dodd disingenuously retorts, 'I don't know that she does pay ... I never pretend to be a business man; My partner appears happy; and the money is all his, as I told you – I only bring the want of business habits' (*Wrecker* 9) – disingenuous because Dodd has formal schooling in business and thus his rejection of the roles and abilities of the businessman is itself a kind of luxury. (At this point in the novel his partner is Carthew.) This disingenuousness is in fact revealed in Dodd's very appearance, sailing up to the bedraggled bohemian company in a yacht with 'walnut bookshelves' and mirrors that are 'genuine Venice' (7), a picture of the out-of-place new-moneyed capitalist, pretending that he does not care about money. Despite Dodd's near-constant rejection of the values of commerce or of speculation, as the novel progresses he is continuously drawn into venture after venture – a series of get-rich-quick schemes that belie his protests that he is a true artist (and, after all, he is not all that good at art). Just as Hirsch found that *The Wrong Box* reflects Stevenson's own biographical sense of the conflicts between artistry and commercialism, so, too, in his study of *The Wrecker* he finds that Stevenson revisits this theme which is frequently found in his essays.[9] Where Galchen has found that 'All this adventure, it is almost explicitly said, eventually makes of him a kind of artist, or at least his life a kind of work of art, if a very pulpy one', this takes at face value Dodd's own self-assessment; it seems closer to the mark to say that he is a mere *poseur*, ashamed of the fact that his real talents and interests lie in the financial world.[10]

When Dodd meets Jim Pinkerton, a wild speculator and journalist based on Sam McClure of the New York *Sun* (*Letters* 6: 13 n.), he is drawn to the romance of the commercial world that Pinkerton represents: 'Reality was his romance' (*Wrecker* 125). The very tropes of adventure fiction for which Stevenson had become famous are exposed for their commercialism; in *The Wrecker* the treasure itself is cynically revealed as the real source of the adventure rather than merely the motivating fact of the narrative as it had been in *Treasure Island*. Dodd describes global economies as more exciting than buried treasure:

> Suppose a man to dig up a galleon on the Coromandel coast, his rakish schooner keeping the while an offing under easy sail, and he, by the blaze of a great fire of wreckwood, to measure ingots by the bucketful on the uproarious beach: such an [sic] one might realise a greater material spoil; he should have no more profit of romance than Pinkerton when he cast up his weekly balance-sheet in a bald office. Every dollar gained was like something brought ashore from a mysterious deep; every venture made was like a diver's plunge; and as he thrust his bold hand into the plexus of the money-market, he was delightedly aware of how he shook the pillars of existence, turned out men (as at a battle-cry) to labour in far countries, and set the gold twitching in the drawers of millionaires. (*Wrecker* 125)

The way in which the characters, even the sympathetic ones, are motivated by capital above all contributes to what Roderick Watson has found is the novel's 'amoral spirit'.[11] As the setting of the novel moves out of American and into the Pacific, Stevenson's critique of capitalism dove-tails with a critique of imperialism: as Philip Steer has argued, *The Wrecker* as well as *The Ebb-Tide* represent 'a concerted attempt to describe the workings of an emerging form of imperial expansion driven more by multinational forms of financial speculation than national political interests', and Hirsch has identified all the crimes of the novel as being economic in origin, arguing that the novel's climactic murder is itself only 'the tragic culmination of the unscrupulous business practices that have circulated through the novel from the beginning'.[12] Lawrence Phillips argues that, unlike the masculinist fiction to which it gestures, the novel's violence has no 'redeeming ideal' and cannot even be 'construed as justifiable by an appeal to the colonial "idea" which might be expected of the adventure genre'.[13] The true romance of the buried treasure is that of 'ingot'; the true adventurer is not the traveller, but rather the global capitalist, whose actions have far-reaching effects, some of extraordinary violence.

It is Dodd's mercenary partnership with Pinkerton, with its associated difficulties, that is the engine of the novel, and which reflects the increasingly belaboured partnership that authored it. Through this partnership, Dodd is brought into a number of misguided schemes and speculations, including a knock-off brandy business and a picnic cruise that involves Dodd singing maudlin popular ballads as master of ceremonies. When Dodd's art career proves difficult, Pinkerton proposes:

> Come back home with me, and let's throw our whole soul into business. I have the capital; you bring the culture. *Dodd and Pinkerton* – I never saw a better name for an advertisement; and you can't think, Loudon, how much depends on a name. (*Wrecker* 79)

It is as one of these wild speculations that the two purchase the wreck of *The Flying Scud* at auction. This collaboration, which symbolises the corruption of art by business, seems destined to go wrong from the start. Stephen Arata, in his reading of *The Wrecker*, has argued that certain key words in the text such as 'figure' or 'value' do double (or triple) duty in the way in which they 'bridge the realms of art, commerce, and adventure in the novel but also . . . bring them into productive conversation with one another'.[14] I would extend Arata's analysis to include the word 'partner'. In *Deacon Brodie* (1880), much earlier in Stevenson's career, the use of the term 'collaborator' had carried the double sense of the *criminal* collaborator. In *The Wrecker*, Stevenson prefers the term 'partner', alluding to its more specific sense as business partner in its full legal meaning, as well as to the partnership of Stevenson himself with Osbourne.

In a lengthy letter discussed below, Stevenson reports that the most difficult part of the novel to write with Osbourne was the chapter entitled 'Cross-Questions and Crooked Answers', which is the chapter that deals most intricately with the moral and legal nuances of partnership. In this chapter, Dodd returns to San Francisco and Pinkerton, where he is confronted by Pinkerton's new wife, Mamie, who suspects that Dodd does not have her husband's best interest at heart. Mamie's voice in the novel represents a threatening challenge to the male partnerships that structure *The Wrecker*. Not only does she undermine the Dodd–Pinkerton partnership, she also asserts her own claim to be Pinkerton's true partner, when she takes on work as a typist to pull the couple out of poverty: 'But we do not want your charity; thank God, I can work for my own husband!' (*Wrecker* 364). Mamie's scepticism is justified, because the men have at this point been working at cross-purposes to each other, as the chapter title indicates. Dodd and Pinkerton have together purchased the wreck of *The Flying Scud*, but Dodd alone has travelled to Midway Island to recover it, as Pinkerton is going on his honeymoon. Pinkerton has put forward the capital, but Dodd has put forth the greater part of the labour. When the partnership is robust, this seems a reasonable division, but as it begins to show signs of strain each man feels he has a greater claim to the profits.

In an earlier chapter, when Dodd arrives in Hawaii to sell the small cache of opium found on the wreck, he is met by letters from Pinkerton explaining that the partners' firm has gone bankrupt. Pinkerton begs Dodd to turn over any profit to an associate for laundering so that it will not consumed by their creditors. Dodd, who never hesitated at opium smuggling, nevertheless is too principled or too frightened to commit bankruptcy fraud, and so he betrays Pinkerton and sells the opium himself. Meanwhile, Pinkerton feels that *he* has betrayed Dodd because he has blamed Dodd for inconsistencies in the company's books, and represented Dodd as an employee rather than a partner, as he explains at the end of 'Cross-Questions and Crooked Answers': 'And there being no deed of partnership, I made out you were only a kind of clerk that I called a partner just to give you taffy; and so I got you ranked a creditor on the estate for your wages and the money you had lent' (*Wrecker* 374). Here Stevenson plays on the double meaning of the word when it turns out that the two men, partners in the colloquial sense, were not partners in a legal sense. This equivocation, as it happens, saves the pair from ruin. When Dodd learns he has inherited seventeen thousand pounds from his Scottish grandfather, he believes it will be eaten up in the bankruptcy, but because Pinkerton has denied the partnership his inheritance is preserved. In their treatment of the partnership between Dodd and Pinkerton, Stevenson and Osbourne give us a kind of reverse prisoner's dilemma. Each man has in his own way denied the other, but circumstances conspire to make those very denials serve the partnership.

The Wrecker was not the first time Stevenson and Osbourne had interrogated the different meanings of partnership. The novel draws on their earlier, abandoned, collaborative work, *Fighting the Ring*, where they had explored the interplay between loyalty and commercialism within business partnerships. It is there that Stevenson and Osbourne first refer to the deed or contract of partnership which is so significant as a plot element in *The Wrecker*. The fragment even features an established old wealthy family by the name of Carthew, the name of the secondary, aristocratic protagonist from *The Wrecker*'s inset narrative. In *Fighting the Ring*, a copper mining firm called Carthew Brothers and Son is embattled with a larger syndicate, when one business partner, Fanshaw, suddenly decides to force his partner to buy him out. (Osbourne's interest in copper mining may have been inspired by his own father Sam Osbourne's failure as the owner of a silver mine.)

Fanshaw's partner, Hilton, is furious, believing the pair to be friends as well as partners, and says he will be ruined, but Fanshaw reminds him that business is business: "'Really, Hilton,' said Fanshaw, "I regard this as a business transaction; if you are bent on being ruined by the French Syndicate I am not, and I intend to retire. There's no call for this sentiment and exhortation."[15] Fanshaw's son Basil has inherited his father's cutthroat attitude, bragging that "'I intend to make money at all events," exclaimed Basil, "even if I carry business principals so far as to put a pistol to the head of Rothschild himself.'"[16] (The Rothschilds are wrapped up in the syndicate.) This unsentimental and business-like attitude will not characterise Dodd and Pinkerton of *The Wrecker*, both of whom are prone to fall into bitter regrets and fits of conscience as they work out their loyalties. Later in the fragment, Hilton is surprised by a mysterious Scot, who can save his business by selling him a store of copper he has found in the Martin Vaz Islands in Brazil, who is pleased to find Hilton now working alone: "'All the better, all the better,' ejaculated MacAlpine nervously. "It's always easier work dealing with singly [sic] parties.'"[17] Since the fragment ends before we learn the motivations of this character, it is impossible to know how we are to understand his critique of partnerships.

Unlike the more cynical *Fighting the Ring*, *The Wrecker* remains committed to its idealisation of partnership through the epilogue. Although the central partnership between Dodd and Pinkerton loses its primacy, Dodd subsequently works closely with first Captain Nares of the *Norah Creina*, and then becomes entangled in the story of Norris Carthew in what Rod Edmond has described as 'a homosocial romance of adventure and quest' in which Dodd has 'a series of emotionally intense relations with men'.[18] In the epilogue, the pairs are reorganised: Dodd explains that his new yacht belongs to Norris Carthew, who, like Pinkerton, has the capital to support such an adventurer. Pinkerton too has surprisingly re-partnered:

> As for Jim, he's right again: one of the best businesses, they say, in the West, fruit, cereals, and real estate; and he has a Tartar of a partner now – Nares, no less. Nares will keep him straight, Nares has a big head. (*Wrecker* 547)

Captain Nares is a more effective 'man of action' for Pinkerton's incessant American scheming than was Dodd, whose romantic and artistic temperament always made a bad match. And Dodd, as an artist, finds a better partner in Carthew, an old money elite with a more relaxed attitude towards the accumulation of capital.

Years after writing the novel, when *The Ebb-Tide* was in press (and thus when his collaboration with Osbourne had effectively ended), Stevenson reflected on the creation of *The Wrecker* in what would be his most extensive discussion of collaboration:

> Yes, it is in the manner of the book, of course, that collaboration shows; as for the manner, it is superficially all mine, in the sense that the last copy is all in my hand. Lloyd did not even put pen to paper in the Paris scenes or the Barbizon scene; it was no good; he wrote and often rewrote, all the rest; I had the best service from him on the character of Nares. You see, we had been just meeting the man, and his memory was full of the man's words and ways. And Lloyd is an impressionist, pure and simple. The great difficulty of collaboration is that you can't explain what you mean. I know what kind of effect I mean a character to give – what kind of *tache* he is to make; but how am I to tell my collaborator in words? Hence it was easy to say 'make him So-and-so'; and this was all right for Nares and Pinkerton and Loudon Dodd, whom we both knew, but for Bellairs, for instance – a man with whom I passed ten minutes fifteen years ago – what was I to say? and what could Lloyd do? I, as a personal artist, can begin a character with only a haze in my head, but how if I have to translate the haze with words before I begin? In our manner of collaboration (which I think the only possible – I mean that of one person being responsible and giving the *coup de pouce* to every part of the work) I was spared the obviously hopeless business of trying to explain to my collaborator what *style* I wished a passage to be treated in. These are the times that illustrate to a man the inadequacy of spoken language. Now – to be just to written language – I can (or could) find a language for my every mood, but how could I *tell* anyone beforehand what this effect was to be, which it would take every art that I possessed, and hours and hours of deliberate labour and selection and rejection, to produce? These are the impossibilities of collaboration. Its immediate advantage is to focus two minds together on the stuff, and to produce in consequence an extraordinary greater richness of purview, consideration, and invention. The hardest chapter of all was 'Cross Questions and Crooked Answers.' You would not believe what that cost us before it assumed the least unity and colour. Lloyd wrote it at least thrice, and I at least five times – this is from memory. And was that last chapter worth the trouble it cost? Alas, that I should ask the question! Two classes of men – the artist and the educationalist – are sworn, on soul and conscience, not to ask it. You get an ordinary, grinning, red-headed boy, and you have to educate him. Faith supports you; you give your valuable hours, the boy does not seem to profit, but that way your duty lies, for which you are paid, and you must persevere. Education has always seemed to me one of

the few possible and dignified ways of life. A sailor, a shepherd, a schoolmaster – to a less degree, a soldier – and (I don't know why, upon my soul, except as a sort of schoolmaster's unofficial assistant, and a kind of acrobat in tights) an artist, almost exhaust the category. (*Letters* 8: 364–5)

Here Stevenson touches lightly on the positives of collaboration, the 'greater richness of purview, consideration, and invention', but spends more time dwelling on its difficulties. In particular, the difficulty rests on a greater reliance on verbal rather than written language. Stevenson's phrase 'The great difficulty of collaboration is that you can't explain what you mean' from this letter is taken from reflections on communication difficulties that he made years earlier in the fourth and final section of his essay on love and marriage, 'Virginibus Puerisque': 'The difficulty of literature is not to write, but to write what you mean; not to affect your reader, but to affect him precisely as you wish',[19] an essay in which he regrets the inadequacy of language to meaning, comparing it to the exercise clothes that skim an athlete's body – almost but not exactly identical with the skin. Where the 'Virginibus Puerisque' example explores the frustration that Stevenson has communicating with readers, in the letter on *The Wrecker* a third party, the co-author, interposes and exacerbates these difficulties.

However, in that essay it is oral communication which is superior, and written literature which, lacking intimacy and body language, is more difficult. In the letter, Stevenson says the opposite: it is the conversation with Osbourne where the truth is hard to get to.

The letter also underscores that the collaborative process is limited. Even as he discusses the difficulties of collaboration, he is careful to maintain that he is the sole author and is in entire control of the work: 'one person being responsible and giving the *coup de pouce* [helping hand] to every part of the work'. As Gordon Hirsch has demonstrated, Stevenson had been reading Walter Besant on collaboration, and his quote here about the *coup de pouce* 'echoes descriptions . . . of collaboration' Besant had made, specifically his claim that 'one of the two must be in authority: one of the two must have the final word: one of the two must be permitted to put the last touches'.[20] Collaboration becomes an inspiration for the author rather than a challenge to his authority, just as in earlier accounts of his creative process Stevenson had described how reading other works, or dreaming, had served to lend his work 'greater richness'.

His use of simile in his comparison of the artist and the educator barely hides his condescension, suggesting that Lloyd is the 'grinning, red-headed boy' whom he has to 'educate', and who 'does not seem to profit'. The analogy here, strictly speaking, is that author is to his novel as the educator is to his pupil, in that both must stay at their task whether it is going well or poorly. But the close link between vehicle and tenor invites crossover – it is unclear whether it is *The Wrecker* or Osbourne himself that is the source of Stevenson's disappointment, and Osbourne is himself both author of the project and the object of the project simultaneously.

Stevenson's depiction of the collaboration is negative, filled with words like 'difficulty', 'hopeless', 'trouble', 'labour'. As Glenda Norquay has pointed out, in Osbourne's description of the composition process, he 'positioned himself and Stevenson as leisured seekers after pleasure'.[21] Here is Osbourne's description of the same period:

> Here [encamped in Apemama] a large part of 'The Wrecker' was written, and in that collaboration, in spite of my cramped legs, I spent many of the pleasantest hours of my life.
>
> It was exhilarating to work with Stevenson; he was so appreciative, so humourous – brought such gaiety, *camaraderie*, and goodwill to our task. We never had a single disagreement as the book ran its course; it was a pastime, not a task, and I am sure no reader ever enjoyed it as much as we did. Well do I remember him saying: 'It's glorious to have the ground ploughed, and to sit back in luxury for the real fun of writing – which is rewriting.'[22]

The two partners' experiences of the collaboration could not be more different. Whereas Stevenson focuses on the struggles of collaboration, Osbourne focuses on its joys; much as Henley had before him, Osbourne seems to bask in the company of his weightier partner, seeing the work as a diversion and overestimating Stevenson's own joy in the process. Osbourne's metaphor of the plough harks back to the folk song of *The Wrong Box*, discussed earlier, 'The Ploughboy'. In Balfour's biography of Stevenson, Osbourne is quoted using the same metaphor: 'I always wrote the first draft, to break the ground.'[23] Ploughing frequently recurs through Stevenson's oeuvre to mean early, sketchy thinking – not always meant in a derogatory way but often as a positive. For instance, in his 1882 essay 'Talk and Talkers', Stevenson argues that 'Natural talk, like ploughing, should turn up a large surface of life, rather than dig mines into geological strata.'[24] But, however necessary such ploughing might be, it does not represent the real labour of art. Where Stevenson here reflects on his own, metaphorical ploughboy as a 'grinning, red-headed boy', it recalls Shield's 'flaxen-headed ploughboy' of the song who becomes the 'tow-headed' carriage driver of *The Wrong Box*. All these boys are naive about their own ambitions, just as Osbourne naively argues that he has made the writing process *easier* for Stevenson. In fact, Stevenson's own reflections show that the barriers of communication, and the additional need to educate the collaborator, serve to make the process *harder*.

Why, then, would Stevenson undertake such a process, making his work more laborious? One answer that he provides is that, by 'focus[ing] two minds together on the stuff', collaboration will produce 'an extraordinary greater richness of purview, consideration and invention'. This predicts his reflections on Butaritari, where he finds in the conflictual relation of the opera a greater aesthetic possibility, but it also prompts him to ask was it 'worth the trouble it cost'? In the context of both *The Wrong Box* and *The Wrecker* the economic framing of this question is significant, because both novels critique the shallow myopism of commercial culture, as Hirsch and Ambrosini have demonstrated in regard to *The Wrong Box* and Hirsch and Steer have demonstrated in reference to *The Wrecker*. In this letter, Stevenson critiques a strictly commercial view of the author's function when he compares the role of the writer, or the artist, to a sequence of other jobs. All the jobs that Stevenson mentions are thematically connected in that the goals of their practitioners are not always completely aligned with economic goals. The people performing them must show the same dedication whether the work turns profitable or not: the teacher, whose purpose he sees himself as here fulfilling with respect to Osbourne; the shepherd, whose regard for his charges exceeds their economic value; and, most importantly, the sailor, whose duties are not directly determined by the profits of his employer. (This last Stevenson and Osbourne will perversely explore in both *The Wrecker* and *The Ebb-Tide*, two novels that often find the duty of the sailor to safely move a ship from place to place is at odds with the economic interests of the men who finance it.) We see Stevenson returning again to the persistent conflict that Norquay and others have found in his work – between the commercial and artistic missions of the artist – and here suggesting that collaborative work on *The Wrecker* served the latter. If *The Wrong Box* was undertaken in a cynically commercial vein, as Stevenson seemed to suggest, there is evidence that the collaboration in *The Wrecker* was more self-consciously experimental, and more artistic, and that Stevenson may have undertaken it *despite* the difficulties that the process posed and the hit to the novel's marketability that his publisher complained about.

Where Stevenson's collaborative methods began to show the most strain in the composition of *The Wrecker* was in character creation. It is, he acknowledges in his letter above, vastly more difficult to conceive characters collaboratively: 'Hence it was easy to say "make him So-and-so;" and this was all right for Nares and Pinkerton and Loudon Dodd, whom we both knew.' He returns to this concern in a letter to Burlingame that accompanied the manuscript of the first ten chapters, worrying and asking for advice about the fact that the characters were so '*devilish recognizable*', and explaining

> This is not as you know my method of work; and has sprung partly from the scope of the book, partly from convenience in collaboration, when it is so ready a thing to say to your collaborator, 'O, make him so and so! I want your advice as to (a) the success and (b) the decency of this method. (*Letters* 6: 376)

Stevenson had sometimes based characters on real people before (such as Henley as Long John Silver in *Treasure Island*), but with his work with Osbourne this begins to emerge as a real artistic challenge posed specifically by collaboration. Osbourne had devised the characters in their earlier collaboration on *The Wrong Box*, basing the character of Michael Finsbury on Stevenson's friend Charles Baxter. However, with *The Wrecker*, Stevenson had a new challenge – how to create a character himself that Osbourne could also depict? 'I, as a personal artist, can begin a character with only a haze in my head, but how if I have to translate the haze with words before I begin?' (*Letters* 8: 364–5). In this way, the impact of the collaboration goes beyond a question of whose influence might be found in this or that section. Rather, this letter shows Stevenson making drastically different artistic decisions right from the earliest stages of thinking about characterisation; decisions that were shaped by the necessity of this mode of composition. Indeed, in Walter Besant's view of collaboration, with which Stevenson was familiar, only story, and not character, can benefit from the compositional process.[25]

Each character in *The Wrecker* has a counterpart in Stevenson's life, making it a stark departure to his other compositions, where he had sometimes used this method and at other times relied on inspiration. Dodd is based on Stevenson's artist friend Will H. Low, although he certainly has traits traceable to Stevenson himself. Pinkerton was Sam McClure, as mentioned above. The Scottish Stennis brothers whom Dodd meets at Barbizon were Louis himself and his cousin Bob.[26] Tommy Hadden, Norris Carthew's first partner, was based on Tin Jack, a passenger on the *Janet Nicoll*, whom Jolly describes as 'handsome, high-spirited, careless, improvident and childish; the maker and butt of jokes; generous, but with a dubious moral sense; in appearance a cross between a gentleman-beachcomber and an island dandy'.[27] Wing is based upon the Stevenson family's cook, Ah Fu. Nares was based on Captain Otis, the captain of the *Casco*, the ship on which the Stevenson family sailed from San Francisco to the Pacific in 1889. Isobel Field (Belle Strong) writes that

> Captain Otis (you will find him as Nares in *The Wrecker*) was very impatient of the proceedings ... with an oath he thumped his fist against the mainmast, and then stood frozen with horror, for his hand sunk into the wood, which was rotten. If the *Casco* had left that day, sailing as it would have done into stormy weather, it might never have reached Honolulu.[28]

This real-life scene prefigures the fate of *The Currency Lass* in *The Wrecker*. After Irishman Mac easily pulls the stateroom door off its hinges, he observes, 'Why, I see what looks like a patch of dry rot up yonder that I bet I could stick my fist into' (*Wrecker* 479). Soon afterwards, the *Currency Lass* loses her mast in a storm, just like the imagined fate of the *Casco*.

The ease with which real-life people could be used as a short hand to make communication easier was again something he had early on discussed in 'Talk and Talkers'. There, he suggests an important function of fictional characters is to bear a world of meaning in a single name: 'If they know Othello and Napoleon, Consuelo and Clarissa Harlowe, Vautrin and Steenie Steenson, they can leave generalities and begin at once to speak by figures.'[29] As we see here, this method also works in reverse, where real and living people may serve as examples of an entire type of character, an effective way to allow him to continue working with Osbourne, a thing he admitted was becoming increasingly difficult.

Whereas in Stevenson's collaborative writing with Osbourne he relies much more heavily on real-life models, a preface to *The Master of Ballantrae* shows him pulling characters out of his imagination

'A kind of partnership business'   165

Figure 5.1 Self-portrait of artist Will H. Low, Stevenson's friend and the original for Loudon Dodd in *The Wrecker*. William H. Low, *Self-Portrait at Montigny*, 1876, oil on canvas, Smithsonian American Art Museum, Bequest of Henry Ward Ranger through the National Academy of Design.

almost fully formed. (In fact, he describes *The Wrecker* as being in 'singular contrast' to *The Master* because of its 'modern face and opposite methods' (*Letters* 6: 377).) In manuscript pages originally written as part of the preface to *The Master*, Stevenson describes the creation of character, and in particular the Byronic James Durie, the Master of the title. His discussion echoes his earlier comments in 'A Chapter on Dreams', where he describes the creation of *Jekyll and Hyde* (discussed in Chapter 2). Stevenson writes:

> With James Durie himself I never had a moment's stick; I had no model in my eye, whatever, he rose before me, and took shape, and justification, as when a whistler unconsciously and note by note recalls a melody. I have been at school and college with Mackellar and with Henry; the chronicle, as I have said, was drawn from the

possibilities of a callow youth who went long since to the bad; my old Durrisdeer was founded on the face of an old gentleman whom I once loved, although I scarcely knew him, but for the Master I had no original, which is perhaps another way of confessing that the original was no other than myself.[30]

Of course, in his own life, Stevenson was conscientious and loyal, and not at all like the mercurial and vindictive Master, so the equivalence is between, perhaps, the Master and that dreaming self, rather than the waking one. Reinforcing Stevenson's return to the world of the dream as the world of inspiration, he identifies the 'story told to Mackellar on board the *Nonesuch*' with 'a dream I had in Papeete, when I supposed myself to be reading a tale of Edgar Allan Poe's',[31] just as in his letters to Myers he had dreamed he was reading a biography of Jonathan Swift.[32] Here, then, we have presented two different ways of creating character: on the one hand, directly pulling from life, by making Michael Finsbury Charles Baxter, for instance, or, in Stevenson's own words, 'Make him So-and-So', and on the other, Stevenson's sense that characters exist, almost independently, in the unconscious. As in Robert Macfarlane's discussion of *inventio*, the mode of artistry which he describes as that 'more pragmatic account of creation as rearrangement',[33] Stevenson's literary bodysnatching takes his acquaintances as its raw material and breathes into them his inspiration, making them into the character that he requires. A similar practice is at work in the case of Osbourne's drafts, when he inspirits the shell of *A Game of Bluff*, thereby giving life to the raw material. His depiction of the creation of James Durie, on the other hand, recalls an older view of the role of the author, the 'brief, noumenal moment of afflatus or inspiration' which Macfarlane labels *creatio*.[34] Not only are these visions of creation incompatible, but Stevenson begins to feel that the unconscious inspiration model may in fact be incompatible with collaboration, the mode in which he had begun to work more and more, although not without difficulty.

The Ebb-Tide

The Ebb-Tide, published the year of Stevenson's death in 1894, was Stevenson's last completed novel. It was begun in 1889 by Lloyd Osbourne under the title *The Pearl Fisher*. *The Ebb-Tide* is the story of three flawed beachcombers: Herrick, a dissipated and depressed Oxford man who functions as the novel's de facto protagonist;

Davis, an alcoholic American sea captain who has killed his last crew and passengers by sailing while drunk; and a Cockney thug named Huish. The novel is in two parts: in the first, 'The Trio', Stevenson follows the characters as they take commission of a plague ship the *Farallone* and plan to steal her cargo of California champagne, but later find the bottles full of water since the previous captains were planning insurance fraud. In the second half of the novel, 'The Quartette', the three desperate men land on an atoll ruled by a creepy and charismatic missionary named Attwater, whom they plan to rob of his pearls. The novel ends with a violent and inevitable confrontation reminiscent of the endings of both *Treasure Island* and *The Wrecker*: a final violent showdown on the beach of an island between adventurers from two different ships. Although the novel was highly controversial among Stevenson's associates, more recent criticism has identified it as one of Stevenson's best, and most important works, with Alan Sandison venturing that it is 'Stevenson's only wholly serious book'.[35]

According to Osbourne, he himself begun *The Ebb-Tide* (then *The Pearl Fisher*) in Waikiki in 1889, even before he and Stevenson undertook *The Wrecker*.[36] In February of 1890 Stevenson noted that Osbourne had a draft 'half done, mine not touched' (*Letters* 6: 306). In August, he wrote that 'none of [*The Pearl Fisher*] had been done yet except by Lloyd; who is of course quite incapable of turning the ugliness of this rugged, harsh and really striking tale' (*Letters* 6: 405). Osbourne later claimed that 'the first four chapters of *The Ebb Tide* [sic] remain, save for the text of Herrick's letter to his sweetheart, almost as I first wrote them'.[37] In his biography of Stevenson, Osbourne details his disappointments and frustrations trying to win his stepfather's approval:

> I went along swimmingly, and earning R L S's undiminished commendation until I reached the end of the present book, which was originally conceived as a prologue to a much longer novel. Then the commendation ceased; try as I would I could not please R L S; I wrote and rewrote, and rewrote again, but always to have him shake his head. Finally at his suggestion and in utter hopelessness I laid the manuscript by, hoping to come back to it later with greater success. But I never did.[38]

When Stevenson's cousin (later biographer) Graham Balfour found the manuscript years later, he persuaded Stevenson to revisit it. Stevenson rewrote the prologue, turning the events in that section into the entire plot of the novel, mercifully abandoning an earlier planned version wherein the characters would have 'left the Pacific islands and returned to England where they would take part in a series of adventures loosely patterned on *The Count of Monte Cristo*'.[39]

Although Osbourne may have begun the novel, Stevenson soon acknowledged that the novel was his alone. On 23 August 1893 he wrote to Colvin requesting that Osbourne's name be deleted, saying that 'he had nothing to do with the last half' and calling it 'rather unfair to couple his name with so infamous a work' (*Letters* 8: 155–6; see further discussion of this letter below). Osbourne, too, admits 'The Paris parts of *The Wrecker* and the end of *The Ebb Tide* [sic] (as it stands) I never even touched.'[40] I read Stevenson's disparagement of his own novel here as politely disingenuous. In my discussion of Stevenson's correspondence with Sidney Colvin about *The Ebb-Tide* I find evidence that Stevenson, far from thinking the novel infamous or likely to hurt Osbourne's reputation, in fact considered it one of his best works. More likely than not, Stevenson very late wished to regain full credit for a novel on which he had done the balance of the work, and was looking for a way to remove Osbourne while protecting his feelings. Nevertheless, it was, as Stevenson seems to have predicted, too late. Osbourne's name remained.

Wayne Koestenbaum has argued that the initial decision to collaborate means that a text is conceived of in a fundamentally different way than a single-authored text, and furthermore, that the decision to list two authors on a title page (as Stevenson and Osbourne did in *The Ebb-Tide*) substantively changes the way we read a novel, and 'confers enormous interpretive freedom' regardless of if 'one writer eventually produces more material'.[41] Thus, while critics have questioned the extent and significance of Osbourne's collaboration on this text, we must yet recognise that at its conception, when Osbourne laid out the initial ideas for the novel, through to its publication, when Osbourne's name was ultimately *not* removed from the novel, Stevenson and Osbourne thought of *The Ebb-Tide* in the collaborative mode.

We do have three pages of Osbourne's *The Pearl Fisher*, which give us some sense of how much Stevenson changed this original draft. Comparing these three pages with the novel as published confirms that Stevenson deserves the credit both for the style of the novel and for its themes, though we also see how the plot points developed dialogically. For instance, in Osbourne's original draft, he attempts to convey the horror of the three main characters as they discover that the bottles of champagne aboard the ship are in truth water.

'A kind of partnership business'   169

Here is Osbourne's version (labelled as part of chapter seven in his manuscript but describing an occurrence from chapter five in the published novel):

> At the sight of the water, at once so inexplicable and extraordinary, the blankest astonishment fell upon them all; and not a word was spoken as the mug passed from hand to hand, tasted in turn by the captain and Herrick. From the mug their gaze wandered to the bottle that Huish still held in his hand with all its glory of gold paper and engraved label, identical in every particular with the bottles they had opened for days past.
> Without a word Huish took another bottle from the case, and drawing the coil put the top to his lips; he spat, and let the liquid trickle from the bottle to the floor.
> 'I don't seem to catch on,' cried the captain. 'Not three hours ago I opened a bottle as like that as two peas, down even to the slush about its being pure, undoctored Californian juice of the grape, and if that isn't common, stale water, I'll eat my hat.'
> 'It seems to me a very laboured form of humour,' said Herrick, 'and smells of complications with the police if we have much more of it on board.'
> 'There are more complications in it that [sic] you have any idea for,' said the captain shortly. 'We must try another case.' He rose and went with Herrick to his cabin where on the floor . . .[42]

Not much of this is preserved in the final version except the 'glory of the gold paper':

> If the voice of trumpets had suddenly sounded about the ship in the midst of the sea, the three men in the house could scarcely have been more stunned than by this incident. The mug passed round; each sipped, each smelt of it; each stared at the bottle, its glory of gold paper, as Crusoe may have stared at the footprint; and their minds were swift to fix upon a common apprehension.[43]

Although the three men discern the fraud in the exact same way, in *The Pearl Fisher* and *The Ebb-Tide* the style and the emotional impact of the passage is completely different. The psychological horror evident in the published version is absent from Osbourne's treatment, where the characters' concern is more strictly and mundanely with 'complications with the police'.

In the next two pages of Osbourne's manuscript, he describes the *Farallone*'s sighting of Attwater's island: the two pages immediately preceding Part II: The Quartette. Here, Stevenson has preserved Osbourne's exact wording on some lines, though not ones of great significance. It does at least show that Stevenson was still consulting Osbourne's manuscript as far along as the very end of Part I. This is in direct contradiction to Stevenson's claim, corroborated by Osbourne, that 'Up to the discovery of the champagne the tale was all planned between us and drafted by Lloyd; from that moment he has had nothing to do with it except talking it over' (*Letters* 8: 158). ('A Cargo of Champagne' is chapter four, and this scene does not occur until the very end of chapter five.) The captain's query 'How long did he say it was before they raised Anaa? Five hours I think' (*Ebb-Tide* 104) comes from Osbourne. Where Osbourne has Herrick reply 'Five hours' the novel has 'Four or five' (104), and a statement that the wind is 'four or five knot' has been corrected to 'six or seven', perhaps in the service of greater realism and exactitude. In Osbourne's original, he continues:

> 'What breeze had you?' bawled the captain to the original discoverer of the island, who was standing in the waist 'What breeze had you when you see Anaa all same that.'
>
>   'Six or seven knot,' said the man. 'No too much wind, and schooner plenty fast.'[44]

These navigational details stand mostly unchanged. The biggest changes come in the treatment of the native crew. In the novel, Osbourne's 'original discoverer of the island' from the quote above becomes Taveeta, a crew member whom the adventurers condescendingly rename Uncle Ned because of his bald head, exerting what Guy Davidson calls 'the colonialist power to name or to misname'.[45] In Osbourne's original he seems not to be a character, but in the final version he is crucial to the novel's moral message, because he allows us a perspective, that of the Pacific Islanders, from which to critique the European and American interlopers. In an angry outburst, he tells Herrick, '"Ah, no call me Uncle Ned no mo'!" cried the old man. "No my name! My name Taveeta, all-e-same Taveeta, King of Islael. Wat for he call that Hawaii? I think no savvy nothing . . ."'[46] Taveeta insists upon his real name and history, not allowing himself to be seen as the caricature that Davis and Huish have made him out to be, insisting on a specificity of identity that the white men do not recognise among the crew. (They see the crew members as being of one culture, when in fact they do not share the same language and must talk to each other in English (*Ebb-Tide* 77).) It is ironic that the namelessness, or lack of identity, that enrages Taveeta in the novel was in fact present in Osbourne's original pages. Osbourne's draft refers to him only as 'the original discoverer of the island', displaying the same complacency about anonymising him that the final version critiques. My point here is not to condemn Osbourne for failing to perceive a possible development in the novel in this, his very early draft. But the elaboration of this character opens up political nuances in the novel that are unavailable in Osbourne's draft.

Osbourne's manuscript also suggests that Herrick, Huish and Davis plan to maroon the crew on the island when they land there, something that is not contemplated in the novel:

> 'They'll be taken off sooner than we'd want 'em to be,' said the captain hopefully. 'You may lay to that what with warships and letters in bottles.'
> Herrick gazed about him with some compunction as his eyes fell on the unfortunate kanakas who would so soon find themselves Crusoes, and tried to share the captain's hopefulness as to their ultimate fate.[47]

This does, but in a very limited way, prompt Herrick's passive and fruitless shame at the treatment of the crew, something that the revisions to the novel develop more fully when Herrick reflects on the moral superiority of the native crew to himself and his associates: 'It was thus a cutting reproof to compare the islanders and the whites aboard the "Farallone"' (*Ebb-Tide* 77). Osbourne writes simply, '"Those poor kanakas," exclaimed Herrick moodily. "I can't look one of them in the face,"'[48] demonstrating Herrick's emotion but not the larger moral point.

Without the humanity of the crew on board the *Farallone* and the islanders whom Attwater has enslaved, *The Ebb-Tide* would lose its angry edge, becoming a violent and morally empty imperial adventure. Indeed, in Vanessa Smith's reading of *The Ebb-Tide* she concludes that 'The novel Lloyd Osbourne begins by rewriting the plot of *The Wrecker* is laid aside, becomes waste material', and that when Stevenson takes it up again, writing the second half, he 'recycles this waste material into a new *bricolage*'.[49] What makes *The Ebb-Tide* stand out in Stevenson's oeuvre, both to his contemporaries and to critics today, is the darkness of its vision, particularly the violent and disgusting effects of white colonists on the Pacific

Islands. *The Ebb-Tide* highlights the practice of blackbirding, or enslaving native islanders, a long-time concern of both Louis and Fanny Stevenson, as the white sailors press-gang the native crew that they take on the *Farallone*. Even more evil is Attwater's use of island 'labour' to get his pearls.[50] It represents the British and American commercial traders and visitors to the Pacific as thugs and criminals, and does not spare the missionary presence in the islands from critique, as Ann Colley finds the charismatic character of Attwater emblematic of the way 'missionaries became part and parcel of the worst of the larger colonial enterprise'.[51] Attwater was in many respects based on the real-life figure of Tembinok', the murderous tyrant of the Gilberts whom the Stevensons befriended, and towards whose violent and dangerous behaviour the Stevensons seemed to turn a blind eye, but in *The Ebb-Tide* he is reinterpreted as a white imperialist, an unusual transformation that is itself worthy of note. But Attwater lacks Tembinok''s humour, or the warmth in depiction that Stevenson grants him. Only his sociopathic qualities remain. More famously, Attwater has links to that most famous sociopathic imperialist-gone-native, Kurtz, from Conrad's *Heart of Darkness*. Like *Heart of Darkness*, *The Ebb-Tide* offers a violent critique of the ethics of empire, and also like that novel it features a madman ruling a native community as the representative of that empire. Linda Dryden has convincingly argued that Stevenson is in many ways the originator of Conrad's imperial critique, that 'both Stevenson and Conrad refused to perpetuate the imperial romance myth of the nobility and rectitude of the European imperial adventurer, opting instead to expose the profiteering and brutality that they had both witnessed in their own travels'.[52] Also like Conrad's novel, *The Ebb-Tide* reflects the waning of the progressive power of British imperialism, political or commercial.

The Wrecker was also dark, and also cynical about whites on Pacific adventures, particularly in its critical association of global capitalism with the treasure hunt. Yet in its bonds between men – first Dodd and Pinkerton and then Dodd and Carthew – Stevenson and Osbourne show hopeful human connections. In *The Ebb-Tide*, on the other hand, such connections are doomed. Herrick, whose point of view dominates the novel, is himself a sort of reflection of Stevenson in that he is sensitive, thoughtful and educated. Rod Edmond calls him a 'straitened, more desperate vision of Carthew'.[53] But unlike Carthew, who finds in Dodd another young man of taste, able to understand and thus forgive his (actually fairly terrible) crimes, Herrick looks in vain for anyone to mirror his better self back to himself. Instead, he is forced to see himself reflected in his companions: Huish, the other Englishman, is a Cockney without taste or understanding, with whom Herrick cannot possibly sympathise.[54] Though a more suitable companion, the American ship captain Davis is so psychologically damaged by guilt and alcoholism as to be incapable of redemption except through his adoption of a terrifying and cult-like evangelism at the end of the novel. *The Wrecker* had been organised by serial homosocial romances, but these take a dark and ironic turn in the later novel. In his reading of homosocial and homoerotic elements in *The Ebb-Tide*, Davidson has found that 'homosociality in the text constitutes a sadomasochistic economy' that is 'figured in terms of humiliation and torture'[55] – a far cry from the comparatively innocent 'partnership business' of Dodd and Pinkerton.

When Huish, at the end of the novel, throws vitriol into the eyes of Attwater in the final conflict, a scene which offended contemporary readers including Sidney Colvin because of the extremity of its violence, Herrick must face that the moral depravity of his countryman and companion reflects back his own moral vacuity. Where Dodd and Carthew remain excited and motivated by the capitalist adventure, Herrick spends the novel consumed with despair and thoughts of suicide. By implication comparing himself to the bottles of supposed Californian champagne, valueless at their final appraisal, Herrick concludes 'I am broken crockery; the whole of my life has gone to water; I have nothing else to believe in, except my living horror of myself' (*Ebb-Tide* 173). He is neither apt to be born again like his fellow traveller Captain Davis, nor able to summon the will to forcefully reject that proposition. As Cannon Schmitt has pointed out, on the last page of the novel, Herrick's '*Bildung*' is 'inconclusive', his last statement a seeming demurral of the religious rebirth that Davis offers him: 'Herrick, aloof to the bitter end, shows no inclination to that or any other decisive step', and Robert Caserio, similarly, notes that 'The ebbing of the importance of action in [*The Ebb-Tide*] makes it a remarkably antinarrative narrative'.[56] Growth is impossible, or at least it will never be effected through any relationship that the novel might depict.

In fact, *The Ebb-Tide* was so dark that it would result in a long argument with Sidney Colvin about its suitability. In his complaints about the novel, Sidney Colvin made the by now familiar critical move – to blame Osbourne for everything he found wrong with the text, just has Osbourne had been similarly blamed for the problems in *The Wrong Box* and *The Wrecker*, and Fanny blamed for sections of *The Dynamiter* (1885). First, Colvin took his complaints to Stevenson's business manager and their mutual friend Charles Baxter, bemoaning the work's lack of both morality and marketability. Writing to Baxter on 21 June 1893, Colvin complains that *The Ebb-Tide* has 'A good many marks of Lloyd. I doubt if it can be popular: and don't feel sure the Ill. L. N. [*Illustrated London News*] will have it. Don't think we can expect as much as per 1000 words as for a Scots or any pleasanter story', and again, only two days later, 'There are powerful things in the story: but it is like a second "Wrecker" with less variety, and I cannot think will be a great success: I don't think we ought to expect as much for it as for work that is [Louis's] own.' On 27 June, desperately, he writes, 'Whatever happens, please don't let it go to press, for serial or other publication, without my revision. I wish he had worked at any thing [*sic*] else but this . . . I don't think we must expect as big a price for the Ebb Tide as for work which is all his own and more attractive in character.' On 22 July, angry that he had received a picture of Fanny in lieu of the wished-for end of the novel, he wonders (again to Baxter) if, after the serial publication of *The Ebb-Tide*, it should be 'suppressed and not appear as a book at all'. After finally reading the novel's violent, climactic scenes, he conceded that 'hatefully ugly & vicious as they are, are nevertheless done with astonishing genius' (22 July), and urged Baxter to 'get the story set up in book form & registered by some publisher to protect the book rights' (2 August). Shortly afterwards he changed his mind again and was again set on suppression: 'This makes many months now that he has been unable to write any fiction (except the Ebb-Tide, which will do him no good, and if it were published as a book would undo much of the effect of Catriona)' (17 September). (*Catriona* (1893) is an alternate title for *David Balfour*, the sequel to *Kidnapped* (1886). One of his Scottish novels, it was just the kind of adventure many of his friends wished he would return to, instead of spending his time on dark moralisings about the Pacific.) All of this plotting to suppress the book publication was, it must be noted, without Stevenson's permission and in opposition to his wishes.[57]

Then, in October, Colvin began assailing Stevenson himself with his complaints about the text, hurting Stevenson's feelings in the process. As to Colvin's supposition that Osbourne was mostly responsible for the book, Stevenson would shortly correct him. Two months later, he refers to Colvin's 'pleasing letter *re The Ebb-Tide*' with sarcasm (the letter was not pleasing but hurtful), and asks him to delete Osbourne's name:

> I propose, if it be not too late, to delete Lloyd's name. He has had nothing to do with the last half. The first we wrote together, as the beginning of a long yarn. The second is entirely mine; and I think it rather unfair to couple his name with so infamous a work. Above all, as you had not read the two last chapters, which seem to me the most ugly and cynical of all. Should there be time to drop his name out, I *direct* that some sentences deleted on the last page shall be replaced; they should be easily decipherable. (*Letters* 8: 156)

Here, Stevenson wonders that Colvin could have been so offended before even reading the most violent passages. Yet at the same time he expresses his intention to reverse some of Colvin's censorship of the last pages of the novel should Osbourne's name be removed – to make it, in other words, still more violent and grim. It is difficult to read Stevenson's intention in this letter. Did he truly wish to protect Osbourne from the association with 'so infamous a work'? Or was Colvin's critique merely a cover for him to resume full credit for a text on which he had done most of the work? I find the second explanation more likely. Stevenson appears to have remained committed to *The Ebb-Tide*. He had written to Colvin in May bragging that 'it seems to me to go off with a considerable bang; in fact, to be an extraordinary work: but whether popular! . . . In short, as you see, I'm a trifle vainglorious' (*Letters* 8: 68), so Colvin's criticisms that followed likely stung. Similarly, he writes to his mother, 'I believe you will think it vile . . . Yet I think it has a certain merit' (*Letters* 8: 79). Only after Colvin's initial criticisms did he become more defensive about the work, but even so, he was greatly pleased when Charles Baxter appeared to like it, admitting that 'Colvin (between ourselves) is a bit of an old wife' (*Letters* 8: 256). Julia Reid has discussed Stevenson's self-deprecating association of the novel with the works of Zola, an author whom Stevenson had long derided, noting that in Stevenson's letters this results not in his rejection of *The Ebb-Tide* but rather in a more positive reappraisal of Zola.[58] Stevenson's own criticisms of what he ironically called (again to Colvin) 'the ever-to-be-execrated *Ebb-Tide*, or Stevenson's Blooming Error' (*Letters* 8: 94) must be taken with a grain of salt. Colvin's response to Stevenson's statement that Osbourne had little to do with the novel is similarly disingenuous. 'What you say about the co-operation is pretty much what I had guessed.'[59] Of course, this is not true, as we have seen in his letter of 21 June he had already written to Baxter blaming Osbourne for the text's problems.

Where he was initially impressed with the power of the last chapters, eventually Colvin would recoil from them the most, even now that he could no longer blame Osbourne's collaborations. He pleaded with Stevenson in the same letter:

> The man who can write Catriona owes a great debt to – what you will, Mankind, or his maker, who knows: he has the power to be one of the great permanent benefactors of the human race & alleviators of human fate: and he goes and commits an outrage like that with a light heart. The last two chapters, now I've had them before me set up, seem more hateful, if not less powerful, than before; and hateful with a kind of levity that is really shocking; I'm not squeamish, but Huish's blasphemies are too much for me.[60]

And, in February of 1894 he even criticises Stevenson for liking his own work:

> Am sorry to hear you like the Ebb-Tide; had much hoped you wouldn't. For I'm d—d if it's good, – or interesting, till you get to the tussle between the rogues and Attwater: and what have you to say in defense of the plot? . . . to leave out of count altogether the general revoltingness, in which you are but one with your age: but then the chief point about you used to be that alone in your generation you had the gift and the instinct for imaginative beauty and charm. Well, well, we must wait for the next thing: – though I supposed revoltingness will be a chief note of the Hanging Judge book, inevitably: but let us hope there will be beauty too.[61]

(The 'Hanging Judge book' would be *Weir of Hermiston*, another novel set in Scotland like *Catriona*, but which Stevenson would not live to finish.) Finally, frustrated with his inability to move Stevenson, he wrote again to Baxter, humorously, and sadly, on 2 April 1894, 'My letter from L. was short, last week, and rather to my distress complacent over the Ebb-Tide, which I had sent him in print, and for which, coming fresh to it, I hoped he would share my aversion.'[62] It is evident to me that this was wishful thinking on the part of Colvin – Stevenson thought it was one of his better works, wished he had worked on it alone, and was frustrated with Colvin's inability to appreciate it.

The new direction that *The Ebb-Tide* represents in Stevenson's literary career was one that he would have had to continue alone, however. The political realism did not align with Osbourne's interests or talents, as Osbourne was always more attracted to the more dandyish formal experiments that had characterised works such as Stevenson's *New Arabian Nights*. Stevenson died at the age of forty-four, leaving two novels unfinished: *Weir of Hermiston* (1896) and *St. Ives* (1897). He also left unfinished his larger geographic and ethnographic work on the Pacific, which owes its stripped-down conversational form to the posthumous editing of Sidney Colvin. No one could ever know for certain what would have happened to Stevenson's writing if his life had not been cut short at that moment, and yet there are some clues. Increasingly, his writing at the end of his life was darker, more political and critical of empire, more realistic, and, significantly, less collaborative, particularly when we look at the arc of his three collaborations with Osbourne on *The Wrong Box*, *The Wrecker* and *The Ebb-Tide*. By the end of *The Ebb-Tide*, Osbourne's contributions had dwindled to nothing, and among the family at Vailima, no one stood ready to take Osbourne's place as a new collaborator.

It was a long way from Stevenson's early attempts at collaborating on plays with Henley, which after all for Stevenson had been more of a diversion. However, as Stevenson grew as an artist, so his involvement in a collaborative process deepened, and informed his view of the creative process. He experimented with ways to decentre his authorial process and create a more dialogic mode of composition, first with Henley, later with Fanny Stevenson, and finally with Osbourne, despite the fact that because of his celebrity one might have expected a self-centred writing practice. Instead, he developed an aesthetic experimentation that would in many ways predict the 'salon culture' called of the early twentieth century. It didn't serve him financially, nor did it help his reputation, either then or now. Yet this lifelong experimentation with collaborative composition both influenced, and was influenced by, related themes found in almost all of his work. We see it in the much-noted prevalence of doubling, most famous in *Jekyll and Hyde* but really found in everything he wrote, and in his fascination with ideas of a divided self or proto-subconscious, again famously in *Jekyll and Hyde* but also in other works such as 'A Chapter on Dreams' and 'Markheim'. However, there was in Stevenson's career another strain – his growing interest in political subjects, especially imperialism and international relations, which is barely detectable at the time he is writing *Jekyll and Hyde*, but becomes, by the time of *The Ebb-Tide*, the governing theme of his thought and writing. This topic, while equally cutting edge, demanded a more serious, realistic consideration, and the formal experiments consequently fell away. As his epigraph to *The Ebb-Tide* has it, 'there is a tide in the affairs of men', and for Stevenson it seems that at the end this collaborative tide had gone out and the experiment had ended.

Notes

1. Charles Scribner to Robert Louis Stevenson, 13 June 1893, Edwin J. Beinecke Collection of Robert Louis Stevenson, GEN MSS 664 box 18 folder 493.
2. Rivka Galchen, 'Borges on Pleasure Island', *New York Times Sunday Book Review* (25 June 2010), http://www.nytimes.com/2010/06/27/books/review/Galchen-t.html Galchen may have in mind an interview with Borges in which he states: 'By the way, there's a book no one seems to have read. He wrote it in collaboration with Lloyd Osbourne, a detective novel or, as he called it, a police-novel – *The Wrecker*. I would like you to read that book; I think it's a very fine book', in Yates, 'A Colloquy with Jorge Luis Borges', p. 152.
3. Phillips, *The South Pacific Narratives*, p. 96.
4. Arata, 'Stevenson's Careful Observances', para. 7, McCracken-Flesher, '*The Wrecker*: Unplacing Space in the South Seas', p. 47.
5. Phillips, *The South Pacific Narratives*, p. 130.
6. The name of Carthew's ship comes from the slang term for a second-generation Australian, a 'Currency Lad' (as opposed to a first-generation Australian, or a Sterling). Currency lads were stereotypically poor, hence their association with paper money, as opposed to the metal money (Sterling) of a recent immigrant. This opposition speaks to the novel's interest in debt and speculation, in both Dodd's and Carthew's stories, as well as to the fact that the ship itself is of inferior quality. Thanks to Amy Potter for this connection.
7. Fanny Stevenson, *The Cruise of the* Janet Nichol *among the South Seas Islands*, ed. Roslyn Jolly, pp. 142–3; see also Fanny Stevenson, preface to Robert Louis Stevenson and Lloyd Osbourne, *The Wrecker*, pp. xix–xx. Future references to this edition will be cited parenthetically as *Wrecker*.
8. Cameron, *John Cameron's Odyssey*.
9. Hirsch, 'The Commercial World of *The Wrecker*', p. 77; see also Vanessa Smith, *Literary Culture and the Pacific*, pp. 145–56.
10. Galchen, 'Borges on Pleasure Island'.
11. Watson, '"The Unrest and Movement of Our Century"', p. 114.
12. Steer, 'Romances of Uneven Development: Spatiality, Trade, and Form in Robert Louis Stevenson's Pacific Novels', pp. 343–4; Hirsch, 'The Commercial World of *The Wrecker*', p. 87.
13. Phillips, *The South Pacific Narratives*, p. 93.

14. Arata, 'Stevenson's Careful Observances', para. 12.
15. Lloyd Osbourne and Robert Louis Stevenson, manuscript of *Fighting the Ring*, Beinecke, p. 4.
16. Ibid. p. 11.
17. Ibid. p. 16.
18. Edmond, *Representing the South Pacific*, p. 178.
19. Robert Louis Stevenson, 'Virginibus Puerisque', p. 41.
20. Hirsch, 'Locating RLS in Relation to Brander Matthews's and Walter Besant's Theories', pp. 103, 100. Hirsch cites Walter Besant, 'On Literary Collaboration', *New Review* 6 (1892): 204–5.
21. Norquay, *Robert Louis Stevenson and Theories of Reading*, p. 182.
22. Osbourne, *Intimate Portrait*, pp. 107–8.
23. Balfour, *Life of Robert Louis Stevenson*, vol. 2, p. 41.
24. Robert Louis Stevenson, 'Talk and Talkers', pp. 268–9.
25. Hirsch, 'Locating RLS', p. 99.
26. William Gray, 'Stevenson's "Auld Alliance"', p. 55.
27. Jolly, Introduction to Fanny Stevenson, *The Cruise of the* Janet Nichol *among the South Seas Islands*, ed. Roslyn Jolly, p. 31.
28. Isobel Field, *This Life I've Loved: An Autobiography* (Lafayette, CA: Great West Books), p. 209.
29. Robert Louis Stevenson, 'Talk and Talkers', pp. 269–70.
30. Robert Louis Stevenson, 'Preface to the *Master of Ballantrae*', p. 227.
31. Ibid. p. 228.
32. See Chapter 1.
33. Macfarlane, *Original Copy*, p. 6.
34. Ibid. p. 6.
35. Sandison, *Robert Louis Stevenson and the Appearance of Modernism*, p. 317.
36. Osbourne, *Intimate Portrait*, p. 94.
37. Quoted in Balfour, *Life of Robert Louis Stevenson*, vol. 2, p. 42.
38. Osbourne, *Intimate Portrait*, p. 98.
39. Kerrigan, introduction to *The Ebb-Tide*, p. xviii; Balfour, *Life of Robert Louis Stevenson*, vol. 2, p. 171.
40. Quoted in Balfour, *Life of Robert Louis Stevenson*, vol. 2, p. 41.
41. Koestenbaum, *Double Talk*, p. 2.
42. Robert Louis Stevenson and Lloyd Osbourne, *The Ebb-Tide* manuscript, Edwin J. Beinecke Collection of Robert Louis Stevenson, GEN MSS 664 box 29 folder 673.
43. Robert Louis Stevenson, *The Ebb-Tide*, p. 93. Future references to this edition will be cited parenthetically as *Ebb Tide*.
44. Stevenson and Osbourne, *The Ebb-Tide* manuscript.
45. Davidson, 'Homosocial Relations', p. 132.
46. Taveeta's association of himself with King David derives from his religious practice: while the officers of the *Farallone* spend their time drinking, the crew is engaged in hymns and Bible reading. The name

also suggests a contrast with Captain Davis, who also bears the name of that king, and whose dramatic but unhinged conversion ends the novel. However, Sandison points out that the name of David/Taveeta 'can only be a missionary conferred name' and is thus in itself a kind of misnaming. Sandison, *Robert Louis Stevenson and the Appearance of Modernism*, p. 334.
47. Stevenson and Osbourne, *The Ebb-Tide* manuscript.
48. Ibid.
49. Vanessa Smith, *Literary Culture and the Pacific*, p. 161.
50. See Jolly, 'Piracy, Slavery, and the Imagination of Empire' for an extensive discussion of blackbirding and slavery in *The Ebb-Tide*.
51. Colley, *Robert Louis Stevenson and the Colonial Imagination*, p. 40. Stevenson later revised this into the more conciliatory figure of Tarleton in 'The Beach of Falesá', according to Colley (p. 41).
52. Dryden, 'Literary Affinities and the Postcolonial in Robert Louis Stevenson and Joseph Conrad', p. 87. See also Sandison, *Robert Louis Stevenson and the Appearance of Modernism*, pp. 317–68 for further discussion of the novel's connections to *Heart of Darkness*.
53. Edmond, *Representing the South Pacific*, p. 181.
54. For class-based readings of *The Ebb-Tide*, and in particular critiques of Stevenson's characterisation of the working class, see Phillips, *The South Pacific Narratives*, pp. 183–4, and Davidson, 'Homosocial Relations', pp. 129–30.
55. Davidson, 'Homosocial Relations', pp. 135–6.
56. Cannon Schmitt, 'Technical Maturity in Robert Louis Stevenson', p. 74; Caserio, 'Narrative and Narratology: The Ebb Tide of Action', p. 84.
57. Sidney Colvin to Charles Baxter, 21 June 1893, 23 June 1893, 27 June 1893, 22 July 1893, 2 August 1893 and 17 September 1893, all Edwin J. Beinecke Collection of Robert Louis Stevenson, GEN MSS 664 box 11 folder 281.
58. Reid, *Robert Louis Stevenson, Science, and the* Fin de Siècle, p. 44.
59. Sidney Colvin to Robert Louis Stevenson, 15 October 1893, Edwin J. Beinecke Collection of Robert Louis Stevenson, GEN MSS 664 box 11 folder 284.
60. Ibid.
61. Sidney Colvin to Robert Louis Stevenson, February, 1894, Edwin J. Beinecke Collection of Robert Louis Stevenson, GEN MSS 664 box 11 folder 286.
62. Sidney Colvin to Robert Louis Stevenson, 2 April 1894, Edwin J. Beinecke Collection of Robert Louis Stevenson, GEN MSS 664 box 11 folder 281.

Bibliography

Manuscript Collections

Edwin J. Beinecke Collection of Robert Louis Stevenson. Beinecke Library, Yale University, New Haven, CT.
Huntington Library, San Marino, CA.
Robert Louis Stevenson Collection, Beinecke Library, Yale University, New Haven, CT.
Robert Louis Stevenson Museum, St. Helena, CA.

Primary Works by Robert Louis Stevenson, Collaborators and Others

Henley. W. E. 'Invictus'. 1875. *Poetry Foundation.* https://www.poetryfoundation.org/poems/51642/invictus (last accessed 31 October 2018).
Horan, Nancy. *Under the Wide and Starry Sky.* New York: Ballantine Books, 2014.
James, Henry. 'Greville Fane'. *The Complete Tales of Henry James*, vol. 8, ed. Leon Edel. Philadelphia: J. B. Lippincott and Company, 1963.
Kizer, Carolyn. 'Fanny', in *Pro Femina. Cool, Calm, and Collected: Poems, 1960–2000* (Port Townsend, WA: Copper Canyon Press, 2001), reprinted at Poetry Foundation, https://www.poetryfoundation.org/poems/42603/fanny (last accessed 31 October 2018).
Stevenson, Fanny Van de Grift. *The Cruise of the* Janet Nichol *among the South Seas Islands: A Diary by Mrs Robert Louis Stevenson*, ed. Roslyn Jolly. Seattle: University of Washington Press, 2004.
—. *The Cruise of the* Janet Nichol *among the South Sea Islands: A Diary by Mrs Robert Louis Stevenson.* New York: Scribner's, 1914.
—. 'The Nixie'. *Scribner's*, March 1888: 277–84.
Stevenson, Robert Louis. *The Beach of Falesá.* In *Island Nights' Entertainments.* London: Hogarth Press, 1987.
—. 'The Body-Snatcher'. In *Selected Short Stories of R. L. Stevenson*, ed. Ian Campbell, 76–92. 2nd edn. Glasgow: Kennedy and Boyd, 2012.

—. 'A Chapter on Dreams'. In *Across the Plains*, 248. New York: Scribner's, 1897. https://archive.org/details/acrossplainswit00stevgoog (last accessed 31 October 2018).

—. 'Child's Play'. *The Cornhill Magazine* 38 (1878): 352–9. http://digital.nls.uk/rlstevenson/browse/archive/78694546 (last accessed 31 October 2018).

—. 'A Gossip on Romance'. In *Selected Poetry and Prose of Robert Louis Stevenson*, ed. Bradford Booth, 55–5. Boston, MA: Houghton Mifflin Co., 1968.

—. *Essays I: Virginibus Puerisque and Other Papers*, ed. Robert Louis Abrahamson. Edinburgh: Edinburgh University Press, 2018.

—. *In the South Seas*, ed. Neil Rennie. New York: Penguin, 1998.

—. *In the South Seas and A Footnote to History*. New York: Scribner's, 1905.

—. *Kidnapped*. New York: Scribner's, 1925.

—. *The Master of Ballantrae*, ed. Adrian Poole. New York: Penguin, 1996.

—. *New Arabian Nights*. New York: Current Literature Publishing Co., 1913.

—. 'Some Portraits by Raeburn'. *Virginibus Puerisque and Other Papers*. London: C. K. Paul & Co., 1881. https://archive.org/details/virginibuspueris00steviala (last accessed 31 October 2018).

—. 'The South Seas: Life under the Equator. Letters from a Leisurely Traveller'. Number 14. *The Sun* (24 May 1891): 23–30. http://chroniclingamerica.loc.gov/lccn/sn83030272/1891-05-24/ed-1/seq-23/ (last accessed 31 October 2018).

—. *Strange Case of Dr Jekyll and Mr Hyde*, ed. Richard Dury. Edinburgh: Edinburgh University Press, 2004.

—. 'Talk and Talkers'. 1882. *Memories and Portraits: The Travels and Essays of Robert Louis Stevenson*, vol. 13, 265–79. New York: Scribner's, 1895.

—. 'Tutuila'. 1891. *Hitherto Unpublished Prose Writings*. Ed. Henry H. Harper. Boston, MA: The Bibliophile Society. 1921. 115–56.

—. 'Virginibus Puerisque'. *The Travels and Essays of Robert Louis Stevenson*, vol. 13, 3–50. New York: Scribner's, 1895.

—. *Weir of Hermiston*, ed. Catherine Kerrigan. *The Collected Works of Robert Louis Stevenson*. Edinburgh: Edinburgh University Press, 1995.

Stevenson, Robert Louis and Fanny Van de Grift Stevenson. *The Hanging Judge*. In *Plays*. New York: Charles Scribner's Sons, 1925.

—. *The Hanging Judge*, ed. Edmund Gosse. London: Printed for Private Circulation by Thomas J. Wise, Hampstead, N.W., 1914.

—. *More New Arabian Nights: The Dynamiter*. New York: Standard Book Company, 1930.

—. *More New Arabian Nights: The Dynamiter*, ed. Edmund Gosse. *The Works of Robert Louis Stevenson*, vol. 6. Pentland Edition. London: Cassell and Company, 1907.

Stevenson, Robert Louis and Lloyd Osbourne. *The Ebb-Tide*. Chicago: Stone and Kimball, 1895.
—. *The Ebb-Tide*, ed. Peter Hinchcliffe and Catherine Kerrigan. *The Collected Works of Robert Louis Stevenson*. Edinburgh: Edinburgh University Press, 1996.
—. *The Wrecker*. New York: Scribner's, 1905.
—. *The Wrong Box*, ed. Edmund Gosse. *The Works of Robert Louis Stevenson*, vol. 7. Pentland Edition. London: Cassell and Company, 1907.
—. *The Wrong Box*, ed. Ernest Mehew. London: The Nonesuch Press, 1989.
Stevenson, Robert Louis and W. E. Henley. *Deacon Brodie*. In *Plays*. New York: Charles Scribner's Sons, 1925.

Letters and Biographies

Balfour, Graham. *The Life of Robert Louis Stevenson*, 2 vols. New York: Scribner's, 1916.
Bell, Ian. *Dreams of Exile: Robert Louis Stevenson: A Biography*. New York: Henry Holt, 1992.
Calder, Jenni. *Robert Louis Stevenson: A Life Study*. New York: Oxford University Press, 1980.
Cameron, John. *John Cameron's Odyssey*, ed. and transcribed by Andrew Farrell. New York: The Macmillan Company, 1928. https://archive.org/details/johncameronsodys00came. (last accessed 31 October 2018).
Cohen, Edward H. *The Henley–Stevenson Quarrel*. Gainesville: University Presses of Florida, 1974.
Field, Isobel. *This Life I've Loved: An Autobiography*. Lafayette, CA: Great West Books, 2005.
Furnas, J. C. *Voyage to Windward: The Life of Robert Louis Stevenson*. New York: William Sloane Associates, 1951.
Henley, W. E. *The Selected Letters of W. E. Henley*, ed. Damian Atkinson. Aldershot: Ashgate, 2000.
Kipling, Rudyard. *Something of Myself: For My Friends Known and Unknown*. London: Macmillan, 1937.
Lapierre, Alexandra. *Fanny Stevenson: A Romance of Destiny*, trans. Carol Cosman. New York: Carroll and Graf, 1995.
Lucas, E. V. *The Colvins and Their Friends*. New York: Scribner's, 1928.
Mackay, Margaret. *The Violent Friend: The Story of Mrs Robert Louis Stevenson*. New York: Doubleday, 1968.
McClure, Samuel S. *My Autobiography*. New York: Frederick A. Stokes Company, 1914.
Osbourne, Lloyd. *An Intimate Portrait of R. L. S.* New York: Scribner's, 1924.
Papers Relating to the Foreign Relations of the United States, Transmitted to Congress, With the Annual Message of the President, 1 December 1884. *Office of the Historian*. https://history.state.gov/

Stevenson, Margaret. *From Saranac to the Marquesas and Beyond: Being Letters Written by Mrs M. I. Stevenson during 1887–88, to her Sister Jane Whyte Balfour, with a Short Introduction by George W. Balfour, M.D., LL. D., F. R. S. E.*, ed. Marie Clothilde Balfour. New York: Scribner's, 1903. https://archive.org/details/fromsaranactomar00stevuoft. (last accessed 31 October 2018).

Stevenson, Robert Louis. *The Letters of Robert Louis Stevenson*, ed. Bradford Booth and Ernest Mehew. New Haven: Yale University Press, 1994–5.

Sturgeon, Mary C. *Michael Field*. London: G. G. Harrap, 1922. https://archive.org/details/michaelfield00sturiala. (last accessed 31 October 2018).

Willis, Laulii. *The Story of Laulii, a Daughter of Samoa*, ed. William H. Barnes. San Francisco: Winterburn and Co, 1889. https://archive.org/details/storyoflauliidau00williala. (last accessed 31 October 2018).

Literary Theory, Criticism and History

Ambrosini, Richard. '"The Man Was at My Mercy (So Far as Any Credit Went)": A Counter-Reading of Mackellar's Book'. In *Letter(s): Functions and Forms of Letter-Writing in Victorian Art and Literature*, ed. Mariaconcetta Costantini, Francesco Marroni and Anna Enrichetta Soccio, 175–211. Studi de Anglistica 15. Rome: Aracne, 2009.

—. 'R. L. Stevenson and the Ethical Value of Writing for the Market'. *Journal of Stevenson Studies* 1 (2004): 24–41.

—. 'Stevenson's Self-Portrait as a Popular Author in the *Scribner's* Essays and *The Wrong Box*'. *Journal of Stevenson Studies* 4 (2007): 151–68.

Arata, Stephen. 'Stevenson and Fin-de-Siècle Gothic'. In *The Edinburgh Companion to Robert Louis Stevenson*, ed. Penny Fielding, 53–69. Edinburgh, Scotland: Edinburgh University Press, 2010.

—. 'Stevenson's Careful Observances'. *Romanticism and Victorianism on the Net* 47 (2007): n.p. doi: 10.7202/016704ar.

Bakhtin, M. M. 'Discourse in the Novel'. In *The Dialogic Imagination*, ed. Michael Holquist, trans. Caryl Emerson and Michael Holquist, 259–422. Austin: University of Texas Press, 1981.

Barthes, Roland. 'The Death of the Author'. In *The Rustle of Language*, trans. Richard Howard, 49–55. Berkeley: University of California Press, 1989.

Beattie, Hilary J. 'Dreaming, Doubling and Gender in the Work of Robert Louis Stevenson: The Strange Case of "Olalla"'. *Journal of Stevenson Studies* 2 (2005): 10–31.

—. 'Fanny Osbourne Stevenson's Fiction: "The Nixie" in Context'. *Journal of Stevenson Studies* 11 (2013): 127–50.

—. 'Father and Son: The Origins of *Strange Case of Dr Jekyll and Mr Hyde*'. In *The Psychoanalytic Study of the Child* 56, ed. Albert J. Solnit, Peter B.

Neubauer, Samuel Abrams and A. Scott Dowling, 317–60. New Haven: Yale University Press, 2001.
Bellanca, Mary Ellen. 'After-Life-Writing: Dorothy Wordsworth's Journals in the Memoirs of William Wordsworth'. *European Romantic Review* 25, no. 2 (April 2014): 201–18.
Bernhard Jackson, Emily A. 'Twins, Twinship, and Robert Louis Stevenson's *Strange Case of Dr Jekyll and Mr Hyde*'. *Victorian Review* 39, no. 1 (2013): 70–86. doi: 10.1353/vcr.2013.0014.
Besant, Walter. 'On Literary Collaboration'. *New Review* 6 (1892): 200–09.
Bleakney, F. Eileen. 'Folk-lore from Ottawa and Vicinity'. *The Journal of American Folklore* 31, no. 120 (1918): 158–69. http://www.jstor.org/stable/534872
Bloom, Lynn Z. '"I write for myself and strangers": Private Diaries as Public Documents'. In *Inscribing the Daily: Critical Essays on Women's Diaries*, ed. Suzanne L. Bunkers and Cynthia A. Huff, 23–37. Amherst: University of Massachusetts Press, 1996.
Bolyanatz, Alexander. *Pacific Romanticism: Tahiti and the European Imagination*. Westport: Prager, 2004.
Brantlinger, Patrick. *Rule of Darkness: British Literature and Imperialism, 1830–1914*. Ithaca: Cornell University Press, 1988.
Buckton, Oliver S. *Cruising with Robert Louis Stevenson: Travel, Narrative, and the Colonial Body*. Athens: Ohio University Press, 2007.
Cairney, John. 'Helter-Skeltery: Stevenson and Theatre'. In *Robert Louis Stevenson Reconsidered: New Critical Perspectives*, ed. William B. Jones, Jr., 192–208. Jefferson, NC: McFarland, 2003.
Caserio, Robert L. 'Narrative and Narratology: The Ebb Tide of Action'. In *Approaches to Teaching the Works of Robert Louis Stevenson*, ed. Caroline McCracken-Flesher, 83–8. New York: Modern Language Association of America, 2013.
Chen, Mingyuan, Carlos Fonesca, Laura McAleese, Alba Morollón Díaz-Faes, Elizabeth Nicholas and Robyn Pritzker. *Deciphering* The Dynamiter: *A Study in Authorship. Attribution*. http://thedynamiter.llc.ed.ac.uk/ (last accessed 31 October, 2018).
Cohen, Milton A. '"To Stand on the Rock of the Word 'We'": Appeals, Snares, and Impact of Modernist Groups before World War I'. In *Modernist Group Dynamics: The Politics and Poetics of Friendship*, ed. Fabio A. Durão and Dominic Williams, 1–26. Newcastle upon Tyne: Cambridge Scholars Publishing, 2008.
Colley, Ann C. *Robert Louis Stevenson and the Colonial Imagination*. Burlington: Ashgate, 2004.
—. 'Robert Louis Stevenson's South Seas Crossings'. *SEL: Studies in English Literature 1500–1900* 48, no. 4 (2008): 871–84. doi: 10.1353/sel.0.0034.
Copper, Thomas. 'Nineteenth-Century Spectacle'. In *French Music Since Berlioz*, ed. Richard Langham Smith and Caroline Potter, 19–52. Burlington: Ashgate, 2006.

Danahay, Martin. 'Dr Jekyll's Two Bodies'. *Nineteenth-Century Contexts: An Interdisciplinary Journal* 35 (2013): 23–40.

Davidson, Guy. 'Homosocial Relations, Masculine Embodiment and Imperialism in Stevenson's *The Ebb-Tide*'. *English Literature in Transition: 1880–1920* 47, no. 2 (2004): 123–41. doi:10.2487/7456-2056-W426-X427.

Davies, Corinne and Marjorie Stone. '"Singing Song for Song": The Brownings in the Poetic Relation'. In *Literary Couplings: Writing Couples, Collaborators, and the Construction of Authorship*, ed. Marjorie Stone and Judith Thompson, 151–74. Madison: University of Wisconsin Press, 2006.

Davis, Michael. '"Incongruous Compounds": Re-reading *Jekyll and Hyde* and Late-Victorian Psychology'. *Journal of Victorian Culture* 11, no. 2 (2006): 207–25. doi:10.1353/jvc.2006.0022.

Dever, Maryanne. '"No Mine and Thine but Ours": Finding "M. Barnard Eldershaw."' *Tulsa Studies in Women's Literature*, 14, no. 1 (1995): 65–75. www.jstor.org/stable/464248

Dowling, David. *Literary Partnerships and the Marketplace: Writers and Mentors in Nineteenth-Century America*. Baton Rouge: Louisiana State University Press, 2012.

Dryden, Linda. 'Literary Affinities and the Postcolonial in Robert Louis Stevenson and Joseph Conrad'. In *Scottish Literature and Postcolonial Literature: Comparative Texts and Critical Perspectives*, ed. Michael Gardiner, Graeme Macdonald and Niall O'Gallagher, 86–97. Edinburgh: Edinburgh University Press, 2011.

Duncan, Ian. 'Stevenson and Fiction'. In *The Edinburgh Companion to Robert Louis Stevenson*, ed. Penny Fielding, 11–26. Edinburgh: Edinburgh University Press, 2010.

Ede, Lisa, and Andrea A. Lunsford. 'Collaboration and Concepts of Authorship'. *PMLA* 116, no. 2 (2001): 354–69. www.jstor.org/stable/463522

Edmond, Rod. *Representing the South Pacific: Colonial Discourse from Cook to Gaugin*. Cambridge: Cambridge University Press, 1997.

Eigner, Edwin M. *Robert Louis Stevenson and the Romantic Tradition*. Princeton: Princeton University Press, 1966.

Elbert, Monika M., Julie E. Hall and Katharine Rodier, eds. *Reinventing the Peabody Sisters*. University of Iowa Press, 2006.

Elwin, Malcolm. *The Strange Case of Robert Louis Stevenson*. London: MacDonald, 1950.

Fielding, Penny. *Writing and Orality: Nationality, Culture, and Nineteenth-Century Scottish Fiction*. Oxford: Clarendon Press, 1996.

Foucault, Michel. 'What is an Author?' In *Language, Counter-Memory, Practice: Selected Essays and Interviews by Michel Foucault*, ed. Donald F. Bouchard, 113–38. Ithaca: Cornell University Press, 1977.

Fuller, Jenn. *Dark Paradise: Pacific Islands in the Nineteenth-Century Imagination*. Edinburgh: Edinburgh University Press, 2016.

Freedgood, Elaine. 'How the Victorian Novel Got Realistic, Reactionary, and Great'. Keynote Address at the Interdisciplinary Nineteenth-Century Studies Conference, Renaissance Hotel, Asheville, NC, 12 March 2016.

Gibson, John S. *Deacon Brodie: Father to Jekyll and Hyde*. Edinburgh: Paul Harris Publishers, 1977.

Gifford, Douglas. 'Stevenson and Scottish Fiction: The Importance of *The Master of Ballantrae*'. In *Stevenson and Victorian Scotland*, ed. Jenni Calder, 62–87. Edinburgh: Edinburgh University Press, 1981.

Gish, Nancy K. 'Jekyll and Hyde: The Psychology of Dissociation'. *International Journal of Scottish Literature* 2 (2007). http://www.ijsl.stir.ac.uk/issue2/gish.htm (last accessed 31 October 2018).

Goggin, Gerard. 'Editing Minervas: William Godwin's Liminal Maneuvers in Mary Wollstonecraft's *Wrongs of Woman*'. In *Literary Couplings: Writing Couples, Collaborators, and the Construction of Authorship*, ed. Marjorie Stone and Judith Thompson, 81–99. Madison: University of Wisconsin Press, 2006.

Gray, William. 'Stevenson's "Auld Alliance": France, Art Theory and the Breath of Money in The Wrecker'. *Scottish Studies Review* 3, no. 2 (2002): 54–65. *MLA International Bibliography*.

Gray, William Forbes. *Some Old Scots Judges: Anecdotes and Impressions*. New York: Dutton, 1915.

Hannah, Matthew N. 'Networks of Modernism: Toward a Theory of Cultural Production'. *ProQuest Dissertations & Theses Global* 77, no. 3 (September 2016).

Hickey, Alison. 'Coleridge, Southey, "and Co.": Collaboration and Authority'. *Studies in Romanticism* 37, no. 3 (1998): 305–49. www.jstor.org/stable/25601342

Hirsch, Gordon. 'The Commercial World of *The Wrecker*'. *Journal of Stevenson Studies* 2 (2005): 70–97.

—. 'The Fiction of Lloyd Osbourne: Was This "American Gentleman" Stevenson's Literary Heir?' *Journal of Stevenson Studies* 4 (2007): 52–2.

—. 'Locating RLS in Relation to Brander Matthews's and Walter Besant's Theories of Literary Collaboration in the Production of Popular Fiction'. *Journal of Stevenson Studies* 8 (2011): 97–107.

—. 'The Stevenson–Osbourne Collaboration'. In *Approaches to Teaching the Works of Robert Louis Stevenson*, ed. Caroline McCracken-Flesher, 162–7. New York: The Modern Language Association of America, 2013.

—. 'Tontines, Tontine Insurance, and Commercial Culture: Stevenson and Osbourne's *The Wrong Box*'. In *Robert Louis Stevenson: Writer of Boundaries*, ed. Richard Ambrosini and Richard Dury, 83–94. Madison: University of Wisconsin Press, 2006.

Hirschfeld, Heather. 'Early Modern Collaboration and Theories of Authorship'. *PMLA* 116, no. 3 (2001): 609–22. www.jstor.org/stable/463501

Hultgren, Neil. *Melodramatic Imperial Writing: From the Sepoy Rebellion to Cecil Rhodes*. Athens: Ohio University Press, 2014.

Jaëck, Nathalie. 'The Greenhouse vs. the Glasshouse: Stevenson's Stories as Textual Matrices'. In *Robert Louis Stevenson: Writer of Boundaries*, ed. Richard Ambrosini and Richard Dury, 48–59. Madison: University of Wisconsin Press, 2006.

James, Henry. 'The Art of Fiction'. In *Essays on Literature; American Writers; English Writers*, 44–65. New York: Library of America, 1984.
—. 'Robert Louis Stevenson'. *Century Magazine*, April 1888. Reprinted in *Essays on Literature; American Writers; English Writers*, 1231–1255. New York: Library of America, 1984.
Jamison, Anne. 'Copyright and Collaboration: Wordsworth, Coleridge, and the Debate over Literary Property'. *Romanticism: The Journal of Romantic Culture and Criticism* 17, no. 2 (2011): 209–21. doi. 10.3366/rom.2011.0025.
Jaszi, Peter. 'On the Author Effect: Contemporary Copyright and Collective Creativity'. In *The Construction of Authorship: Textual Appropriation in Law and Literature*, ed. Martha Woodmansee and Peter Jaszi, 29–56. Durham, NC: Duke University Press, 1994.
Jolly, Roslyn. 'Piracy, Slavery, and the Imagination of Empire in Stevenson's Pacific Fiction'. *Victorian Literature and Culture* 35, no. 1 (2007): 157–73. http://www.jstor.org/stable/40347129
—. *Robert Louis Stevenson in the Pacific: Travel, Empire, and the Author's Profession*. Surrey: Ashgate, 2009.
—. 'South Sea Gothic: Pierre Loti and Robert Louis Stevenson'. *English Literature in Transition, 1880–1920* 47, no. 1 (2004): 28–49. MLA International Bibliography.
—. 'Stevenson's "Sterling Domestic Fiction," "The Beach Of Falesá"'. *Review of English Studies: A Quarterly Journal of English Literature and the English Language* 50, no. 200 (1999): 463–82. MLA International Bibliography.
—. 'Women's Trading in Fanny Stevenson's *The Cruise of the "Janet Nichol"'* . In *Economies of Representation: 1790–2000: Colonialism and Commerce*, ed. Helen Gilbert and Leigh Dale, 143–55. Farnham: Ashgate, 2007.
Kenna, Shane. Interview with Cathal Brennan and John Dorney. *The History Show* 16. NearFM, Dublin, Ireland. 2013. https://soundcloud.com/nearfm/the-history-show-episode-16 (last accessed 31 October 2018).
—. *War in the Shadows: The Irish-American Fenians Who Bombed Victorian Britain*. Co. Kildaire, Ireland: Merrion, 2014.
Kiely, Robert. *Robert Louis Stevenson and the Fiction of Adventure*. Cambridge, MA: Harvard University Press, 1964.
Koestenbaum, Wayne. *Double Talk: The Erotics of Male Literary Collaboration*. London: Routledge, 1989.
—. 'The Shadow on the Bed: Dr Jekyll, Mr Hyde, and the Labouchère Amendment'. *Critical Matrix* (1988): 31–55.
Kucich, John. *Imperial Masochism: British Fiction, Fantasy, and Social Class*. Princeton: Princeton University Press, 2007.
Kurnick, David. *Empty Houses: Theatrical Failure and the Novel*. Princeton: Princeton University Press, 2012.

Laird, Holly A. '"A Hand Spills from the Book's Threshold": Coauthorship's Readers'. *PMLA* 116, no. 2 (2001): 344–53. www.jstor.org/stable/463521

—. *Women Coauthors*. Chicago: University of Illinois Press, 2000.

Lang, Anouk. 'Style and the Stevensons', *Digital Textualities, Textual Cartographies, Networked Geographies* (blog), 13 July 2016, http://aelang.net/wordpress/2016/07/13/stylostevensons/ (last accessed 31 October 2018).

Levine, Philippa. *Prostitution, Race, and Politics: Policing Venereal Disease in the British Empire*. New York: Routledge, 2003.

Linehan, Katherine Bailey. 'Taking up with Kanakas: Stevenson's Complex Social Criticism in "The Beach of Falesá"'. *English Literature in Transition, 1880–1920* 33, no. 4 (1990): 407–22. Project Muse. EBSCOhost.

London, Bette. *Writing Double: Women's Literary Partnerships*. Ithaca: Cornell University Press, 1999.

Lumsden, Alison. 'Stevenson, Scott, and Scottish History'. In *The Edinburgh Companion to Robert Louis Stevenson*, ed. Penny Fielding, 70–85. Edinburgh University Press, 2010.

McCracken-Flesher, Caroline. *Doctor Dissected: A Cultural Autopsy of the Burke and Hare Murders*. Oxford: Oxford University Press, 2011.

—. '*The Wrecker*: Unplacing Space in the South Seas'. In *Robert Louis Stevenson and the Great Affair: Movement, Memory, and Modernity*, ed. Richard J. Hill. New York: Routledge, 2017.

Macfarlane, Robert. *Original Copy: Plagiarism and Originality in Nineteenth-Century Literature*. Oxford: Oxford University Press, 2007.

McGann, Jerome. *The Textual Condition*. Princeton Studies in Culture/ Power/ History. Princeton: Princeton University Press, 1991.

Maixner, Paul, ed. *Robert Louis Stevenson: The Critical Heritage*. London: Routledge and Kegan Paul, 1981.

Manfredi, Carla. 'Pacific Phantasmagorias: Robert Louis Stevenson's Pacific Photography'. In *Oceania and the Victorian Imagination: Where All Things are Possible*, ed. Richard D. Fulton and Peter H. Hoffenberg, 11–29. Farnham: Ashgate, 2013.

Martin, Maureen M. *The Mighty Scot: Nation, Gender, and the Nineteenth-Century Mystique of Scottish Masculinity*. Albany: SUNY Press, 2009.

Masten, Jeffrey. *Textual Intercourse*. Cambridge: Cambridge University Press, 1997.

Menikoff, Barry. '*New Arabian Nights*: Stevenson's Experiment in Fiction'. *Nineteenth-Century Literature* 45 (1990): 339–62.

—. *Robert Louis Stevenson and 'The Beach of Falesá': A Study in Victorian Publishing with the Original Text*. Stanford: Stanford University Press, 1984.

Miller, Elizabeth C. *Framed: The New Woman Criminal in British Culture at the Fin de Siècle*. Ann Arbor: University of Michigan Press, 2009.

Millim, Anne-Marie. *The Victorian Diary: Authorship and Emotional Labour*. Burlington, VT: Ashgate, 2013.
Murfin, Audrey. 'Victorian Nights' Entertainments: Elizabeth Gaskell and Wilkie Collins Develop the British Story Sequence'. *Romanticism and Victorianism on the Net* 48 (2007). https://www.erudit.org/en/journals/ravon/2007-n48-ravon1979/017440ar/ (last accessed 31 October 2018).
Norquay, Glenda. *Robert Louis Stevenson and Theories of Reading: The Reader as Vagabond*. Manchester: Manchester University Press, 2007.
O'Malley, Seamus. 'R. L. Stevenson's "The Beach of Falesá" and the Conjuring-Tricks of Capital'. *English Literature in Transition, 1880–1920* 57 (2014): 59–80. MLA International Bibliography.
Pearson, W. H. 'European Intimidation and the Myth of Tahiti'. *The Journal of Pacific History* 4 (1969): 199–217. http://www.jstor.org/stable/25167994
Pettitt, Clare. 'The Law and Victorian Fiction'. In *A Concise Companion to the Victorian Novel*, ed. Francis O'Gorman, 71–90. Malden, MA: Blackwell, 2005.
—. *Patent Inventions: Intellectual Property and the Victorian Novel*. Oxford: Oxford University Press, 2004.
Phillips, Lawrence. *The South Pacific Narratives of Robert Louis Stevenson and Jack London : Race, Class, Imperialism*. New York: Continuum Literary Studies, 2012.
Pinkston, C. Alex Jr. 'The Stage Premiere of Dr Jekyll and Mr Hyde'. *Nineteenth Century Theatre Research* 24 (1986): 21–43.
Pound, Ezra. 'Patria Mia', *New Age* 11 (17 October 1912).
Pratt, Mary Louise. *Imperial Eyes: Travel Writing and Transculturation*. London: Routledge, 1992.
Rainey, Lawrence. *Institutions of Modernism: Literary Elites and Public Culture*. Harvard: Yale University Press, 1998.
Rajan, Tilottama. 'Framing the Corpus: Godwin's "Editing" of Wollstonecraft in 1798'. *Studies in Romanticism* 39, no. 4, (2000): 511–31. http://www.jstor.org/stable/25601470.
Reid, Julia. *Robert Louis Stevenson, Science, and the* Fin de Siècle. New York: Palgrave Macmillan, 2006.
Richardson, Ruth. 'Robert Louis Stevenson's *The Body Snatcher*'. *The Lancet* 385 (2015): 412–13.
Riewald, Jacobus Gerhardus. *Max Beerbohm's Mischievous Wit: A Literary Entertainment*. Assen, The Netherlands: Van Gorcum, 2000.
Roughead, William, ed. *Trial of Deacon Brodie*. Notable Scottish Trials. Glasgow: William Hodge and Co., 1906.
Salmon, Richard. '"Farewell Poetry and Aerial Flights": The Function of the Author and Victorian Fiction'. In *A Concise Companion to the Victorian Novel*, ed. Francis O'Gorman. Oxford: Blackwell Publishing, 2005: 134–55.

Sandison, Alan. *Robert Louis Stevenson and the Appearance of Modernism: A Future Feeling.* New York: St. Martin's Press, 1996.
—. 'A World Made for Liars: Stevenson's *Dynamiter* and the Death of the Real'. In *Robert Louis Stevenson Reconsidered: New Critical Perspectives*, ed. William B. Jones, Jr., 140–62. Jefferson, NC: McFarland, 2003.
Schmitt, Cannon. 'Technical Maturity in Robert Louis Stevenson'. *Representations* 125 (2014): 54–79. doi: 10.1525/rep.2014.125.1.54.
Scott, Patrick. 'Anatomizing Professionalism: Medicine, Authorship, and R. L. Stevenson's "The Body Snatcher"'. *Victorians Institute Journal* 27 (1999): 113–30.
Showalter, Elaine. *Sexual Anarchy: Gender and Culture at the Fin de Siècle.* New York: Penguin, 1990.
Smith, Vanessa. *Intimate Strangers.* Cambridge: Cambridge University Press, 2010.
—. *Literary Culture and the Pacific: Nineteenth Century Textual Encounters.* Cambridge: Cambridge University Press, 1998.
Smith, Victoria Ford. 'Toy Presses and Treasure Maps: Robert Louis Stevenson and Lloyd Osbourne as Collaborators'. *Children's Literature Association Quarterly* 35, no. 1 (2010): 26–54. Project Muse. EBSCOhost.
States, Bert O. *Great Reckonings in Little Rooms: On the Phenomenology of Theater.* Berkeley: University of California Press, 1985.
Steer, Philip. 'Romances of Uneven Development: Spatiality, Trade, and Form in Robert Louis Stevenson's Pacific Novels'. *Victorian Literature and Culture* 43 (2015): 343–56.
Steinitz, Rebecca. *Time, Space, and Gender in the Nineteenth-Century British Diary.* New York: Palgrave, 2011.
Stewart, Garrett. *Dear Reader: The Conscripted Audience in Nineteenth-Century British Fiction.* Baltimore: The Johns Hopkins University Press, 1996.
Stiles, Anne. *Popular Fiction and Brain Science in the Late Nineteenth Century.* New York: Cambridge University Press, 2012.
Stillinger, Jack. *Multiple Authorship and the Myth of Solitary Genius.* Oxford: Oxford University Press, 1991.
Stone, Marjorie, and Judith Thompson. 'Contexts and Heterotexts: A Theoretical and Historical Introduction'. In *Literary Couplings: Writing Couples, Collaborators, and the Construction of Authorship*, ed. Marjorie Stone and Judith Thompson, 3–40. Madison: University of Wisconsin Press, 2006.
Swearingen, Roger G. *The Prose Writings of Robert Louis Stevenson: A Guide.* London: Macmillan, 1980.
Thomas, Ronald R. 'The Strange Voices in the Strange Case: Dr Jekyll, Mr Hyde, and the Voices of Modern Fiction'. In *Dr Jekyll and Mr Hyde after One Hundred Years*, ed. William Veeder and Gordon Hirsch, 73–106. Chicago: University of Chicago Press, 1988.

Veeder, William. 'Children of the Night: Stevenson and Patriarchy'. In *Dr Jekyll and Mr Hyde after One Hundred Years*, ed. William Veeder and Gordon Hirsch, 107–60. Chicago: University of Chicago Press, 1988.

Walkowitz, Judith. *City of Dreadful Delight: Narratives of Sexual Danger in Late-Victorian London*. Chicago: University of Chicago Press, 1992.

Wallace, Anne D. 'Home at Grasmere Again: Revisiting the Family in Dove Cottage'. In *Literary Couplings: Writing Couples, Collaborators, and the Construction of Authorship*, ed. Marjorie Stone and Judith Thompson, 100–23. Madison: University of Wisconsin Press, 2006.

Wallace, Lee. *Sexual Encounter: Pacific Texts, Modern Sexualities*. Ithaca: Cornell University Press, 2003.

Wallace, Tara Ghoshal. *Imperial Characters: Home and Periphery in Eighteenth-Century Literature*. Lewisburg: Bucknell University Press, 2010.

Warner, F. B. '"The Hanging Judge" Once More before the Bar'. *The Papers of the Bibliographical Society of America* 70 (1976): 89–95. ProQuest.

Watson, Roderick. 'Modernism'. In *Approaches to Teaching the Works of Robert Louis Stevenson*, ed. Caroline McCracken-Flesher, 69–75. New York: Modern Language Association of America, 2013.

—. '"The Unrest and Movement of Our Century": The Universe of *The Wrecker*. *Journal of Stevenson Studies* 4 (2007): 114–28.

Welsh, Louise. 'Robert Louis Stevenson and the Theatre of the Brain: An Exploration of Creativity and the Unconscious in a Pre-Freudian Age', A lecture presented at The Glasgow School of Art, University of Glasgow, Scotland, 26 February 2013. http://vimeo.com/60546840 (last accessed 31 October 2018).

Whelehan, Niall. *The Dynamiters: Irish Nationalism and Political Violence in the Wider World, 1867–1900*. Cambridge: Cambridge University Press, 2012.

Woodmansee, Martha. 'On the Author Effect: Recovering Collectivity'. In *The Construction of Authorship: Textual Appropriation in Law and Literature*, ed. Martha Woodmansee and Peter Jaszi, 15–8. Durham, NC: Duke University Press, 1994.

Worrall, Nick. *The Moscow Art Theatre*. Theatre Production Studies Series. London and New York: Routledge, 1996.

Yates, Donald. 'A Colloquy with Jorge Luis Borges'. In *Jorge Luis Borges: Conversations*, 149–63. Jackson: University of Mississippi Press, 1998.

York, Lorraine. 'Crowding the Garret: Women's Collaborative Writing and the Problematics of Space'. In *Literary Couplings: Writing Couples, Collaborators, and the Construction of Authorship*, ed. Marjorie Stone and Judith Thompson, 288–308. Madison: University of Wisconsin Press, 2006.

Index

All writings are by Robert Louis Stevenson unless otherwise described. Figure are indicated by *italic* page numbers.

'A Chapter on Dreams', 14–15, 16, 22, 43–8, 49, 136, 165–6, 177
A Game of Bluff see Osbourne
'A Gossip on Romance', 56, 145–6
'A Samoan Scrapbook' proposed photojournalism project (with Joe Strong), 108
Admiral Guinea play (with W. E. Henley), 21, 31, 33, 62
Aguero, Carlos, 58
Ah Fu (Chinese cook in Samoa), 109, 164
Ajax planned play (with W. E. Henley), 37, 122
Amalaisa (Atafu trader's wife), 104
Ambrosini, Richard, 126, 129, 131, 136, 145, 162
Arabian Nights (*Tales from 1001 Nights*), 22, 23, 55–6, 57, 62, 69
Arata, Stephen, 45, 46, 152, 156
author
  as celebrity, 2, 3, 20, 76, 177
  and commercial marketplace, 16–17, 18, 27n, 28n, 76, 81, 88, 136, 154, 162
  as 'solitary genius', 5, 11, 16, 17, 22
author control, 6, 50, 90, 113, 120, 140, 143, 160
author-function, 4, 13, 20, 45, 82, 125, 162

author intention, 4, 7, 86, 98, 107–8, 175
authorship
  in 'A Chapter on Dreams', 44, 45, 47–9
  decentring, 31, 49, 177
  dialogic, 16, 18, 120, 168, 177
  see also collaboration; divided/conflicted self

Bakhtin, M. M., 4
Balfour, Graham, 37, 39–40, 53, 65, 66, 70, 73, 109, 167
Ballantyne, R. M., *The Coral Island*, 15
Barnard, Marjorie *see* Eldershaw, M. Barnard
Barnes, William H., 112, 113
Barrie, J. M., 87
Barthes, Roland, 4
Baxter, Charles, 76, 94, 126, 134, 139, 163, 174, 175, 176
Beattie, Hilary, 10, 43, 46, 70, 75, 80n, 139
Beau Austin play (with W. E. Henley), 21, 31, 33, 35, 62, 129
Beaumont and Fletcher, 10
Beerbohm, Max, 125
Bell, Ian, 9, 71
Besant, Walter, 160, 163

Black and White magazine, 83, 116n, 124
Bloom, Lynn Z., 86
Booth, Bradford, 109
Borges, Jorge Luis, 151, 178n
Bradbury, Malcolm, 17, 18, 27n
Bradley, Katherine *see* Field, Michael
Britten, Benjamin, 133
Brodie, William, 31
Brontë, Emily, 143
Buckton, Oliver, 83, 99, 116n, 125, 134
Bull, Johnny (Manihiki island boy), 99
Bulwer-Lytton, Edward, *Paul Clifford*, 73
Burke, Thomas Henry, 58
Burlingame, Edward L., 151, 152, 163
Burton, Richard, 56

Cairney, John, 72
Calder, Jenni, 8, 43, 74
Cameron, John, 153
Carroll, Lewis, 48
Caserio, Robert, 173
Catriona (or *David Balfour*), 18, 137, 174, 176
Cavendish, Lord Frederick, 68
character creation, 163–6
Child's Garden of Verses, 37
'Child's Play', 14, 37
Cohen, Edward, 75
Cohen, Milton A., 13, 17
Cole, William, 61
Coleridge, Samuel Taylor, 14, 16
collaboration: theory and practice, 1–26, 49
    acknowledgement of, 5–8; *see also* double signature
    benefits and advantages, 3, 21, 160, 161, 162
    and character creation, 163–6
    conflictual, 14, 21, 22, 23, 38, 43, 44, 50, 76, 88, 89, 162
    and copyright law, 11–12, 18
    difficulties and disadvantages, 3, 14–15, 21, 25–6, 32, 33, 50, 150, 159–60, 161–2, 163, 167
    distinguished from editing, 6–7, 8
    end of, 25–6
    and equality, 9–12, 23, 25
    examples in literature (other than Stevenson), 8, 10, 12–13, 14, 16, 66, 112–13
    and feminism, 5–6, 7
    limits, 160–1
    male/male, 4
    and marriage, 22–3, 62–3, 78n
    and mutuality, 8
    operatic, 14, 16, 23, 88–90, 91, 162
    and plagiarism, 8, 12, 15, 77
    and separability, 12–16
    theatrical, 22, 37
    see also partnership theme
Colley, Ann C., 105, 114n, 172
Collins, Wilkie, 56, 143
Colvin, Sidney, 24, 34, 36–7, 54, 63, 70, 71, 73
    as editor rather than collaborator, 6–7, 8
    and Pacific islands writings, 81, 82, 84, 85, 88, 93, 94, 99–100, 108, 121, 145, 168, 177
    and *The Ebb-Tide*, 19, 173–6
Conrad, Joseph, *Heart of Darkness*, 172
Cooper, Edith *see* Field, Michael
Cox, Robert, 61

Danahay, Martin, 39
David Balfour see Catriona
Davidson, Guy, 170, 173
Deacon Brodie play (with W. E. Henley), 14, 21, 34, 41–2, 44, 49, 72
    and criminality, 35–6, 42, 156
    and double face of actor, 38
    and end of friendship, 32, 36
    and male partnership, 31, 35–6

and *Strange Case of Dr Jekyll and Mr Hyde*, 22, 35
and *The Wrecker*, 25
Dever, Maryanne, 13
diaries, as public or private documents, 86–7; *see also* Pacific islands
Dickens, Charles
Bleak House, 11
David Copperfield, 17
divided/conflicted self, 36, 41, 42, 43, 46, 47, 50, 177
double signature, 6, 75, 77
doubling, 177
Dowling, David, 11
dreams *see* 'A Chapter on Dreams'
Dryden, Linda, 172
duality, 31, 35, 37, 38, 40, 43, 45, 47, 144
Duncan, Ian, 142
Durão, Fabio A., 17

Ede, Lisa, 21
Edmond, Rod, 84, 158, 172
Eigner, Edwin, 9
Eldershaw, Flora, 13
Eldershaw, M. Barnard, 13
Eliot, George, 35
Ellis, Havelock, 12, 66
Elwin, Malcolm, 53, 65

Fani (Manihiki island girl), 97–9, 102, 106, 111
Field, Isobel *see* Strong, Belle
Field, Michael, 12, 66
Fielding, Penny, 140
Fighting the Ring (proposed collaboration with Lloyd Osbourne), 121, 122, 157–8
Foucault, Michel, 4, 20, 62, 82
Freedgood, Elaine, 38
Freud, Sigmund, 46, 47
Furnas, J. C., 65

Galchen, Rivka, 151, 154
Galland, Antoine, 55

Gaskell, Elizabeth, 56
Gladstone, W. E., 61
Godwin, William, 16
Gordon, General, 61
Gosse, Edmund, 63, 64–5, 71, 131
Gray, William Forbes, 73
Greene, Graham, 127, 147n

Haggard, H. Rider, 135
Hawthorne, Nathaniel, 16
Hawthorne, Sophia, 16
Henley, Teddy, 38
Henley, W. E., 3, 8, 9, 29–31, *30*, 53, 91
  end of friendship with Robert Louis Stevenson, 23, 32, 36, 74–5
  In Hospital poems, 9, 30
  'Invictus' poem, 30
  plays (with Robert Louis Stevenson) *see Admiral Guinea*; *Ajax*; *Beau Austin*; *Deacon Brodie*; *Macaire*; *Three Plays*
Herman, Henry, 35
Hickey, Alison, 14
Hills, G., 120, 131, 146–7n
Hirsch, Gordon, 10, 109, 123, 131, 154, 160, 162
Hirschfeld, Heather, 16
Horan, Nancy, 54
Hunt (white man on Samoa), 112

In the South Seas, 16, 23, 81, 83, 85, 86, 88–9, 90, 91, 92–3, 95, 96, 98, 99–100, 101, 105, 111, 116n, 148n
Irving, Henry, 38
Irving, Washington, 8, 15

Jaëck, Nathalie, 141
James, Henry, 35, 38, 64, 67, 124, 143
  The Private Life, 1
  The Real Thing and Other Tales, 1–2
Jaszi, Peter, 11

Jolly, Roslyn, 27n, 84, 88, 90, 91, 106, 137, 164
Jones, Henry Arthur, 35
Jones, Henry Arthur and Herman, Henry, *The Silver King*, 35
Joyce, James, 35

Kidnapped, 18, 70, 137, 144, 174
Kiely, Robert, 69
Kipling, Rudyard, 125
Kizer, Carolyn, 54
Koestenbaum, Wayne, 4, 6, 42, 43, 53, 66, 82, 168
Kucich, John, 140
Kurnick, David, 35, 37–8

Laird, Holly, 4
Lane, Edward, 56
Lang, Anouk, 12
Lapierre, Alexandra, 54
LeFanu, Sheridan, 72
Linehan, Katherine Bailey, 105
Lombroso, Cesare, 60
London, Bette, 4, 8, 63
Loti, Pierre
  Madame Chrysanthème, 107
  The Marriage of Loti, 106–7
Low, Will H., 154, 164, *165*
Lumsden, Alison, 142
Lunsford, Andrea A., 21

Macaire play (with W. E. Henley), 21, 31, 62
McClure, Sam, 99, 124, 154, 164
McCracken-Flesher, Caroline, 41, 152
Macfarlane, Robert, 15, 45, 77, 166
McGann, Jerome, 5, 7, 108
Machen, Arthur, *The Great God Pan*, 74
Mackay, Margaret, 54, 65–6
MacQueen, Robert, Lord Braxfield, 72–3
Madame Butterfly (Puccini), 107
male friendship/partnership, 4, 35–6, 42–3

Mansfield, Richard, *39*
'Markheim', 177
Marrero, Federico Gil, 58
Masters, Jeffrey, 16
Mattos, Katharine de, and 'The Nixie', 8, 23, 74–5, 76–7, 85
Mehew, Ernest, 11, 109, 128
Meiklejohn, John, 62
Menikoff, Barry, 6–7, 57, 105, 107–8
Miller, Elizabeth C., 60
Millim, Anne-Marie, 86
More New Arabian Nights: The Dynamiter (with Fanny Stevenson), 3, 4, 7, 10, 12, 15, 17–18, 19, 22–3, 33, 54, 55, 57–62, 63–9, 70, 76–7, 91, 120, 122, 131, 140, 174
'My First Book', 8, 15, 123
Myers, F. W. H., 44, 46, 47, 50, 166

New Arabian Nights, 18, 32, 55, 56–7, 64, 126, 140, 177
Norquay, Glenda, 47, 136, 161

Oliphant, Mrs, 137
O'Malley, Seamus, 107
Osbourne, Fanny Van de Grift / Vandegrift (later Fanny Stevenson), 53, 120
Osbourne, Hervey, 120
Osbourne, Isobel, 120
Osbourne, Katharine Durham, 109, 123, 127
Osbourne, Lloyd, 3, 4, 9, 33, 34–5, *121*
  A Game of Bluff (draft for *The Wrong Box*), 15, 24, 124, 127, 131, 133, 135, 136, 147n, 166
  collaborations with Robert Louis Stevenson (proposed) *see Fighting the Ring*, *The Beachcombers*; *The Gaol Bird*, *The Goldenson Mystery*; *The Last of the Yeomen*; *The White Nigger*

collaborations with Robert Louis Stevenson (undertaken) *see The Ebb-Tide*; *The Wrecker*; *The Wrong Box*
literary reputation, 120, 131, 137, 173–4, 176
Pacific diary, 110–11
The Pearl Fisher (origin of *The Ebb-Tide*), 151, 166–7, 168–71
Osbourne, Sam, 53, 74, 157
Otis, Captain, 164

Pacific islands
and censoring of sexualised descriptions, 94, 95, 97–8
and Colvin's editorial work, 81, 82, 84, 88, 93, 94, 108, 121, 145, 168
cruises to, 83
diaries: Lloyd Osbourne, 86, 110–11; Fanny Stevenson, 87, 93–6, 98, 101–2, 104, 108; *see also The Cruise of the* Janet Nichol; Margaret Stevenson, 86; Robert Louis Stevenson, 86–7, 92; *see also In The South Seas*; *and under The Cruise of the* Janet Nichol
and fiction works *see The Beach of Falesá*; *The Ebb-Tide*; *The Wrecker*
locations: Atafu, 103–4; Manihiki, 95–9; Nassau, 102–3; Niue, 92–4; Olosega, 92, 115n; Penrhyn, 99–102, 116n; Samoa, 108–10, 112–13; Tahiti, 110–11; Tutuila, 116n
and non-fiction works *see A Samoan Scrapbook*; *Black and White* magazine; *In the South Seas*; *Sun* (New York): letters to
and sexual exploitation of young women, 23–4, 81, 85, 97–9, 104, 110–12, 113, 116n; *see also The Beach of Falesá*

Park, Mungo, 115–16n
partnership *see* collaboration
partnership theme
in *Deacon Brodie*, 31, 35–6
in *Fighting the Ring*, 157–8
in *Strange Case of Dr Jekyll and Mr Hyde*, 42–3
in 'The Body Snatcher', 40
in *The Wrecker*, 4, 25, 155–7, 158
Pettitt, Clare, 11, 12
Phillips, Lawrence, 155
Pinkston, C. Alex, 39
plagiarism, 8, 12, 15, 77
plays
collaboration with Fanny Stevenson *see The Hanging Judge*
collaborations with W. E. Henley *see Admiral Guinea*; *Ajax*; *Beau Austin*; *Deacon Brodie*; *Macaire*; *Three Plays*
failure of, 22, 23, 31, 34, 35, 38–40, 71
Poe, Edgar Allan, 166
Pollock, W. H., 57
Pound, Ezra, 13, 17
Pratt, Mary Louise, 84, 115n
Pritzker, Robyn, 12

Quiller-Couch, Sir Arthur, 8

Randall, David, 127–8, 147n
Reid, Julia, 175
Richardson, Ruth, 42
Richardson, Samuel, *Clarissa*, 145
Rossa, O'Donovan, 58
Rubiera, R., 59

St. Ives (unfinished, completed by Sir Arthur Quiller-Couch), 8, 122, 177
Salmon, Richard, 17
Sandison, Alan, 17, 57, 66, 69, 141
Schmitt, Cannon, 173
Scott, Patrick, 40

Scott, Sir Walter, 17
Selia (first husband of Laulii Willis), 112
Shelley, Mary, 63
Shelley, Sir Percy, 63
Shield, William, 133
Showalter, Elaine, 42
Sitwell, Fanny, 60, 61
Smith, Vanessa, 108, 171
Smith, Victoria Ford, 123
'Some Portraits by Raeburn', 72, 73
Southey, Robert, 14, 16
States, Bert, 38
Steer, Philip, 155, 162
Steinitz, Rebecca, 86
Stevenson, Fanny, 3, 4, 7, 9, 53–4, 55, 83
  collaborations with Robert Louis Stevenson *see More New Arabian Nights*; *The Hanging Judge*
  literary reputation, 53–4, 63–4, 65–6, 70, 71–2, 76
  More New Arabian Nights: The Dynamiter (with Robert Louis Stevenson), 3, 4, 7, 10, 12, 15, 17–18, 19, 22–3, 33, 54, 55, 57–62, 63–9, 70, 76–7, 91, 120, 122, 131, 140, 174; 'The Destroying Angel' (presumed authorship), 66, 76; 'The Explosive Bomb' (presumed authorship), 66; 'The Fair Cuban' (presumed authorship), 65, 66, 76
  own works *see The Cruise of the* Janet Nichol; 'The Nixie' and supposed plagiarism *see* 'The Nixie'
  The Black Man and Other Tales (proposed collaboration with Robert Louis Stevenson), 54–5
  The Cruise of the Janet Nichol *among the South Sea Islands*, 7–8, 19, 23, 82, 83–4, 92, 93, 94, 95, 96–7, 98–9, 100, 102, 103–4, 114n; Robert Louis Stevenson's contribution to, 84–5, 92, 93, 103
  The Hanging Judge play (with Robert Louis Stevenson), 23, 54, 70–4, 76, 80n
  'The Nixie' (controverted collaboration with Katharine de Mattos), 23, 54, 74–7, 85
Stevenson, Margaret, 63, 83, 86–7
Stevenson, Robert Alan Mowbray, 3, 164
Stevenson, Robert Louis
  collaborations *see under* Henley, W. E.; Osbourne, Lloyd; Stevenson, Fanny
  end of friendship with W. E. Henley, 23, 32, 36, 74–5
  political views, 18–19, 102; in The Dynamiter, 58–61, 68–9; in *The Ebb-Tide*, 170–2, 177; in *The Wrecker*, 19, 69, 81, 83, 140, 172, 177; in *The Wrong Box*, 139–40
  as proto-modernist, 17, 27n
  as romancer, 17
  as writer for popular market, 18, 28n; *see also* author: and commercial marketplace
Stewart, Garrett, 47
Stillinger, Jack, 5, 7, 16, 49
Stone, Marjorie, 16, 20
Strange Case of Dr Jekyll and Mr Hyde, 14, 16, 18, 31, 41, 91
  and collaboration, 29, 49–50
  composition described in 'A Chapter on Dreams', 22, 43–7, 165
  and *Deacon Brodie*, 31, 35–6
  and doubling, 177

dramatic versions, 22, 29, 39–40
and duality, 22, 37–8, 42–3, 47
partnership theme in, 42–3
revision of, 53
Strong, Belle (Isobel Field), 73, 80 n, 86, 108, 109, 164
Strong, Joe, 108, *121*
Sun (New York), letters to, 87, 95, 99, 100–1, 105, 124
Swift, Jonathan, 48–9, 166
Symonds, John Addington, 61

'Talk and Talkers', 90, 161–2, 164
Tembinok' (Gilbert Islands tyrant), 172
Tennyson, Alfred Lord, 96
Thackeray, W. M., 35
The Beach of Falesá, 6–7, 23, 24, 81, 83, 104–8
The Beachcombers (proposed collaboration with Lloyd Osbourne), 151
The Black Man and Other Tales (proposed collaboration with Fanny Stevenson), 54–5
'The Body Snatcher', 31, 40–2, 44, 49, 55
'The Cruise of the Equator' photograph album, 89
'The Destroying Angel' (attributed to Fanny Stevenson) in *More New Arabian Nights*, 57–8, 64, 65, 66, 67, 69, 71, 76
The Dynamiter (with Fanny Stevenson) *see More New Arabian Nights*
The Ebb-Tide (with Lloyd Osbourne), 3, 9, 18, 19, 25–6, 55, 81, 83, 95, 100, 119, 120, 136, 140, 159, 162, 166–78
defects in blamed on Osbourne, 173–4, 176
origin in Osbourne, *The Pearl Fisher*, 151, 166–7, 168–71

Stevenson requests deletion of Osbourne's name as author, 168, 175
Stevenson's political views in, 170–2, 177
violence in criticised by Colvin, 173–6
'The Explosive Bomb' (attributed to Fanny Stevenson) in *More New Arabian Nights*, 64, 65, 66
'The Fair Cuban' (attributed to Fanny Stevenson) in *More New Arabian Nights*, 58, 64, 65, 66, 67–8, 69, 71, 76
The Gaol Bird (proposed collaboration with Lloyd Osbourne), 122
The Goldenson Mystery (proposed collaboration with Lloyd Osbourne), 120–1, 122
The Hanging Judge play (with Fanny Stevenson), 23, 54, 70–4, 76, 80n
The Last of the Yeomen (proposed collaboration with Lloyd Osbourne), 121, 122–3
The Master of Ballantrae, 18, 19, 24, 119, 131, 136, 137–45, 152, 164, 165
fictional editing in, 141–3, 146
politics in, 139–40
relation to *The Wrong Box*, 138–9, 144–5
'The Merry Men', 55
The Pearl Fisher see Osbourne
'The Ploughboy' song, 133, 148n, 161–2
'The Shadow on the Bed', 55
The South Seas (intended work), 88
'The Suicide Club' in *More New Arabian Nights*, 55
'The Superfluous Mansion' in *More New Arabian Nights*, 59–60, 61

The White Nigger (proposed collaboration with Lloyd Osbourne), 120, 121–2
The Wrecker (with Lloyd Osbourne), 2, 4, 25, 36, 96, 97, 119, 120, 129, 136, 150–60, 162–5, 167, 173, 177
   collaboration on described, 3, 9, 18, 161
   factual origin of story, 153
   Osbourne blamed for defects, 174
   partnership theme in, 4, 25, 155–7, 158
   political views in, 19, 69, 81, 83, 140, 172, 177
The Wrong Box (with Lloyd Osbourne), 3, 9–10, 19, 24–5, 119, 140, 142, 146n, 147n, 150, 154, 163, 177
   and *A Game of Bluff* draft, 24, 124, 129–30, 131–3
   as commercial project, 136, 162
   fictional collaboration in, 133–4
   negative aspects of collaboration on, 2, 18, 120, 151
   Osbourne blamed for defects, 174
   political views in, 154, 162
   and railway novel, 134–5
   relation to *The Master of Ballantrae*, 138–9, 144–5
theatre of the mind, 43, 50
theatrical collaboration, 22, 37
Thomas, Ronald R., 49
Thompson, Judith, 16, 20
'Thrawn Janet', 55

Three Plays (with W. E. Henley), 21, 31
Tin Jack (Jack Buckland, passenger on the *Janet Nicoll*), 164
Travels with a Donkey, 32
Treasure Island, 8, 15, 18, 30, 123, 155, 163, 167
'Truth of Intercourse', 15

Veeder, William, 42, 43
Virginibus Puerisque, 15, 72, 160

Walkowitz, Judith, 114n
Wallace, Lee, 99
Wallace, Tara Ghoshal, 139
Watson, Roderick, 155
Weir of Hermiston (unfinished), 18, 67, 73, 80n, 176, 177
Whelehan, Niall, 58
Williams, Dominic, 17
Willis, Alexander, 111, 112, 113
Willis, Laulii, 111–13
Wollstonecraft, Mary, 16
Woodmansee, Martha, 11
Wordsworth, Dorothy, 7, 16
Wordsworth, William, 7, 16
writing
   as *creatio*, 15, 166
   as *inventio*, 15, 77, 166

York, Lorraine, 12, 66

Zola, Émile, 175
Zosephina (Sosophina) (Samoan attendant), 108–9, *110*, 111

EU representative:
Easy Access System Europe
Mustamäe tee 50, 10621 Tallinn, Estonia
Gpsr.requests@easproject.com

www.ingramcontent.com/pod-product-compliance
Lightning Source LLC
Chambersburg PA
CBHW070356240426
43671CB00013BA/2521